Advance praise for *Oil's Deep State*

"Kevin Taft's powerful book, *Oil's Deep State*, is compelling because it is drawn from his personal experience as a politician. In order to understand why governments at the federal and provincial levels have been so reticent in taking action to get us off fossil fuels, we must see that money has undermined democracy. There is no place for ethics or morality when the sole drive of corporations is to make money, the more and faster, the better, and that means getting rid of all obstacles to unbridled growth, even if the future of generations to come is in jeopardy. Unless corporations are reined in, environmental destruction and climate change are certain to happen. **Read this book, get mad, then take action to restore democracy.**"

— David Suzuki

"For progressives everywhere, it has been painful and bewildering to see the Alberta NDP government take the same line as the Conservatives it toppled on the province's defining industry: that what's good for big oil is good for Alberta. This revelatory book explains how decades of patient work by the fossil fuel sector and its operatives made this almost inevitable. Do we really have a 'Deep State' of petro interests in Canada?

Kevin Taft lays out a meticulous and convincing case that we most certainly do. When the oil industry has captured powerful levers in our democracy – not just the political class, but the regulatory system, academia, the courts and more – this provocative term is precisely the right one to use. **Taft delivers a gripping read for anyone who wonders why, despite a broad consensus for ambitious action in the face of the climate crisis, our country is hurtling in the wrong direction.**"

— Avi Lewis, journalist and filmmaker

"**Taft's book is a must-read for voting-age Canadians who smugly believe that the political idiocy unfolding in the USA can't happen in Canada.** Taft has done a meticulous, scholarly job of documenting how democracy in Canada and Alberta has been corrupted by petropolitics. His book is a combination of history and a handbook on how to avoid our democracy being 'hornswoggled' by industrial and political soothesayers."

— David Schindler, environmental scientist

"**Kevin Taft, the ultimate the insider / outsider, deftly peels back the cover over what Big Oil doesn't want you to see.** How they attempt to 'capture' governments and subvert democracy to preserve their huge profits and delay our needed transition to a zero carbon future. Read the fascinating stories of how powerful, behind-the-scenes oil operatives use corporate money, influence, networking, and disinformation to prolong the era of fossil fuels. And learn how exposing them and rescuing democracy from their tentacles are needed to save the planet from global warming."

— Gordon Laxer, founding director
of Parkland Institute at the University
of Alberta and author of *After the Sands:
Energy and Ecological Security for Canadians*

"Taft's examination of how the petroleum industry successfully manipulated governments in Alberta, Canada and the U.S to downplay the threat of global warming despite all the scientific evidence is **a must read for anyone who wants to save democracy and the planet at the same time.**"

— Gillian Steward, *Toronto Star* columnist

Oil's Deep State

How the petroleum industry undermines democracy and stops action on global warming — in **Alberta**, and in **Ottawa**

KEVIN TAFT

James Lorimer & Company Ltd., Publishers
Toronto

James Lorimer & Company Ltd., Publishers acknowledges the support of the Ontario Arts Council (OAC), an agency of the Government of Ontario, which in 2015-16 funded 1,676 individual artists and 1,125 organizations in 209 communities across Ontario for a total of $50.5 million. We acknowledge the support of the Canada Council for the Arts, which last year invested $153 million to bring the arts to Canadians throughout the country. This project has been made possible in part by the Government of Canada and with the support of the Ontario Media Development Corporation.

Cover design: Tyler Cleroux
Cover images: Shutterstock

Library and Archives Canada Cataloguing in Publication

Taft, Kevin, 1955-, author

Oil's deep state : how the petroleum industry undermines democracy and stops action on global warming in Alberta, and in Ottawa / Kevin Taft.

Includes bibliographical references and index.
Issued in print and electronic formats.
ISBN 978-1-4594-0997-2 (hardcover).--ISBN 978-1-4594-0999-6 (EPUB)

1. Petroleum industry and trade--Political activity--Canada.
2. Global warming--Political aspects--Canada.I. Title.

HD9574.C22T34 2017   338.2'72820971   C2017-903829-X
                                            C2017-903830-3

James Lorimer & Company Ltd., Publishers
117 Peter Street, Suite 304
Toronto, ON, Canada
M5V 0M3
www.lorimer.ca

Printed and bound in Canada.

Contents

Preface

While this book occasionally dwells on the science of global warming — because it is the driving force behind many of the issues we will explore — it is primarily about democracy and politics. Most writing on the impacts of global warming is by scientists, academics, or journalists. My perspective, on the other hand, is that of an elected politician, one who had an eyewitness view of the effects of the fossil fuel industry, especially the oil industry, on democracy. For eleven years I was a member of the Legislative Assembly of Alberta for the Alberta Liberal Party, including an almost five-year term as Leader of the Opposition through two general elections. I was part of a team of people who devoted their lives with dogged passion to democracy, politics, and governance.

My position gave me an unusually deep and broad perspective on the machinery of democracy. I listened to thousands of voters. In the public chambers and private rooms of the legislature, I saw how the cantankerous equipment of politics and policy was worked: by premiers, cabinet ministers, elected members of government and opposition, political staff, and civil servants. I served on committees that selected auditors-general, chief electoral officers, and ethics commissioners. I dealt daily with the media and attended to political parties, both my own and others, with almost life-or-death interest. Being in Alberta, I met constantly with people from the oil and gas industry, some of whom became friends, and I had to raise money — or at least try to — largely from oil and gas corporations. I was in court twice, once for the judicial recount of an election and once to file a *Charter of Rights and Freedoms* challenge over the conduct of an election, and I was sued once for defamation, although the case fell apart before it went to court. In short, I got up close and personal with many of the institutions of democracy.

In this book, I intend to use this experience to reflect on the strengths and frailties of modern democratic societies as they struggle to respond effectively to global warming, an issue that could be their undoing.

Two years after leaving politics in 2012, I was invited to spend three weeks at the Whitlam Institute at Western Sydney University in Australia. Australia, like Canada, was going through a prolonged export boom of fossil fuels; while the resource in Canada was primarily bitumen, in Australia it was coal and liquid natural gas. The Whitlam Institute wanted me to speak and write about what happens to democracy in societies that become huge exporters of fossil fuels, especially in light of global warming. They arranged a feature interview for me on a national radio program, and the interviewer, as good interviewers do, challenged my concern that the fossil fuel industry was shaping politics in Alberta. "Canada is a democracy, and in Alberta there are democratic elections," she said.[1] I responded to her with examples of my concerns, but I also found myself thinking, "Does it automatically follow that if there are elections, there is democracy?" I realized I needed to go deeper into the matter.

Two other conversations also returned to my mind as I worked on this book. One was with a senior energy industry official in 2007, a bright, verbal man with a direct and sometimes sharp tongue with whom I enjoyed parrying. I met him several times, especially about our party's stance on raising royalties, which he and his organization strongly opposed. Our party had held our position despite intense pressure, and he finally turned to me and said, as I recall, in a quietly threatening tone: "If you don't get with our program, there will be no holds barred in the future, no more Marquis of Queensbury rules. We can do things you'll never know. You won't even know what hit you." I took it as a declaration of total political war, in which our small caucus and tiny resources were completely outgunned. I never saw him again, but the stories and results from the 2008 Alberta general election, and subsequent events in other parties, lead me to conclude he was as good as his word. Darth Vader had raised his anger and let me know that looming behind him was the Emperor.

About a year later, after the 2008 Alberta election, I met one-on-one for the first and only time with one of the heavyweights of Canada's petroleum industry. It was a quiet meeting, friendly in a clinical sort of way, and one of our topics was Alberta's future. "Alberta should give up on economic diversification," he told me, "and commit itself completely to oil sands production. It should become an oil sands province with an oil sands economy." He spoke as if he already knew what the future held, as if the script for his vision had been written and endorsed long before our meeting, and he was simply reciting a foregone conclusion. In the following five years, $131 billion of capital was invested in Alberta's oil sands.[2]

Years later, I realized these conversations were in some way connected, but I needed to understand how. This book reflects that exploration.

There are many terrific volumes about the impacts of global warming. Some are written for popular audiences and tend to tell compelling stories while avoiding theory, while the books written for academic readers are often too arcane for popular audiences. My hope is that this book can bridge the divide, that it can be both a good read and a presentation of credible and accessible social theory. I lightly draw on theory in order to better explain what is happening to democracy due to the actions of the fossil fuel industry. I draw upon analyses by historians, political scientists, and economists, and I approach the topic of democracy using the work of journalists and investigators, as well as my own experience.

Perhaps most importantly, I bring together two areas of political analysis, one concerning "institutional capture," in which public institutions become instruments of private interests, and the other concerning "deep states," the state-within-a-state that arises when several key public institutions are captured and held for a long period by the same private interest. I argue the oil industry has captured and held enough different public institutions for a long enough time that a deep state has formed in Alberta and to a lesser degree across Canada, which by nature resists meaningful action on global warming. Naming, defining, and identifying "institutional capture" and "oil's deep state" enables us to understand and counter these processes, and to defend democracy and the environment.

★ ★ ★

Global warming caused by burning fossil fuels is not a comfortable or happy truth for me. I've spent my life in one of the world's great fossil fuel regions. Most of Canada's fossil fuels come from where I live: Alberta, home of the Athabasca oil sands and a major hub for the oil and gas industry. It is also home to several of Canada's biggest coal-fired power plants, fed by mines working thick seams of coal. Exploiting fossil fuels provides good employment, rich profits, high incomes, and low taxes in Alberta, across Canada, and in places far beyond. This book is an act of bearing witness to the environmental and political costs of these benefits.

With a century-long history and the opportunity to develop one of the planet's great carbon reserves, Canada's petroleum industry has a lot of influence in Alberta. An impressive portion of the industry is headquartered in Alberta, and it is active in major oil and gas fields around the world.[3] It may be Canada's most successful industry, forming a fully integrated sector of advanced research, software development, geo-engineering, equipment design, manufacturing, financing, production, upgrading, refining, transportation, and marketing. Different individuals and groups within the industry have differing priorities, attitudes, and politics. But this is a diversity united by a common commitment to fossil fuels. The fulfillment of its purpose is to find, produce, and sell oil and natural gas, bringing the industry into direct conflict with the need to slow global warming.

Global warming will force Alberta and all of Canada to change. There is a risk that, rather than abandoning fossil fuels and strengthening democracy, we will hang on to fossil fuels and begin to abandon democracy. Fossil fuels have made some people extraordinarily rich and powerful, and in defending their positions, some of them can be expected to place their personal privilege above the public good, no matter what the cost.

Many people helped with this book, and I thank them all. Glenn Rollans, who suffered with the patience of Job through many drafts, asked questions that always sent me back to my writing with a better focus. He has a vast knowledge of books, editing, and publishing, and I am lucky to call him a great friend. Anna Yeatman and Eric Sidoti of the Whitlam Institute at Western Sydney University in Australia created the opportunity that got me thinking more deeply about the topics explored herein. Kathryn Topinka was invaluable in digging up material on the Bruce Carson trial. David Cooper, Sheila Pratt, Paul Precht, and Tom Radford reviewed late drafts to help with clarity, accuracy, and depth. William McMillan encouraged me through early drafts. Martin Sharp, Jennifer Klutsch, and Jim Morrow advised me on the science of global warming. Grant Dunlop provided assistance at crucial moments, and Allan Wachowich and Marie Carlson helped sort out background details. I must also thank the wonderful librarians who repeatedly found material and dug up answers to my questions. Finally, I thank Jim Lorimer, whose enthusiastic response to a draft manuscript led to this book getting published. To the many others who assisted me, I am forever grateful.

The foundation for all my work is my wife, Jeanette Boman, and our sons Jordan and Spencer. They provide the support, encouragement, and clear-eyed feedback that is the lifeblood of writing. I cannot thank the three of them enough.

Despite the help of all these people, there are many imperfections in this book, all of which are my responsibility.

A note on terminology is needed. I use several terms that apply to hydrocarbon fuels, especially "fossil fuels," "oil," "petroleum," "natural gas," "coal," and "bitumen." If the context specifically requires one of these, I use it. In more general contexts, I choose the term that seems to fit best with the wording and meaning of the sentence or paragraph. My primary emphasis is on "the oil industry," which includes oil, natural gas, and bitumen extracted from the oil sands. The coal industry is also an important factor, especially in the United States, and in the American context I often use the term "fossil fuels."

Introduction
An unwitting experiment

In the calendar of world events, September 1992 had its share of noteworthy moments. The Toronto Blue Jays had a late season surge on their way to World Series victory the following month. Mariel Hemingway broke taboo by appearing nude on a television series. Natural disasters of various kinds struck Hawaii, France, Nicaragua and Pakistan; the siege of Sarajevo entered its sixth month and would continue for forty-one more; China conducted a nuclear test; and two Kurdish opposition leaders were assassinated. But as the decades passed, a different reason emerged to make September 1992 remarkable: It was the last ever cooler-than-average month.

NASA, the organization that put Neil Armstrong on the moon and ran the space shuttle program, takes great interest in the conditions and temperatures of the atmosphere, for understandable reasons. Working with organizations around the world, NASA has compiled average global temperatures at the surface of the Earth for every month since January 1880. They use the average of the period from 1951 to 1980 as a baseline and calculate global temperatures as either cooler or warmer than that baseline. January 1900, for example, was 0.38°C cooler than the baseline, and January 2000 was 0.26°C warmer.[4]

A careful look at the monthly data shows a stark pattern. From 1880 to 1900, the temperature was colder than the baseline more than nine months out of ten, and the world got even chillier from 1901 to 1920, when all but two months were colder than the baseline. Then the pattern started to change. Decade by decade, the number of warm days increased and the number of cool days declined. From 1961 to 1980, there was a near perfect split of 120 months cooler, 117 months warmer, and three months exactly on the baseline, with a decided shift toward warm months in the 1970s.

After that, it was no contest. Cool months simply faded away: The records show only four months after 1980 cooler than the baseline. Which brings us to September 1992, the last month the global average temperature was below the baseline, by just a hundredth of a degree Celsius.[5] From then on, the global records for heat were broken with numbing frequency; by 2015, the temperatures sometimes rose so fast they seemed to lift off the page and threaten to combust.

This should not be a surprise. In 1965, the science advisory committee to the president of the United States delivered a paper to President Lyndon B. Johnson, titled "Atmospheric Carbon Dioxide," which the president made public. It was written by five of America's leading climate scientists and was based on work stretching back to 1899. The scientists weighed the historic data, examined the best theories, and presented detailed computations. They concluded with a warning: "Through his worldwide industrial civilization, Man is unwittingly conducting a vast geophysical experiment. Within a few generations he is burning fossil fuels that slowly accumulated in the earth over the past 500 million years." This burning of fossil fuels emitted so much carbon dioxide that it "may be sufficient to produce measurable and perhaps marked changes in climate" that could be "deleterious from the point of view of human beings,"[6] including global warming, melting ice caps, and rising sea levels.

The warning of the committee was confirmed by growing bodies of research throughout the 1970s and 1980s, the results of which were so compelling they led to what is perhaps the largest gathering of world leaders in history: the 1992 Rio Earth Summit, formally called the United Nations Conference on Environment and Development.

Hosted by Brazil and with Canadian Maurice Strong as its secretary-general, the Rio Earth Summit reflected the scale of international concern about environmental issues. Governments from more than 150 countries participated, including 108 heads of state.[7] An estimated 2,400 representatives of non-governmental organizations, 10,000 journalists, and 17,000 other people travelled from around the world to witness presidents, prime ministers, and national leaders of all kinds endorse a range of agreements, including the *United Nations Framework Convention on Climate Change* (UNFCC). Article 4 of the UNFCC required countries to develop "policies and measures" to reduce "emissions of carbon dioxide and other greenhouse gases" to their 1990 levels.[8]

Despite the agreement at Rio and a number of subsequent treaties, coal, oil, and natural gas continued to be burned in record amounts. The 1965 US advisory committee had based its warning on a projection of CO_2 levels in the atmosphere rising 25 per cent from the mid-1800s to the year 2000. The actual rise was 30 per cent, and by 2015, it passed 40 per cent.[9] Carbon dioxide in the atmosphere reached levels unknown since long before humans existed and, as the science predicted, there was global warming, melting ice caps, and rising sea levels.

More than half a century has passed since the science advisory panel to President Johnson presented its forecast, and it has proven to be true. The causes of rising temperatures were clear — primarily the increase in atmospheric carbon dioxide from the burning of fossil fuels. So was the main solution: reducing emissions by curtailing the use of fossil fuels. Such was not to be. We understood the problem, we knew the solution, but we failed to act.

* * *

This book addresses the question, "why have democratic governments failed to act to reduce carbon emissions despite dire warnings and compelling evidence of a profound and growing threat of global warming?" There might be several reasons. Polling shows that many people believe the science is unsettled. In fact, the first detailed calculations to show that increasing carbon dioxide levels in the atmosphere would raise global temperatures were done in the 1890s by Swedish chemist Svante Arrhenius, an eventual Nobel prize winner.[10] Decades of scientific debate and analysis followed. By 1965, the basic points of the science were largely understood, and by 1990, the core causes of global warming were effectively settled.

A different argument made for inaction is that the human brain is not "wired" to deal with long-term threats like global warming.[11] For people who take this view, it is a matter of human biology. Yet people and governments deal with long-term issues all the time. To pick one example, Alberta's oil sands industry developed a twenty-five-year plan to expand oil sands production in 1995, which proved extraordinarily effective.

For other people, global warming is a matter for God, not for human beings. American Senator James Inhofe referred to the account of God's creation of Earth in the book of Genesis and claimed, "The arrogance of people to think that we, human beings, would be able to change what He is doing in the climate is to me outrageous."[12] Inhofe chaired the powerful US Senate Committee on the Environment and Public Works from 2003 to 2007 and returned to that position in 2015.

I take a different view. The reason governments have failed to respond to climate change by reducing carbon emissions is that the fossil fuel industry has worked very hard, both directly and indirectly, to oppose effective government responses. This book examines the capture of democratic institutions such as political parties, government bureaucracies, regulators, and universities, so that those institutions increasingly serve the interests not of democracy, science, or the public, but the interests of the fossil fuel industry, especially the oil industry.

* * *

This book ranges widely, from the minutes of backroom meetings made public through police investigations to the spectacular destruction of the Deepwater Horizon disaster. It describes the basic science of global warming and provides political context from Alberta, Ottawa, and Washington. If you want to go straight to the action, you can skip to Chapter One now. If you want a sense of where the journey leads and the theory behind it, read the next three paragraphs.

While the icon of democracy is elections, its substance is a system of institutions that makes democratically accountable government possible. Prominent among those institutions are parliaments and congresses, political parties, courts, civil services, universities, an unhindered media, and many others. To be effective, those institutions need the resources and independence to pursue their own mandates in the public interest, and they must be substantially autonomous; they should not become instruments of private interests or outside groups. Courts, for example, should be free from political meddling, and civil servants should be non-partisan in their work. In the unending contests of democracy, however, democratic institutions sometimes *do* become instruments of specific private interests. In other words, they are "captured." In a healthy democracy, the few captured institutions are restored to autonomy by the many institutions that remain autonomous. The police investigate the senate, for example; a judicial inquiry probes the activities of a political party; or an opposition party defeats a governing party that has lost touch with voters.

But what happens when a whole series of institutions falls under the sway of one outside interest? A central premise of this book is that when a number of institutions are captured and held long enough by the same interest, the capacity of the system to correct itself is paralyzed. This would happen, for example, when the governing party, the opposition party, the civil service, universities, and regulators are all following the lead of the same private interest. These captive institutions reinforce each other's captivity, and the ability of democracy to function in the public interest is impaired. Democracy falls into the grip of private interests that work the machinery of government for their own ends, powerful and enduring enough to form a state within the state: a deep state.

This book presents the argument that the petroleum industry in Canada, and especially in Alberta, has captured and held enough democratic institutions for long enough that it has formed a deep state, a hybrid public-private state-within-a-state that pursues its agenda regardless of the public interest. Global warming has been a catalyst for the rise of this deep state, because combatting it requires governments to reduce and then eliminate the burning of fossil fuels. Global warming is a death sentence for the fossil fuel industry, and to delay that sentence, the industry has spent untold millions of dollars and many years capturing key democratic institutions.

★ ★ ★

There are seventeen chapters in this book, divided into four parts. Part One (Chapters 1 to 5) opens with a trial in an Ottawa courtroom that exposed the strategies used by the oil industry to shape government policy and public discourse. It then links the Canadian experience to the United States, revealing some of the industry's ties to the George W. Bush government and exploring the implications of the 2010 Deepwater Horizon disaster in the Gulf of Mexico. It closes with an analysis of the ties between the fossil fuel industry and the hard right political movement that carried Donald Trump to the White House in 2016. Part Two (Chapters 6 to 8) provides a brief analysis of how a modern democracy functions through its institutions and introduces the concept of institutional capture. Part Two then presents a theory of the deep state and closes with a chapter on how an economy heavily dependent on oil production sets the stage for a deep state. Part Three (Chapters 9 to 16), the longest section of the book, exposes both the depth and the breadth of oil's deep state in Alberta, and uses first-hand accounts to contrast the efforts of Peter Lougheed's government to assert control over Alberta's oil industry with the descent into capture during the Klein government. Part Four (Chapter 17) provides a review and concludes with a call to action for concerned citizens, illustrating how we can protect both our democracy and our environment.

PART ONE
BREAKDOWN

Chapter 1
EPIC: The oil industry comes to call

In 2011, the commercial crimes unit of the RCMP in Ottawa began an investigation into the lobbying activities of Bruce Carson. Known as "the mechanic" in federal Conservative circles for fixing political problems[13] and likened to a "secret sauce" for his ability to connect the petroleum industry to the Harper government,[14] Carson was well acquainted with both sides of the law.[15] He had a law degree from the University of Ottawa and a master's degree in constitutional law from the University of Toronto. He began practising law in the 1970s and, for many years, held senior staff positions with Conservative caucuses in the Ontario legislature and the Canadian parliament. From 2004 to 2006, he worked as the director of policy research for federal Leader of the Opposition Stephen Harper. On the day Harper was sworn in as prime minister in 2006, Carson went to work in the Prime Minister's Office (PMO) as legislative assistant and then senior advisor to the prime minister. He was at the heart of power. Three years later, he went from the PMO to the University of Calgary to head a multi-million–dollar research centre on energy and the environment. He travelled as a guest speaker, advisor, and advocate, and mixed constantly with cabinet ministers, diplomats, the highest civil servants, and the most powerful CEOs in Canada's surging petroleum industry. In 2014, he published a book on the success of the conservative movement in Canada with the prestigious McGill-Queen's University Press.[16]

It was a glorious ride. It was also a notorious ride.

Carson couldn't stay out of trouble. As a young lawyer in 1977, he and his then-wife were sued by a developer to recover an Ottawa house. In the next few years, he was in court for bouncing cheques, defaulting on a mortgage, and failing to make lease payments on a car. In 1983, he was convicted on two counts of theft, sentenced to eighteen months in jail, and lost his licence to practise law. In 1990, he pleaded guilty to defrauding two different banks and a car rental company and, as a condition of his sentence, was required to undergo psychiatric treatment. For the next two decades, Carson stayed out of court.

Then his life blew up on the front pages. A major story by the Aboriginal Peoples Television Network in 2011 alleged that Carson, now sixty-five, was wrongly using his extensive government connections to help his twenty-two-year-old girlfriend and her mother secure contracts for their water treatment business. The story was spiced by the age difference between Carson and his girlfriend and by her past work as an escort, complete with racy photos. Carson's powerful positions and close ties to Stephen Harper were well known, and his long history of legal troubles was resurrected by reporters. Under pressure from the opposition, Carson's long-time ally Harper asked the RCMP to investigate, and in July 2012, Carson was charged with influence-peddling. With trials and appeals, the case took years to work through the courts. In February 2017, Ontario's highest court reversed the decision of a lower court and found him guilty.[17] This case, however, was only half of Carson's legal troubles. The other half was much more revealing.

Sparked by formal complaints and aided by evidence from the federal ethics commissioner, a second line of investigation into Carson was opened by the RCMP in late 2011, one that had nothing to do with his girlfriend. Police found evidence that, in the years after Carson left the PMO, he engaged in what could be illegal lobbying by repeatedly connecting the energy industry to a range of public officials. Charges were laid under the *Lobbying Act*, and in May 2016, Bruce Carson, seventy years old and in failing health, was put on trial in the handsome, stone-clad Ottawa provincial courthouse.

In September, Madam Justice Catherine Kehoe delivered her verdict: guilty on all three counts.[18] Two months later, Justice Kehoe, saying "the public interest is high" and Carson's "blameworthiness could not be more clear,"[19] sentenced him to pay a total of $50,000 in fines. Carson's lawyer said his client was destitute and filed an appeal on both the guilty verdict and the sentence. At the time of writing, the appeals had not been decided.

The hundreds of pages of evidence presented in Carson's illegal lobbying trial shed light on the permanent campaign by Canada's oil industry to influence government. In Canada, evidence presented in trials is almost always available to the public, so the Carson trial opened a rare glance into the backrooms of power for those who really wanted to look. Police seized computers, searched emails, studied documents, and conducted intense interviews with prominent people unaccustomed to such scrutiny. The police investigation, the dozens of documents filed in court, and Justice Kehoe's ruling, when combined with media investigations and material obtained through access to information requests by watchdog groups, gave insight into how the oil industry pursued public institutions. They showed boundaries between organizations had broken down, and relationships among private and public interests that should have been arm's length became group hugs.

Ironically, the *Lobbying Act* under which Carson was charged was enacted by the same government he served. Its purpose was to let the public know which lobbyists were meeting with which public officials for what reasons. The *Act* prohibited people who held senior government positions, such as Carson's, from being paid to lobby for five years after they left their positions.

The *Lobbying Act* is like border surveillance: Public and private interests are separate arenas, and citizens have a right to know and control who crosses the border from one to the other. Strong organizational boundaries around public institutions keep them from falling under the sway of any particular private interest and provide a democratic society with a variety of independent voices. The *Lobbying Act* recognizes that democratic institutions need to be kept separate from private interests; the two should interact, but they must not merge. In a democracy they serve different masters.

Two of the three charges against Carson involved his activities with an organization called the Energy Policy Institute of Canada (EPIC), and the third charge involved the Canada School of Energy and Environment (CSEE). It is important to note here that no one else involved with EPIC or CSEE was investigated for anything illegal.

EPIC was established to represent a substantial group of Canada's largest energy corporations, including Canadian Natural Resources Limited (CNRL), Suncor, Imperial Oil, Enbridge, TransCanada, and more than two dozen others. As Justice Kehoe wrote in her ruling, EPIC's "sole purpose was to bring together major private oil, gas and energy producers and later consumers." EPIC was not cheap to join: membership fees were $50,000 to $100,000 a year, depending on the nature of involvement.[20]

EPIC was incorporated on October 7, 2009, became the centre of an intense flurry of activity, and closed shop at the end of July 2014.[21] Its incorporation papers listed three directors: Douglas Black, David Emerson, and Gerard (Gerry) Protti,[22] who were among a roster of impressive people involved in EPIC during its short life.

• **Douglas Black**, a founding director and a president of EPIC, was a prominent Calgary lawyer with expertise in corporate, commercial, and energy law. Appointed to the University of Calgary Board of Governors in 2007,[23] he became its chair in 2011 and stepped down in October 2012. An active member of the federal Conservative Party, he was appointed to the Senate by Stephen Harper in January 2013, after winning a non-binding Alberta election for the position.

• **David Emerson**, a founding director and a chair of EPIC, had a PhD in economics.[24] He had worked as deputy minister of finance in B.C., CEO of a bank, and CEO of a large forest products company. First elected to parliament as a Liberal in Paul Martin's government in 2004, he crossed the floor to join Stephen Harper's Conservative cabinet two weeks after the 2006 election, stirring voter outrage. He left politics in 2008, choosing not to test his fortune with voters another time.

• **Gerry Protti**, a founding director of EPIC, was an extremely well-connected veteran of Alberta's energy industry.[25] Trained as an economist, Protti had been an assistant deputy minister at the Alberta Department of Energy before crossing into the petroleum industry. For many years he worked with EnCana and other companies, and was the founding president of the industry's most powerful interest group, the Canadian Association of Petroleum Producers (CAPP). Protti was on the University of Alberta Board of Governors from 2004 to 2010.

While Black, Emerson, and Protti had their names on EPIC's incorporation papers, they were joined by other key figures.

• **Larry Clausen** served as EPIC's communications consultant and secretary-treasurer.[26] Clausen had spent his career in

public relations in Calgary. In January 2010, three months
after EPIC was founded, he became senior executive at
the Calgary office of public relations firm Cohn & Wolfe.[27]
The office address on EPIC's incorporation papers was the
same Calgary address eventually occupied by the firm.
Cohn & Wolfe was part of a massive public relations and
communications network tied to a company called WPP.

WPP affiliates worked with many of the world's largest
corporations, including Exxon/Mobil, the largest shareholder
in Imperial Oil. In its 2010 *Annual Report*, WPP, referring to
its affiliate Hill and Knowlton as "the firm," said,

> The firm assisted the Canadian Association of
> Petroleum Producers (CAPP) on industry-wide
> programs around Responsible Canadian Energy,
> driving an international conversation around Canada's
> oil sands by bringing together serious-minded
> business, environmental, sustainability, academic,
> aboriginal and community leaders.[28]

• **Thomas D'Aquino**, first chair of EPIC,[29] was president of the
Canadian Council of Chief Executives from 1981 to December
31, 2009. In 2009, this council was composed of 150 of
Canada's most powerful CEOs. According to at least one claim,
it was "the world's most effective CEO-based organization
dedicated to public policy development and solutions."[30]

• **Daniel Gagnier**, vice-chair, president, and committee
member of EPIC,[31] had worked as a deputy minister of energy
in Ontario and a chief of staff to Liberal Premier Jean Charest
in Quebec and Liberal Premier David Peterson in Ontario.
He had worked for thirteen years as a senior executive with

mining and aluminum company Alcan. Gagnier would be caught in controversy in October 2015 when, while serving as co-chair of the federal Liberal election campaign, he wrote an email to several officials at TransCanada Corporation advising them on how to approach a new federal government.[32] The email concluded:

> An energy strategy for Canada is on the radar and we need a spear carrier for those in the industry who are part of the solution going forward rather than refusing to grasp the implications of a changing global reality. The last point is critical as Federal leadership and a discussion with Premiers will take place early. This is where we can play and help them get things right. Glad to answer any questions. Dan[33]

It is difficult to know from the context just who the "we" playing with the federal government would be.

• **Frank McKenna**, a co-chair of EPIC, is best known to the public as the Liberal premier of New Brunswick from 1987 to 1997 and Canada's ambassador to the United States in 2005–06. New Brunswick was home to Canada's largest oil refinery, owned by the billionaire Irving family, and McKenna was a keen supporter of both the family and their refinery.[34] The Irving refinery was the eastern terminus for TransCanada's planned Energy East pipeline, delivering Alberta oil and bitumen to the east coast. McKenna had served many years on the board of directors of CNRL, one of the largest petroleum companies in Canada, and was deputy chair of TD Bank Financial.

These and other people within EPIC were spectacularly connected through interlocking corporate and professional positions, social circles, and political affiliations. They formed an all-star network for the oil industry that could plug in to Conservative and Liberal circles; federal and provincial interests; B.C., the Prairies, Ontario, Quebec, and Atlantic Canada; corporate and government figures; and elected and appointed officials. Few calls from this group were likely to go unanswered.

★ ★ ★

It is not clear when the idea to form EPIC was hatched, but it did not materialize out of thin air. Interests with serious intent and deep pockets pushed it into being. When its founding meeting was held on August 13, 2009, a twenty-page package of sophisticated by-laws was presented, which defined, among other things, the role of a "strategic advisory board" and named Black as president and D'Aquino and Carson as co-chairpersons.[35] The minutes for the meeting,[36] obtained by police, noted that "A preliminary budget of $2.9 million was reviewed. It was felt this was reasonable but it was noted further review would occur . . ." The minutes give no indication of who prepared the budget or where the $2.9 million would come from. At the meeting, Carson[37] and D'Aquino were awarded honoraria of $60,000 per year, and Black was appointed president for a two-year term at $10,000 a month. This is also when Clausen became secretary-treasurer.

EPIC's "Founding Charter" was finalized a month later, on September 9, 2009. In an interview with RCMP, D'Aquino explained that "EPIC's goal was to develop an Energy Strategy for Canada . . ."[38] This was a goal of remarkable ambition. EPIC and its backers, primarily the oil industry, weren't lobbying to change a particular policy or get support for a specific project. They weren't looking for a tax break or a change in environmental standards. Their goal was to do something that would be led by national governments in other democracies: develop an energy strategy — oil, gas, coal, electricity, nuclear, pipelines, renewables — for all of Canada. In effect, EPIC was founded with the ambition of capturing the energy policy of a nation, with the oil industry *de facto* in a privileged position. If it succeeded, every resident, government, and business in the country would be affected.

D'Aquino told RCMP investigators that EPIC's strategy had four points. The first was to get "all the private sector leaders engaged and on board." Given the people and money behind EPIC, this was in hand before the organization was even launched. Second was "to build support by engaging the academic community, the ones writing about energy." Third was to build "public sensitivity" through newspapers and magazines, and fourth was to "take their ideas for an energy strategy . . . to municipal, provincial and federal governments."[39]

The investigation by police shows how quickly and effectively EPIC moved. It was able to jump, as it were, onto a train that had been put in motion well before the organization was set up. And that train was already hurtling down the track.

Universities had been early to get on board, well ahead of EPIC's creation and nicely in line with the strategy of "engaging the academic community." The University of Calgary led the way, with the University of Alberta and others coming right along.

In September 2006, three years before EPIC was incorporated, the University of Calgary sent President Harvey Weingarten and scientist David Keith to meet with Bruce Carson in his position at the PMO and to pitch the idea behind the Canada School of Energy and Environment (CSEE). The vision for CSEE was to connect academics and scholars worldwide through a powerful, web-based information system hosted in Alberta. As the University of Alberta, one of CSEE's eventual partners, described it, "This will enable Canadians and researchers around the world to have easy access to materials from a range of academic disciplines in a variety of formats . . ."[40] CSEE would become a virtual meeting place where the brightest minds in the fields of energy and environmental issues could instantly share information.

Weingarten and Keith must have been convincing when they met Carson. It likely helped that they were from Calgary, home of Carson's boss, Stephen Harper, who had been elected prime minister just nine months earlier. When Harper's Minister of Finance Jim Flaherty delivered the federal budget the following March, he also delivered $15 million for CSEE, which would have branches operating under different names at the universities of Calgary, Alberta, and Lethbridge. No doubt it was a joyful day for Weingarten and Keith. The joy would not last.

The following year, on August 14, 2008, Carson himself took the helm of CSEE, even though he kept his position at the PMO until the end of October and took an unpaid leave to return there for another month in January 2009.[41]

A month before he headed to CSEE, in his capacity as senior advisor in the PMO, Carson had met with the president of Shell Canada, David Collyer. Collyer followed proper procedure and registered the meeting with the federal commissioner of lobbying.[42] The subject matter listed for the meeting was only one word, "environment," so it's impossible to know the details of their meeting. A month later, in August 2008, Carson went to CSEE. In September, Collyer left Shell to become head of the powerful Canadian Association of Petroleum Producers (CAPP). In October, EPIC was launched, fully formed and well financed. Carson and Collyer would be spending a great deal of time together with EPIC, working on a fossil fuel future for Canada.

Carson's offer of employment with the University of Calgary provided him with a base salary of $258,000 per year, a car allowance of $900 per month, and a package of other benefits.[43] It also granted him an adjunct appointment in the newly formed School of Policy Studies at the University of Calgary,[44] reporting to its director, Dr. Jack Mintz. The School of Policy Studies, soon renamed the School of Public Policy, had been launched just a few months earlier with a $4 million endowment from one of Calgary's top oil investors and an early grant of $1 million from Imperial Oil. Mintz himself was on the board of directors of Imperial Oil; indeed, we'll see Dr. Mintz again later in this book.

Carson was neither a scientist nor an academic, but he was in charge at CSEE. He soon hired as deputy director Zoe Addington, who had worked closely with two members of the Harper cabinet — Tony Clement and Jim Prentice — and who would eventually leave CSEE to work for the petroleum giant CNRL. In September 2014, she moved to the office of Alberta's new premier, Jim Prentice, to become deputy chief of staff for policy coordination.[45]

Carson acted quickly in his new job. He revamped the mandate of CSEE, a change that exasperated CSEE's first scientist, David Keith. In frustration, Keith moved to Harvard and eventually wrote about his experience with CSEE in the *Toronto Star*:

> I assumed Carson would take his new mandate seriously and we could maintain an independent, university-based centre that could serve as a neutral convening ground for a wide variety of perspectives from the oil patch to environmental advocates. I was wrong . . . It soon became clear that Carson was simply using his academic post to further the interests of the Conservative government and a narrow segment of the energy industry . . . Carson worked closely with industry leaders to produce meetings and reports that had the patina of stakeholder representation while in fact aiming to avoid meaningful public debate. Leaders of Alberta's universities did nothing substantive to manage the problem until Carson's scandal forced their hands. Even then, they failed to act decisively to ensure that public money was used for research that supported broad public interests.[46]

The make-up of the CSEE board gave an indication of the organizational entwining underway. The six-person board included the presidents of the universities of Alberta, Calgary, and Lethbridge, plus the chairman of the board of governors of the University of Lethbridge. It also included Douglas Black, who was a member of the University of Calgary Board of Governors and who would become the founding president of EPIC. The chair of CSEE was Brian

Heidecker, who was also the chair of the University of Alberta Board of Governors and a former vice-president of the Alberta Progressive Conservative Party. It was under Heidecker's watch that Carson was hired to CSEE, and it was left to Heidecker to explain the hiring when Carson resigned in disgrace.

★ ★ ★

Throughout 2009 and 2010, CSEE and EPIC worked tirelessly to bring universities, public servants, and politicians together on a single agenda for the energy industry. The boundaries separating these organizations began to break down, and it was soon hard to tell where one ended and the next began. CSEE, based in universities, had overlapping staff and board members with industry-based EPIC, as well as board members with strong ties to the Alberta Progressive Conservative Party and the federal Conservative Party, both of which formed governments that were aggressively advocating oil sands, pipeline, and fossil fuel development. As CSEE's executive director, Carson was paid over a quarter million dollars annually to head a major university institute, while he was simultaneously collecting substantial pay from EPIC. His pay from EPIC jumped from $5,000 per month when he started, to $10,000 per month between February 2010 and February 2011.[47] CSEE worked closely with the Canadian Association of Petroleum Producers (CAPP) on drafting reports to politicians and CEOs,[48] and was fully engaged with federal and provincial civil servants through a very active working group.

Not everyone approved. The federal conflicts of interest and ethics commissioner was taking an interest in Carson's role; some reporters and opposition MPs were starting to take note; and even Guy Giorno, Stephen Harper's chief of staff from 2008 to 2010, raised concerns. The Canadian Association of University Teachers was also concerned and published an article about CSEE in May 2011, titled "Collaborations: Are Universities Sacrificing Integrity?"[49] By then, formal investigations into Carson were underway by the ethics commissioner and then the police, and he had resigned. His bright but brief university career was over.

Chapter 2
The civil service falls in line

No doubt the federal civil servants involved with Carson, CSEE, and EPIC were pressed hard by the political staff and ministers of the Harper government. It would be easy for civil servants to turn a blind eye to global warming and other risks when thousands of jobs and billions of dollars of investment and government revenue were on offer. Perhaps they were also daunted by the wealth, size, and sheer forcefulness of the oil industry, which was overwhelmingly headquartered in Calgary, where Harper made his home and where voters repeatedly elected him to parliament. Harper was born and raised in Toronto, where his father worked as an accountant for Imperial Oil. Harper moved to Alberta as a young man; graduated from the University of Calgary; and cultivated deep roots with prominent political science, history, and economics professors there. For two decades, he had worked the front rooms and backrooms of Calgary's well-financed and unusually active conservative political scene, and as his political power grew, so did his prominence with oil, gas, coal, and pipeline companies.

Whatever the reasons, by 2009, top civil servants were falling into line for a fossil fuel future in Canada. The plan behind EPIC was unfolding much as Thomas D'Aquino would later indicate in his police interview: The energy industry was taking its strategy to governments through both elected politicians and some of the highest civil servants in the land.[50]

In the spring of 2009, Carson was head of CSEE and on the brink of taking his role with EPIC.[51] In April, he accompanied federal environment minister Jim Prentice to Washington, DC. He joined Prentice, Canadian ambassador Michel Wilson, and two staff in a meeting with American Secretary of Energy Steven Chu. When questioned about Carson's presence at the meeting, Environment Canada described him as "an unpaid adviser to the deputy minister of environment."[52] Curiously, during this period, the deputy minister of environment wrote a letter to the federal ethics commissioner registering concerns about Carson's role.[53] Wires seemed to be getting crossed somewhere.

The documents presented in court during Carson's trial peeled away the covers on the activities of the oil industry, EPIC, CSEE, and governments. By June, governments and industry had agreed to establish an "Oil and Gas Working Group."[54] The federal government commonly used working groups to address issues; the striking thing about this one was the power of its members. It included a senior member from the Canadian Association of Petroleum Producers (CAPP), whose name was blacked out in police documents; deputy ministers of environment from the federal, Alberta, and Saskatchewan governments (deputy ministers are the most powerful civil servants); and Bruce Carson as chair.[55]

One of the working group's tasks was to lay the groundwork for a meeting on June 5, 2009, between environment minister Prentice and "Key Oil and Gas Industry Representatives." "Good progress has been achieved to date by the Working Group," said the background note to the meeting.[56]

Three days after the meeting between Prentice and key industry representatives, a CAPP official emailed Carson at CSEE and copied two other CAPP officials (all CAPP names are struck out in the police documents). The email showed CAPP's leading role in the working group: "Attached is a draft outline of the work plan," said the CAPP official. "The last couple of pages pastes work plan elements into the format of the original list of issues for discussion as a check that we are covering them off . . ."[57]

Carson's assistant then forwarded the email from CAPP, along with the work plan, to the federal deputy minister of environment, the most powerful environmental official in the country; an assistant federal deputy minister of environment; and the deputy ministers of environment for Alberta[58] and Saskatchewan. The cover note by Carson's assistant gives a sense of how seamlessly CAPP's approach to the work plan was given to civil servants: "Hello, Bruce was asked to circulate this to the group. He has not had time to read it yet today but wanted you to have it ASAP."[59]

The four pages of the work plan address the concerns of the oil and gas industry. The first bullet point under item one speaks to emissions: "Growth: Accommodated as it occurs (i.e. no overall cap) through free allocation to facilities."[60] The parenthetical clarification, "(i.e. no overall cap)," is in the original. The implication was that the option of capping emissions would be precluded from the start; the oil industry was working to engineer the very DNA of government climate change policy to its advantage.

Industry was particularly focused on the federal government's Department of Natural Resources. In her ruling, Justice Kehoe spent several paragraphs discussing the relationship between Carson and the most senior civil servant in that department, Deputy Minister Cassie Doyle.[61] Kehoe noted Carson and Doyle had worked "very closely" in previous positions, and that Doyle "knew that Mr. Carson, as a result of his years with the prime minister's office, had extensive connections with the federal public service, including connections with the clerk of the privy council office and access to deputy ministers." She noted that Doyle, from her position inside the civil service, advised Carson "as to how to proceed and whom he should contact" in various emails that discuss meetings with federal, provincial, industry, and university officials.

In June 2009, an email sent by Doyle indicated the close relationship between her department and the oil industry. Doyle had just received an email from Dave Collyer, the president of CAPP, listing CAPP's desired participants at an upcoming June 12 meeting between Clerk of the Privy Council Kevin Lynch and nine of Canada's most powerful oil executives.[62] Doyle replied to Collyer with this message:

> Dave, as we discussed earlier today, please feel free to invite others to ensure full representation of CAPP's oil sands committee. This will ensure that we're fully aligned and issues raised by Murray[63] are resolved.[64]

It is worth taking stock here. The clerk of the privy council is the highest civil servant in the country. Privy councils predate parliaments and can be traced to the "private councils" that worked in the inner sanctums of royal courts in early England, advising kings and queens. The clerk of the privy council is its chief. In Canada, all federal civil servants ultimately report to the clerk through their deputy ministers, and the clerk in turn reports to the prime minister.

Remember those boundaries that protect the independence of democratic institutions? As a symbol of the separation of the civil service from party politics, the clerk of the privy council is chosen by the prime minister, but actually hired by the governor-general, because the governor-general, as the monarch's representative and the head of state, stands apart from party politics.

When a deputy minister such as Cassie Doyle wants to ensure "full alignment" among a group including the clerk of the privy council (her boss); the most senior officials in the federal department of natural resources (her subordinates); the largest corporations in the oil sands industry; and industry organization CAPP, it seems fair to say the boundaries separating the government and the oil industry are breaking down.

The records of the June 12, 2009, meetings[65] suggest this breakdown continued. The meeting notes taken by a federal official list the names of the energy industry leaders, all from oil companies, who met with Clerk of the Privy Council Kevin Lynch and Deputy Minister Cassie Doyle. After several blanked out lines, the notes say, "The effort is critical given the crucial role the oil sector plays in the Canadian economy today and into the foreseeable future." After several more redacted lines, the notes continue, referring to the federal Department of Natural Resources as "NRCan": "It also needs to be a concerted and on-going effort that runs for a year to 18 months. It was agreed that Doyle/NRCan and Carson/Canada School would be part of an upcoming meeting of the CEO working group on oil sands/energy."

The notes from that day also record a meeting in the afternoon among Lynch, Doyle, Carson, and the presidents of the universities of Alberta, Calgary, and Saskatchewan, discussing the need to focus university research on "clean energy/GHG reductions." (The term *clean energy* is commonly used in these emails and notes, although it generally refers to fossil fuels, including from the oil sands.) Lynch, with his immense influence over federal budgets and policies, weighed in on institutional priorities for the university presidents:

> The discussion focused on the need to better understand and
> co-ordinate university research being done on clean energy/
> GHG reductions. The Clerk said the focus should be on:
> what do we know and have learned; what more do we need
> to know; and, what areas are we deficient and where are we
> strong in terms of research.

The notes close with this plan: "Next steps will be for Carson/Canada School to set an agenda for a subsequent meeting with CEOs, governments and universities which would define where research should focus its efforts on clean energy"[66]; the final lines have been blanked out. Bruce Carson, soon to be on the payroll of the petroleum industry's EPIC, was literally setting the agenda for clean energy research in Canada. With major universities in two provinces and the federal government on board, the pieces were starting to come together nicely for the oil industry.

Once again it is worth taking stock. The most powerful civil servant in Canada stepped into an afternoon meeting with the presidents of three major public universities. Though the universities were large, they were financial dust mites in that room. The federal government's budget that year was 170 times larger than the budget of the largest of these universities.[67] The clerk of the privy council could whisper a few directives and arrange enough crumbs from the federal budget to deliver a glorious feast to the universities.

The clerk had just spent the morning in a closed session with nine of the most powerful corporate heads of Canada's oil industry. His deputy on the file supported the oil industry, as did his boss, the prime minister. It was time to act. No matter that universities, as provincial creations, were not under his jurisdiction. No matter that they had boards of governors of their own, and that academics liked to think they, not heads of corporations and powerful civil servants, set research agendas.

By the summer of 2009, CAPP was working closely with environment and energy officials in the federal, Alberta, and Saskatchewan governments on writing a report from the working group to ministers and CEOs on energy policy, to be delivered July 22. An email from a CAPP official to civil servants said, "Thanks for picking up most of our comments on the earlier draft. There are two areas where we have outstanding concerns regarding the draft . . ."[68] The first was about the way greenhouse gas standards were defined and described, and the email asked for a change: "(i.e. don't single out oil sands in the design of the framework)." The second was for the report to "address the issue of competitiveness. We had proposed language in our earlier comments that addressed this issue, but would be open to other wording." The final paragraph of the email said,

> My preference would be to issue the final version of this report to CEOs and Ministers on a confidential basis in advance of the meeting on Wednesday. It is a comprehensive description of the results of our work activity and I think it is important that the group go into the meeting with a common basis for the discussion. Thanks, [name redacted].

This confidential report may have appeared fresh and new to various federal and provincial ministers, but it would have been old hat to industry CEOs. They and their representatives had been directly involved in preparing it; it was almost like they had been writing a report to themselves, with the friendly cooperation of federal and provincial civil servants. Messages of support for the fossil fuel industry would have bounced back and forth among corporations, CAPP, CSEE, universities, and federal and provincial civil servants. The ministers who needed to make the final decisions and sell it to the public were caught in a policy echo chamber where every voice resonated with the same pro–fossil fuel messages. At this point, the boundaries separating the civil service, universities, and the industry seemed almost to have disappeared.

* * *

All this was achieved before EPIC was formed, and it cleared a political path for that organization to follow. Introducing EPIC to the situation was like introducing a catalyst to a chemical reaction: The close cooperation of civil servants with industry seemed to accelerate. One morning in March 2010, for example, three of CAPP's highest officials hosted a meeting attended by three top civil servants from Alberta and two from

Ottawa. The minutes of the meeting say its purpose "was to discuss a proposal that CAPP had for the oil sands CEO task force on 'upping their game' on oil sands outreach and communications as part of a renewed strategy."[69] Department of Natural Resources (NRCan) officials were keen: "NRCan's role in this work was noted but others identified that Environment Canada is a critical player. Deputy Minister Doyle acknowledged this and noted how closely we were working together."

The meeting discussed the federal–provincial–industry working group and a separate steering committee of deputy ministers and CEOs, and reviewed the work of a different steering committee of assistant deputy ministers and CAPP. After lunch, the meeting held a conference call with Alberta's Minister of Environment Rob Renner just before he attended Question Period in the Alberta Legislature in Edmonton, where he was grilled by the Official Opposition (I was there, and we were unaware of the conference call) on a proposed "downgrading" of environmental impact assessments.[70] After the conference call, the meeting continued at CAPP headquarters, high in the towers of downtown Calgary, where Deputy Minister Doyle told the meeting, "NRCan has been working with CAPP on this for some time and it is now time to up our game."

While the civil servants were "upping their game" for the oil industry, EPIC was more than pulling its weight. By September 2011, it produced four substantial documents, including the forty-page "Strategy for Canada's Global Energy Leadership Framework" and a twenty-two-page presentation to the July 2011 conference of ministers of energy. EPIC and its allies also had a hand in a series of high-profile events across the country. These followed the approach Hill and Knowlton had described for CAPP, which was to drive a "conversation around Canada's oil sands by bringing together serious-minded business, environmental, sustainability, academic, aboriginal and community leaders." Hill and Knowlton, recall, is a branch of WPP, the corporate family that included Cohn & Wolfe, the company that employed Larry Clausen, EPIC's secretary-treasurer.

This "conversation" hopscotched across Canada like a kind of travelling circus. It started in October 2009 with a meeting of carefully selected think tanks in Winnipeg, which found there was a "consensus" about Canada's energy future. It continued in April 2010 in Banff, when "65 leaders met and reached a broad consensus on the need for a pan-Canadian energy strategy."[71] The conversation returned to Winnipeg that August to be discussed by all Canada's premiers at the Council of the Federation. From there, it went to Montreal in September, where the annual meeting of energy ministers from across the country worked on it and their deputies were "mandated to follow up." The following spring, it was back to Winnipeg again, with "80 leaders finding common ground and more work to do." In summer 2011, the conversation moved to the annual meeting of energy ministers at the resort of Kananaskis, Alberta, and in November, it travelled to Halifax for more "dialogue."

This parade of meetings was just a fraction of the efforts of the fossil fuel industry to shape public policy. From July 2008 to November 2012, oil industry CEOs, lobbyists, and associations such as EPIC had 2,733 meetings or communications with federal government officials, ministers, and members of parliament — almost six times as many as occurred with environmental groups on similar topics.[72] The effort was worthwhile. Many of EPIC's recommendations to ease approval processes for oil sands, pipelines, and other projects were adopted by the federal *Canadian Environmental Assessment Act 2012* and the National Energy Board, sometimes word for word.[73] EPIC acknowledged as much in one of its final reports:

> While all EPIC recommendations were presented as a work in progress, some were so compelling that they were accepted and acted upon. Notably, the Honourable Joe Oliver, Minister of Natural Resources, announced significant improvements to the country's regulatory framework, much of which was reflective of our regulatory document and recommendations.[74]

The fossil fuel industry was helping write the government's rules.

Justice Kehoe's ruling on Carson filled in the picture of EPIC: "The intent of EPIC was to help design regulatory processes and make recommendations on regulatory reform," she wrote.[75] Later in her ruling, she noted that every key element of EPIC's Canadian Energy Strategy carried a set of recommendations for action, and she found that EPIC was "proposing regulations or changes to regulations and regulatory processes for federal, provincial, territorial and municipal government." The first example of an EPIC recommendation she noted was to "Design a Canadian energy strategy as a federal-provincial-territorial-municipal construct."[76] This begs the question: In a healthy democracy, is that properly the task of an industry group?

During his trial, Carson's lawyers argued he was acting on his own and therefore was not lobbying. Justice Kehoe didn't buy it. She concluded Carson was part of a much larger process:

> I reject the submission by the defence that Mr. Carson was acting on his own . . . He was working on behalf of EPIC and its membership. From the outset the sole purpose and mandate of EPIC was to develop a national and/or global energy strategy for Canada.[77]

A few pages later, Kehoe, having culled from seized emails a list of people and organizations with whom Carson and EPIC communicated, wrote:

> The emails prove that the Executive Committee of EPIC knew who, why and how Mr. Carson was communicating with . . . and approved of Mr. Carson's communications and the progress he was making moving EPIC's policy development forward . . .[78]

The list of seized emails included ones from three federal departments, two provincial governments, the clerk of the privy council, the prime minister's chief of staff, and energy ministers from across the country.

In her sentencing report, Kehoe took the EPIC process to task:

> It is especially egregious in the case of EPIC where Mr. Carson was representing a non-profit corporation set up to represent numerous major private Oil and Gas Energy Companies whose sole purpose was to develop energy policy for Canada for the commercial benefit of the companies while the public including other interested companies, environmentalists, etc. *had no knowledge of what was transpiring behind the scene with Ministers, Deputy Ministers, and other very senior officials in government, both federal and provincial.*[79] [italics added]

In a Shakespearian twist, one of Carson's final email exchanges from his positions with EPIC and CSEE was with Nigel Wright. Wright had recently left a senior position with Onex Corporation to become chief of staff to Prime Minister Harper. Onex, incidentally, was an associate member of EPIC, and Wright would eventually return to Onex after resigning in disgrace from the PMO during the Mike Duffy scandal in May 2013.[80, 81] Carson, working late on the wintry evening of January 21, 2011, emailed Wright:

> Nigel — I don't think we have ever met — but we have a few mutual friends — so firstly good luck with this great adventure you have taken on — and secondly thought I would share with you a report I just finished on energy — would also like to talk to you about some work I am doing on energy with Shawn Atleo — the AFN National Chief — would love to meet with you at your convenience — bc[82]

The following afternoon, Wright found time to reply:

Bruce,
I've heard a lot of good things about you. Feel free to give me a call at any time. I'll read the report over the weekend.
Nigel[83]

How the mighty would fall.

Bruce Carson's 2011 resignation barely caused a flutter in industry's campaign to establish an energy strategy for Canada. With or without him, the drive for a fossil fuel future continued, and the federal government gave full support. The Harper Conservatives curtailed regulatory processes and stifled the voices of federal scientists who might have dissenting views.[84] They rewrote legislation to reduce environmental and First Nations' requirements affecting pipelines, oil sands expansion, and other fossil fuel projects, and weakened the autonomy of the country's main energy regulator,[85] the National Energy Board (NEB). In 2015, political scientist Lorna Stefanick called it "neutralizing dissent," and it was comprehensive and aggressive:

> . . . the federal government passed Bill C-38 in 2012, a massive omnibus bill that included a completely new environmental assessment law, repealed the Kyoto Protocol Implementation Act, weakened protection of at-risk species, decreased opportunities for public participation in environmental decision-making, weakened accountability by allowing more decisions to be made by cabinet and individual ministers, allowed cabinet to override decisions made by the National Energy Board, and contained an entirely new environmental assessment law that sets timelines for environmental

assessment hearings and narrows the range of projects that
will come under review.[86]

In October 2012, this was followed by Bill C-45, which weakened
standards in both the *Navigation Protection Act* and the *Environmental
Protection Act*, which might slow oil and gas development.[87] The government
pushed the bills through parliament using procedural tactics that
undercut opposition and gave little time for public response. Although the
bills overhauled environmental and other laws, they were actually budget
bills, each over four hundred pages long. The changes to environmental
and other laws were folded in among a vast range of budget provisions
and so never faced the parliamentary committees that specialized in
environmental legislation. It was a procedural end-run.

Environmental and First Nations groups were alarmed while the oil
industry was pleased. An analysis by the Canadian Press compared the
new legislation to a presentation in 2011 by the Canadian Energy Pipeline
Association. The pipeline industry presentation made seven key requests
to senior government officials, from modifying laws and regulations
right down to an 811 hotline for construction companies to "call before
you dig." The Canadian Press found that "In the end, they [the pipeline
industry] got almost everything they wanted except the 811 hotline. Federal
regulators ruled that idea out, mainly because the number is already used by
telephone-health services in many provinces."[88]

The Harper government also took the hammer to environmental
agencies. It stopped funding the Canadian Foundation for Climate
and Atmospheric Sciences and terminated Environment Canada's
Adaptation to Climate Change Research Group. It shut down
the National Roundtable on the Environment and Economy and
cancelled funding for the Canadian Environmental Network.

The political distortion was so complete that even while the federal
government was chopping its environmental protection system and
Department of Natural Resources civil servants were working closely
with CAPP and its members, Minister of Natural Resources Joe Oliver

was delivering angry speeches against "environmental and other radical groups . . . that threaten to hijack our regulatory system to achieve their radical ideological agenda."[89] The regulatory system was getting hijacked all right, but not by environmental groups. On other occasions, Oliver was dismissive: "I think that people aren't as worried as they were before about global warming of 2 degrees. Scientists have recently told us that our fears on climate change are exaggerated."[90]

At the top of the government's priority list was the Keystone XL pipeline from Alberta to refineries in the southern United States. In 2011, Prime Minister Harper told reporters in New York that the American decision to approve the Keystone XL pipeline, which rested ultimately with President Obama, should be a "complete no-brainer." Returning to New York in 2013, Harper told an audience of business leaders that when it came to the Keystone XL pipeline, "my view is you don't take no for an answer." Asked what would happen if the United States said no, Harper replied, "We haven't had that but if we were to get that, that won't be final. This won't be final until it's approved and we will keep pushing forward."[91]

As if these efforts weren't enough, in 2013 and early 2014 the Canadian government ran a major advertising campaign in the United States to raise support among American "decision makers/influencers and opinion leaders"[92] for Canadian oil and energy resources. The cost was an astonishing $24 million in taxpayer money for advertisements online and in newspapers, magazines, and subway stations, primarily in the Washington, DC, region. Canada's government was in lockstep with the fossil fuel industry.

The fossil fuel industry had to work hard because it faced stiffening resistance. Aboriginal land claims, local land use issues, pipeline leaks, and oil spills raised public alarms, and looming over all these was the evidence of global warming. While the federal, Alberta, and Saskatchewan governments were betting the country's future on fossil fuels, much of the rest of the world was beginning the shift to solar, wind, and other low-carbon energies.

* * *

In September 2014, Alberta's fossil fuel–friendly Progressive Conservative government chose a new premier, former federal environment minister Jim Prentice. Prentice was well known to the oil industry through, among other things, the federal–provincial–industry working group, and he seemed certain to maintain the PC Party's uninterrupted forty-four-year reign in the province.

Even the best laid plans go awry. Albertans had been dismayed by a succession of controversies involving the PC government. Prentice initially regained public confidence with his performance as premier and the PCs swept four by-elections. Then, perhaps overcome with his early success, he engineered a move that stunned observers: He convinced most of the Wildrose caucus to abandon their positions as the Official Opposition to join his government. Wildrose leader Danielle Smith justified her move this way: "If you are going to be the official opposition leader you have to really want to take down the government. I don't want to take down this premier. I want this premier to succeed."[93] It was unprecedented for an opposition leader and most of her caucus to cross the floor, and for a brief moment, it seemed the notion of political opposition in Alberta had been gutted in the backrooms of the legislature.

The offence to democracy was too much for voters, who felt insulted, manipulated, and angry. They got in the mood for revenge. When Prentice called an early election and then ran a poor campaign, voters rejected both the PCs and the Wildrose and turned in an unexpected direction. On May 5, 2015, the political ground under Canada's petroleum industry shuddered when a new governing party was elected in Alberta for the first time in forty-four years. The New Democratic Party won a majority in the legislature under its leader, Rachel Notley, the new premier. The NDP platform included tougher action on global warming.

Compounding the political change, Stephen Harper's federal government was defeated in October 2015 by the Liberals under Justin

Trudeau, who also promised tougher action on global warming. To add to the apparent setbacks, a month later President Obama said "no" to the Keystone XL pipeline because of environmental concerns.

The events of 2015 looked like a step backward for fossil fuels in Canada and a step forward for low-carbon alternatives. But while the political landscape had changed, the interests of the fossil fuel industry were unrelenting. The big message at Rachel Notley's first news conference as premier was to tell her "partners in the energy industry" that "they can count on us to work collaboratively with them."[94] And while the federal Liberals committed Canada to limit carbon emissions under the Paris Climate Agreement and imposed a national price on carbon emissions, they also approved the Kinder Morgan Trans Mountain pipeline and supported the Keystone XL pipeline, both of which aided oil sands expansion.

In the United States, President Obama's decision against the Keystone XL pipeline soon faced a formal challenge under NAFTA, launched by Calgary-based EPIC supporter TransCanada Corporation. Before long, however, that was moot. In November 2016, Donald Trump was elected president on a platform that included approving the Keystone XL pipeline and reviving the coal industry.[95] The morning after Trump's victory, Stephen Harper, now a civilian consultant, tweeted, "Congratulations to Donald Trump on his impressive victory. Canada/US partnership is strong. There is much to do, incl moving ahead with KXL [Keystone XL]." Three days after being sworn in as American president, Donald Trump invited TransCanada to resubmit its application for the Keystone XL pipeline.[96]

The struggle of the fossil fuel industry with global warming was far from over.

Chapter 3
Global warming: What industry knew and when they knew it

The fossil fuel industry's efforts in Canada were not happening in isolation. Canada's industry was deeply integrated with the United States, where it sent 99 per cent of Canada's oil and natural gas exports,[97] and there was frequent contact by Canadian government and industry officials with their counterparts south of the border. On April 23 and 24, 2009, for example, platoons of officials from the Canadian government worked with the Canadian Association of Petroleum Producers (CAPP) to arrange an "oil sands workshop and outreach program" in Washington, DC. The blind courtesy copy list at the end of one email included eighty-two federal officials in dozens of offices. One of the meetings they arranged was with the CEO and other executives of the American Petroleum Institute.[98]

The American Petroleum Institute (API) is CAPP's much bigger and older American cousin. It bills itself as a trade association for America's oil and gas industry, but that barely indicates the scope of its work. API is structured somewhat like a government. It has a substantial political branch that lobbies politicians and officials, funds interest groups, and works to shape the public agenda to favour oil and natural gas. What sets API apart from typical lobby groups are its massive administrative, regulatory, and scientific activities. It produces an astounding 300,000 documents a year on everything from offshore drilling safety standards to weekly production levels of kerosene jet fuel. It sets standards for motor oils and develops software for tracking groundwater flows. It is a partner in research and development with universities, governments, corporations, and private laboratories.[99]

API has long reflected the intensely scientific world of petroleum production. Drilling wells in deep oceans and cracking crude in refineries takes billions of dollars in research. One of the harsh ironies of the global warming issue is that an industry with such scientific sophistication would turn its back on the science of climate change. It wasn't always this way. API and others in the industry undertook careful scientific analysis of global warming in the 1970s and 1980s. Legal researchers and journalists have uncovered remarkable inside information on this and have posted the results of their work on the Internet, including images of the original documents.[100, 101] Their efforts often support a growing list of investigations, including by the New York Securities Exchange Commission and the New York attorney-general,[102] into the possibility that the fossil fuel industry has misled the public and investors about the hazards of climate change, downplaying risks that it knew were serious.

* * *

Perhaps the first scientist inside the petroleum industry to study global warming was James F. Black at Exxon.[103] Black, whose bespectacled and friendly face made him look the part of the wise uncle, had studied global warming since the 1960s, when he contributed to a US National Academy of Sciences report on climate. As a senior scientist at Exxon, he began concentrating on global warming in the 1970s as an issue of strategic importance to the company and to the planet. In various presentations and reports in 1977 and 1978, Black informed officials at Exxon headquarters that there was "general scientific agreement" that the global climate was warming because of emissions from the burning of fossil fuels, and while some countries would benefit, "others would have their agricultural output reduced or destroyed."[104] There were many uncertainties, said Black, but the clock was running fast: "Present thinking holds that man has a time window of five to ten years before the need for hard decisions regarding changes in energy strategies might become critical," he wrote to company officials in 1978.[105]

To their credit, Exxon executives took the message seriously and supported a long-term, multi-million–dollar research program into the issues. Scientists, mathematicians, and specialists in computer modelling were hired. A supertanker was equipped to collect data on carbon dioxide (CO_2) in the oceans and atmosphere as it plied the waters between the Gulf of Mexico and the Persian Gulf. The burst of knowledge and activity generated dozens of peer-reviewed scientific papers, many written in collaboration with government and university scientists.[106]

In September 1982, a memo from a director of one of Exxon's major science laboratories to Exxon headquarters on the Avenue of the Americas in New York summarized the research to date, and while it acknowledged uncertainty, its core message was clear:[107]

> . . . over the past several years a clear scientific consensus
> has emerged . . . that a doubling of atmospheric CO_2 from
> its pre-industrial revolution value would result in an average
> global temperature rise of 3°C (+/-1.5°) . . . There is unanimous
> agreement in the scientific community that a temperature
> increase of this magnitude would bring about significant
> changes in the earth's climate . . .

The American Petroleum Institute (API) ran its own "CO_2 and Climate Task Force" from 1979 to 1983, involving senior scientists and engineers from several corporations, including some with major operations in Canada. The minutes of a task force meeting from February 1980, held in a rented boardroom at LaGuardia Airport in New York, give a sense of the magnitude of the issues being considered.[108] The task force heard a presentation on "The CO2 Problem" from Dr. J. A. Laurman, who API described in its minutes as "a recognized expert in the field of CO2 and climate." Laurman began by describing the difficulties and uncertainties with the issue because of its complexity and size. The opening slides of his presentation were serious, but cautious: "The physical facts agree on the probability of large effects 50 years away, but with large probable error." Under the subheading "Reasons for increased concern with the CO2 problem," Laurman stated there is "Scientific consensus on the potential for large future climatic response to increased CO2 levels," which he indicated came "mostly from fossil fuel combustion." In effect, he was telling the task force that although there was uncertainty over details, the scientific consensus was that burning fossil fuels put so much CO2 into the atmosphere that big changes were coming to the climate.

Then, as Laurman reached his conclusion, he delivered statements that must have brought the meeting to a standstill:

Likely impacts:

• 1°C rise (2005): barely noticeable.

• 2.5°C rise (2038): major economic consequences . . .

• 5°C rise (2067): globally catastrophic effects.

And, on the final slide, this:

At a 3% per annum growth rate of CO2, a 2.5°C rise brings world economic growth to a halt in about 2025.

The minutes do not record the mood in that rented airport boardroom when Laurman's presentation ended. Being told that your line of work could halt world economic growth and then bring global catastrophe must have been disquieting. Was there long silence as they took in the message? Dismay? Denial? Anger? No doubt that time frame of fifty years looked different in 1980 than now. Still, if the people in the room had children or grandchildren, it was well within reach. Perhaps the message was simply overwhelming.

Shell Oil also took up the global warming banner. It conducted its own research and produced a documentary film for public release, titled *Climate of Concern*.[109] The film opens with aircraft and ships collecting research data on the atmosphere and the oceans, and the narrator soon introduces the film's main theme: "Our energy consuming way of life may be causing climatic changes with adverse consequences for us all." It describes the basic science of global warming, accepts that the research has uncertainties, and delivers the message that CO_2 and other emissions are likely causing the climate to change "too fast, perhaps, for life to adapt without severe dislocation." Shell accepted the mainstream science: A serious warning about climate change was "endorsed by a uniquely broad consensus of scientists in their report to the United Nations at the end of 1990," says the film, before it lists some of the hazards, including tropical islands "obliterated beneath the waves" and "wetland habitats destroyed by intruding salt." After images of widespread drought and famine, it asks, "In a crowded world subject to such adverse shifts of climate, who would take care of such greenhouse refugees?" The film's final words are spoken over images of crowded streets panning out to a shot of the planet from space: "The problems and dilemmas of climate change concern us all."

Shell made the film in 1991.

* * *

The fundamentals of global warming can be summarized in a handful of paragraphs.

1. All objects warmer than absolute zero (an impossibly cold −273.15°C) radiate energy: campfires, clouds, human bodies, farmers' fields, even ice cubes. Hot objects radiate more energy than cool objects. The Sun, being very hot (6,000°C), radiates large amounts of many kinds of energy, including ultraviolet energy; infrared energy; and visible light energy, which our eyes perceive as sunlight.[110] The Earth absorbs a portion of all those energies from the Sun, but being cooler, radiates them back out in just one form: infrared energy. We feel infrared energy as warmth, but cannot see it (unless we're looking through an infrared camera).[111] Because Earth converts these different forms of energy into infrared, it radiates a lot of infrared energy. Think of Earth as an infrared concentrator.

2. Each form of energy passes through some materials, but is absorbed by others. We live with this reality every day. Microwave energy passes through the cup, but is absorbed by the water in the coffee. X-ray energy passes through our muscles, but is absorbed by the calcium in our bones. Ultraviolet energy passes through the atmosphere, but is absorbed by sunscreen (or if we forget the sunscreen, by our skin). Similarly, infrared energy passes through the nitrogen and oxygen that make up 99 per cent of the atmosphere, but is absorbed by the carbon dioxide, water vapour, and other trace gases that make up the last 1 per cent of the atmosphere, which causes those gases to warm. Those gases then re-radiate the energy back to the surface of the Earth, giving it another dose of warming infrared.

If it weren't for this thin blanket of CO2 and other trace gases, the Earth's infrared energy would radiate through the atmosphere into space, and the planet would be frozen in permanent winter. These gases create a kind of greenhouse effect, so they are called "greenhouse gases."

3. The amount of CO_2 in the atmosphere is rising dramatically, mostly from burning coal, oil, and natural gas, which releases carbon from deep underground into the air. When carbon burns to form CO_2, it gains weight because each atom of carbon joins with two atoms of oxygen. As a result, the emissions can weigh more than the fuel.

- Burning one tank of gasoline in a typical sedan produces about 150 kilograms (330 pounds) of CO_2.[112] In 2015, there were about 1.2 billion motor vehicles worldwide.[113]

- One passenger flying economy class on a round-trip flight from Vancouver to Toronto produces about 477 kilograms (985 pounds) of CO_2.[114] In 2013, more than eight million people flew *every day*.[115]

- The electricity used in an average Canadian home in a year would produce about 10,422 kilograms (23,000 pounds) of CO_2 if that electricity were generated by coal-fired power plants.[116, 117] Most Canadian provinces do not rely heavily on coal-fired power plants, but the rest of the world does. In 2014, there were 19,745 coal-fired generators of at least one megawatt capacity in the United States.[118]

Scientists have become very good at tracking the historic levels of CO_2 in the atmosphere. For the past 800,000 years, until the Industrial Revolution of the eighteenth century, levels ranged between 180 and 280 parts per million (ppm), and in the past twenty million years, levels have probably never been above 300 ppm. By burning fossil fuels at a frenetic rate, we are sending that level up like a rocket. In 2016, levels surpassed 400 ppm, a rise of 40 per cent above pre-industrial levels.[119]

Four hundred parts per million doesn't seem like much, but life is filled with things that make an impact in tiny amounts. For example, in a human, a blood alcohol level of 280 ppm is barely noticeable, but 400 ppm reduces concentration and brings on a pleasant warmth. At 800 ppm, a person is legally impaired. At current rates of CO_2 increase, our atmosphere is headed for 800 ppm of carbon dioxide by the end of this century. If we do nothing to stop the increase, we will be living under a wild and drunken sky.

4. Carbon dioxide lasts in the atmosphere for centuries, and a portion of it for millennia, so our emissions just keep piling up. This is different from other greenhouse gases. Water vapour cycles in and out of the atmosphere every several days as evaporation turns into precipitation. Methane, another important greenhouse gas, breaks down in a few decades (albeit into CO_2), so if we were to shut down all human-induced methane emissions today, its level would return to historic norms in half a human lifetime. Not so with CO_2. Most of the emissions from cars, airplanes, and furnaces will still be in the air centuries from now.

David Archer, a scientist at the University of Chicago who studies global warming and the oceans, writes that the timescale for CO_2 emissions to be absorbed by the oceans, plants, and land is centuries or longer, and that "When this centuries-long climate storm subsides, it will leave behind a new, warmer climate state that will persist for thousands of years." The results of what we are doing, he cautions, will "last longer than Stonehenge. Longer than time capsules, longer than nuclear waste, far longer than the age of human civilization so far."[120]

There are other causes of climate change, including variations in Earth's orbit around the Sun, volcanic activity, and sunspots. These will continue to have their effects as usual, but with one major change: Those effects are now happening in an atmosphere unlike anything human beings have encountered before.

★ ★ ★

Among the organizations studying global warming, the most authoritative is the Intergovernmental Panel on Climate Change (IPCC), which includes top scientists from agencies around the world. They report on what we can expect, depending on how much CO_2 we release.[121] Their low-emissions forecast assumes stringent steps are quickly taken to reduce CO_2 emissions, in which case by 2100, global warming would likely rise less than 2°C compared to the period 1850–1900, and keep trending upwards thereafter. There is no sign that stringent steps will be taken quickly enough, so this is an unlikely scenario.

Their medium forecast assumes fewer and slower but still very significant cuts are made to emission rates. By the end of this century, CO_2 levels would reach 650 ppm and the global average temperature would rise 3°C; it will continue to increase for centuries after that. The high forecast assumes emissions continue to rise as they did early in the twenty-first century. CO_2 levels would reach 1,000 ppm by century's end and the rise in global average temperature would approach 4°C compared to 1850–1900, and continue soaring higher for centuries.

In the medium and high scenarios, we will be dealing with a dramatically different atmosphere and climates that will be unrecognizable. We have piled on the blankets and can't get them off. The best we can do now is to stop piling on more of them.

An increase in global average temperature of 4°C doesn't sound alarming. In fact, local temperatures often vary more than that over the course of several hours. The difference is local temperatures vary around an average, where each high is counterbalanced by a low. When that average moves up or down, the entire range moves with it, with huge implications. Think of this in terms of our body temperatures: our extremities can go from the heat of a sauna to a plunge in ice water, but if our core body temperature goes up or down four degrees we will likely die.

Another way to understand this is to compare today's climate with the ice ages, when much of the world was covered in ice sheets. Ice sheets have expanded and receded several times in the past three million years, mostly as a result of very long-term variations in the shape of Earth's orbit around the Sun.[122] The last time this happened, sheets of ice thousands of metres thick covered much of what is now North America, Europe, and Russia. Massive glaciers flowed out of the Alps into southern Europe and out of the Himalayas into India. The ice held so much water that, at times, ocean levels were more than 100 metres lower than they are today.[123] Early people could walk from Papua New Guinea to Australia and from Siberia to Alaska over what today is ocean floor. These sheets of ice gradually retreated from about 20,000 to 12,000 years ago.

How much colder was the world's temperature during this last great glaciation compared to now? The best estimate is that the global average temperature then was only 4 or 5°C colder.[124] That average downward shift of four or five degrees tipped some regional climates into downward spirals that drove temperatures down by much more than the global average decrease[125] and led to a build-up of ice sheets that covered continents.

Through the same dynamics, an upward shift of four or five degrees in global average temperature can cause an *upward* spiral that will have dramatic impacts. The top scientific reports suggest this shift will be one of the impacts of rising CO_2 levels: "If the rise in CO_2 continues unchecked, warming of the same magnitude as the increase out of the ice age can be expected by the end of this century or soon after."[126] It is as if humanity is engineering a reverse ice age, and doing it hundreds of times faster than natural processes. If fire is the opposite of ice, then we are driving our planet into a "fire age" that will be as different from the twentieth century as the twentieth century was from the last ice age.

* * *

Human-induced global warming has already left a trail of clear marks across the planet, and scientists are working intensely to forecast where that trail will lead. Global warming leaves nothing untouched.

Water

The glaciers that crown many mountain ranges are receding as their ice turns to water, and many are likely to vanish this century. These glaciers contribute to hundreds of rivers, including some of the world's great ones: the Indus, Ganges, Yangtze, Mekong, Columbia, and others. Without glaciers, their flows will be disrupted and reduced, especially in dry seasons when the water is needed most.[127]

The Greenland and Antarctic ice caps are also melting, the former with particular speed. These ice caps are far bigger than glaciers and will last much longer. Their drainage, like that from glaciers, is pushing up sea levels and changing ocean chemistry.[128]

Average ocean temperatures are climbing, especially near the surface. Water expands as it warms, so a warmer ocean is a larger ocean, thrusting inland through tidal surges, flooding, and submersion. This expansion is the largest contributor to rising sea levels. The oceans deepened about twenty centimetres in the twentieth century, and will rise another fifty to 100 centimetres this century, flooding low-lying coastlands. Scientists say it is "virtually certain" the oceans will continue rising in subsequent centuries as they absorb more heat and as the remaining glaciers and ice caps melt. Sea levels will eventually rise many metres, depending on the level of emissions,[129, 130] and because warm water holds less oxygen than cold water, the oxygen available for many forms of aquatic life will be reduced.

The oceans draw gases from the air, including a third of the CO_2 released by fossil fuels so far.[131] Carbon dioxide forms a mild acid in the ocean, and rising CO_2 levels mean rising ocean acidity. Research by marine biologists, including large-scale experiments, indicates the increasing acidity will push the oceans over a tipping point by the end of this century, at which time a wide variety of mollusks, sponges, corals, fish, and seaweeds will not survive.[132]

Land and Weather

In general, temperatures are expected to rise more over land than over oceans, and to rise more in higher latitudes than near the equator. Northern Canada, Alaska, Scandinavia, and Russia face the biggest increases, up to 10°C by the end of the century if emissions continue on their current course.[133] The unprecedented voyage of the giant cruise ship *Crystal Serenity* from the Pacific to the Atlantic through Canada's Northwest Passage in August 2016 was a historic marker of a climate threshold being crossed. Global warming has the Arctic ecosystem as we know it on a death march, with the only suspense being how long the march takes.

It isn't just the Arctic, however; land the world over will get warmer. Countries with cold climates may see improved agricultural production, but lands that are already warm will become punishingly hot, including much of the United States, South America, Africa, Asia, southern Europe, and Australia. Research by the Government of Australia predicts the city of Darwin will have over 300 days a year with temperatures above 35°C by the end of the century if emissions continue rising at current rates.[134] At the beginning of the century, the average number of such days was nine.

Rainfall patterns will also change. In general, dry regions will get less rain while wet regions will get more. The IPCC's best forecasts show extreme rainfalls are very likely to become more intense and frequent in mid-latitude and wet tropical regions. In other areas, droughts will be longer and more severe.[135]

Plants and Animals

In the first decade of the twenty-first century, biologists began speaking of "the sixth mass extinction."[136] Five mass extinctions show up in the geologic records. The sixth extinction is not in the geological record; it is happening now, caused by humans. Some of it is caused by people destroying habitats, over-hunting, and spreading diseases and invasive species, but its most powerful driver is carbon emissions. Elizabeth Kolbert summarizes the situation with brutal brevity:

> It is estimated that one-third of all reef-building corals, a third of all freshwater mollusks, a third of sharks and rays, a quarter of all mammals, a fifth of all reptiles, and a sixth of all birds are headed toward oblivion. The losses are occurring all over: in the South Pacific and the North Atlantic, in the Arctic and the Sahel, in lakes and on islands, on mountaintops and in valleys.[137]

Climate change shows its effects on plants and animals in many ways other than extinction. Sunfish, at home in tropical waters, are turning up off the coast of Alaska.[138] Atlantic lobsters are moving their range north as they track changing ocean temperatures.[139] Diseases and pests that were once held at bay by severe winters are now taking hold in northern forests. The mountain pine beetle has ravaged the lodgepole pine forests of Western Canada, in part because winters are no longer cold enough to keep them in check.

The IPCC does not pull punches in its warnings about the impact of climate change on Earth's plants and animals:

> A large fraction of species face increased extinction risk due to climate change during and beyond the 21st century . . . Most plant species cannot naturally shift their geographical ranges sufficiently fast to keep up with current and high projected rates of climate change in most landscapes; most small mammals and freshwater mollusks will not be able to keep up . . . Marine organisms will face progressively lower oxygen levels and high rates and magnitudes of ocean acidification . . . Coral reefs and polar ecosystems are highly vulnerable. Coastal systems and low-lying areas are at risk from sea-level rise . . ."[140]

Humanity

This adds up to a big pile of trouble for humanity, and the pile gets bigger as emissions rise and the decades advance. There is a high risk, the IPCC warns, of disease and social and economic disruption from storm surges, rising sea levels, flooding, and extreme heat.[141] Warmer and more humid weather will extend the range of malaria to hundreds of millions of more people.[142] Coastal flooding will submerge areas that are home to hundreds of millions of people in Asia, the United States, and beyond, destroying roads and infrastructure, squeezing the insurance industry, and forcing important urban areas to be vacated. Gulf of Mexico states are already losing land to the sea, from the wetlands of Louisiana[143] to Miami Beach in Florida.[144]

In the Pacific and Atlantic Oceans, warming is causing cyclones and hurricanes to generate more extreme rain and wind.[145] Sydney, Australia, is on the front line: "If you look at some of our most vulnerable areas," said Will Steffen, part of a team studying the dangers for Australia, "and the Sydney region is one of those, you would say toward the end of this century that a one-in-a-hundred-year flood is going to be happening every few days. Now, that's an impossible situation to cope with."[146] Port cities around the world are paying increasingly urgent attention to these risks.

Not surprisingly, food and water supplies are endangered, as Exxon's scientist James Black predicted to the company in 1978. In most regions, production of wheat, rice, and maize (corn) is predicted to decline due to global warming. Water supplies for drinking and irrigation will decline. Suffering caused by the problems of global warming will be worst among the poorest people, especially in Asia and Africa.[147] The rivers, aquifers, forests, fields, and oceans of the world will provide less usable water, less fresh air, less food, less flood protection, and less of the things that we and the rest of the living world have come to count on over thousands of lifetimes.

I will stop there, for the list of troubles can be overwhelming. As the American Petroleum Institute's task force on CO2 and climate was informed in 1980, the effects will be globally catastrophic if urgent action is not taken.

★ ★ ★

The Atmosphere as a Commons

On top of the environmental challenges posed by global warming are the economic ones. The air we breathe — the atmosphere — is nothing like consumer products that we buy and sell. We all use the atmosphere, but no one owns it. We don't buy air like we buy groceries or drinking water. In economic terms, the atmosphere is called a "commons." A commons is a resource widely and freely available to all, which is vulnerable to damage or failure when it is overused or abused.[148] A classic example of a commons is the community pastures on the edges of villages in medieval Europe. Peasants used these pastures to graze their animals. As long as every peasant grazed only a few animals, the pasture was viable. But if some peasants tried to get ahead by grazing as many animals as possible, the pasture was soon overloaded. The grass would be stripped, the soil turned to mud, and the pasture destroyed. If any one person overused the pasture, then everyone would end up poorer. Medieval societies worked out rules so peasants could share community pastures fairly, and both pastures and peasants could survive.

What the community pasture was to the medieval village, the atmosphere is to the modern world. Because no private interest owns the atmosphere, its use is free to everyone. There is no incentive for anyone to limit their use of the atmosphere, including as a dump for carbon emissions. To protect a commons such as the atmosphere, societies often need to impose strict limits on private interests, such as regulations and carbon taxes.

This is of both political and economic importance, as will soon become clear. Protecting the atmosphere from carbon emissions requires government regulations and taxes, so the fossil fuel industry (which produces those emissions) becomes a natural supporter of anti-government, anti-regulation, and anti-tax political movements. Fossil fuel interests and certain right-wing political movements naturally mix with each other, creating a potent compound.

* * *

The human world was built in the old climate. We established our farms to work in ranges of temperatures and rainfall that we knew. We built our homes, cities, roads, bridges, ports, and railways on land we thought was safe, to function in normal conditions and to survive one-in-a-hundred-year extremes. We made laws and institutions for a given set of conditions. That old climate is gone, and it is not coming back.

Our carbon emissions have turned the established baselines of climate into historic artifacts, like abandoned fortresses and forsaken deities. There is no new baseline. Each decade will likely be warmer than the last for centuries to come. Weather extremes are likely to get more extreme for centuries to come. Sea levels will keep rising for centuries to come.

The baseline has been replaced by an upward trajectory that began taking off in the second half of the twentieth century and is steepening as we continue on this journey, for which we do not know the destination. If we work hard and make tough decisions, we can level off the trajectory. The question is, when will we? If the fossil fuel industry has its way, it won't be any time soon. And, as tragic as it is, they have many ways to secure their positions.

Chapter 4
"The debate is closing": The carbonizing of American politics

Clear and simple lines run through the complications that mark society's responses to global warming. One of these lines is a straightforward tale of self-interest and corporate greed. This story opens with a rich and powerful industry coming to realize its product poses grave public dangers, weighing whether it should responsibly respond to these dangers or ignore the warnings and continue apace, and deciding it is easier and more profitable to carry on with business as usual. This was the tragic tale of the tobacco and asbestos industries, and it will be writ largest of all on the fossil fuel industry.

If one moment in the story of the fossil fuel industry foreshadows its tragic turn, it might be April 1, 1982, the date of an internal Exxon report titled "CO2 Greenhouse Effect, A Technical Review,"[149] prepared by the "Coordination and Planning Division, Exxon Research and Engineering Company." A covering memo written seven months later says the report "has been given wide circulation to Exxon management . . . However, it should be restricted to Exxon personnel and not distributed externally." The forty-page report became public through legal investigations three decades after it was written.[150]

The report stays true to the science, identifying the rise in carbon dioxide levels in the atmosphere as a result of "fossil fuel combustion and the clearing of virgin forests." This rise is "of concern since it can affect global climate." The report is cautiously worded, presents many uncertainties, and does not advocate any action other than further study — hardly surprising given it was written in 1982 by employees of a petroleum company. It points out there is a twenty-year lag between an increase in global CO2 levels and an increase in global temperature, making predictions more difficult. (This is like the lag between pulling up the blankets on a chilly evening and actually feeling warmer, and it means the staggering threefold rise of emissions from China during the period 1996–2016[151] — making it far and away the largest CO2 emitter in the world — won't be fully felt until 2036.)

For all the hedging in this report, it is like a flashing yellow light near a dangerous intersection warning that serious hazards lie ahead. Among the potential hazards are a "drying out" of the American Midwest and changes in rainfall patterns that would have "dramatic impact" on global agriculture. There are also "some potentially catastrophic events that must be considered," including "flooding of much of the U.S. East Coast, including the State of Florida and Washington D.C." over a period of several centuries. Then the report makes a chillingly grim attempt at perspective: "this problem is not as significant to mankind as a nuclear holocaust or world famine."

The foreshadowing of tragedy is not in the report's ominous science, for tragedy is not found in the facts of a situation, but in the human response to those facts. The foreshadowing of tragedy is in the response of Exxon to the predicament repeatedly posed by the report: "Mitigation of the 'greenhouse effect' would require major reductions in fossil fuel combustion."[152] The report put the fossil fuel industry on notice: Either face the prospect that the world needs to reduce fossil fuel combustion, or continue business as usual and risk the possibility that the planet will pay dearly. The report even indirectly hinted at an alternate way forward, saying solar or nuclear energy could displace fossil fuels over a forty- to fifty-year period. (Imagine what the world might be like today if the fossil fuel industry had thrown its resources behind solar power in the 1980s.)

The industry took its time to respond to this dilemma — and then made its dreadful choice.

★ ★ ★

In 1983, three years after its own scientists warned that CO2 emissions from fossil fuels were likely to have globally catastrophic effects, the American Petroleum Institute (API) disbanded its climate task force. Exxon continued researching global warming for a few more years, but the mood of the industry was changing. Even as researchers around the world strengthened the science of global warming, the petroleum industry that had once led the field began back-pedalling. At the 1992 Rio Earth Summit, the industry pressured American President George H. Bush to water down the summit's commitments to reduce carbon emissions. A few years later, when President Clinton was working to have Congress ratify the Kyoto Protocol, the fossil fuel industry stood in active opposition, and their efforts escalated from there.

The first impact of the collision between the fossil fuel industry and the science of global warming was felt in 1988 and 1989. US Senate hearings into global warming heard testimony from James Hansen, a senior scientist at NASA, who said global warming was real and it was 99 per cent likely that human greenhouse gas emissions were the cause. Senators, reporters, and voters across the United States took notice, as did Bush Sr., who was in the midst of an election campaign for president. "The green house effect," he announced in August 1988, would be met by "the White House effect,"[153] and action would be taken.

When Bush Sr. settled into the White House in 1989, a different effect was being felt. Top government officials were getting visits from members of the George C. Marshall Institute, who were contradicting the mainstream science.[154] This institute had been formed in 1984 to support immense new defence initiatives. It included a handful of prominent scientists who used their reputations to open government and media doors and argue on issues that supported the tobacco, defence, and fossil fuel industries. By the time the George C. Marshall Institute closed its doors in 2015, substantial funding ties to these industries had been revealed.

The Marshall Institute was soon joined by much more muscular players. In 1989, a group of major business interests formed the Global Climate Coalition (GCC), including Exxon, Shell, BP, Chevron, the American Petroleum Institute, the National Coal Association, and many other corporations and associations. The Global Climate Coalition didn't deny the science; its strategy was to disrupt progress on enacting solutions. It stirred up controversies about climate change reports that damaged public confidence in the science, opposed President Clinton's actions on climate change, and spent at least $13 million on advertising to oppose the Kyoto Protocol.[155] One of its primary arguments was that action on climate change should be shared "equitably by all nations," effectively meaning that until every nation acts, none will — an automatic brake on action that suits the industry. The GCC concentrated on the United States and was also active in Canada.[156] In the late 1990s, the GCC began to lose industry support because of its more controversial tactics. It wound down in 2001, claiming victory after President George W. Bush withdrew the United States from the Kyoto process.[157]

The scale and nature of the industry's opposition to action on global warming were revealed in a leaked American Petroleum Institute (API) memo obtained by the *New York Times* in April 1998. The memo presents API's "Global Climate Science Communications Action Plan."[158] The plan's purposes are clear from the opening paragraphs, which speak of "so-called green house gases" and the "weaknesses in scientific understanding," and claim that "it's not known for sure whether (a) climate change actually is occurring, or (b) if it is, whether humans really have any influence on it." James F. Black, the climate scientist who retired from Exxon in 1983 and died in 1988, must have been weeping in his grave.

API's communication plan quickly came to its central premise: "The advocates of global warming have been successful on the basis of skillfully misrepresenting the science and the extent of agreement on the science . . ." If API and the industry "can show that science does not support the Kyoto treaty . . ." then President Clinton and the American government wouldn't have the mandate to commit to emission reductions.

As part of its plan, API had commissioned a study of public opinion that found most Americans thought "climate change to be a great threat," but also found that if they were told that scientists did not think the evidence was clear, then a majority would come to oppose the Kyoto treaty. "Victory will be achieved," says the plan, when "those promoting the Kyoto treaty on the basis of extent science appears to be out of touch with reality." Reality, it seems, would be turned into fantasy, and fantasy into reality.

The strategies and tactics of the plan included recruiting scientists "who do not have a long history . . . in the climate change debate" to use as commentators sowing doubt on the global warming science. They would be supported by media information kits and orchestrated campaigns producing "steady streams" of letters-to-the-editor, op-ed columns, workshops, and paid advertising on "scientific uncertainties." That was just the beginning. A "Global Climate Science Data Center" would be set up in Washington, DC, as a non-profit educational foundation staffed with professionals on loan from corporations, to become a "one-stop-shop" for members of Congress, the media, industry, and all others concerned. This was to be augmented by a "National Direct Outreach and Education" plan to "educate members of Congress, state officials, industry leadership, and school teachers/students about the uncertainties in climate science." The plan covered eight pages and proposed an initial $5.9 million in spending, not including advertising. API confirmed to reporters that the plan was genuine, but said it had not yet been approved and financed. If the plan can be judged by the vote in Congress, it was an astounding success, for in July 1997, the Senate voted *not* to ratify Kyoto by a margin of ninety-five to none.

American Vice-President Al Gore had played a central role in assembling the initial Kyoto treaty and was dismayed when it was not ratified by the Senate. When Clinton's term was over, Gore ran for president against George W. Bush in the 2000 election. In an exceedingly close and controversial vote, Bush defeated Gore. Bush, a former governor of Texas, ushered in a flourishing eight years for the fossil fuel industry, accompanied by an unprecedented climb in atmospheric carbon dioxide and a string of the warmest years ever recorded to that date. The fossil fuel industry committed heavily to the Bush Republicans over the Gore Democrats in the 2000 election cycle: The oil and gas industry and its supporters directed 78 per cent of their political donations to the Republicans, and the coal mining industry directed 87 per cent of its donations, for a total of $30.5 million.[159] This pattern was maintained through future election cycles using much larger amounts of money, with the fossil fuel industry directing the large majority of its rapidly growing political funds to the Republicans over the Democrats. In the 2016 campaign, every Republican presidential candidate was a global warming skeptic, including the eventual presidential winner Donald Trump.

* * *

As warmly as the Harper government in Canada welcomed the fossil fuel industry into the house of state, it had nothing on the government of George W. Bush. If the former laid out a welcome mat, the latter flung open the doors. Four of the most powerful members of the Bush government had held senior positions in petroleum corporations. Bush himself grew up in the industry. His father was an oil company executive in Texas in the 1950s and 1960s, and Bush served as an executive, board member, and promoter of a number of oil companies before he became governor of Texas. His vice-president, Dick Cheney, was secretary of defense when Bush's father engaged in the First Gulf War in 1991, and from 1995 to 2000 was chairman and CEO of Halliburton Company, one of the world's largest petroleum services companies. While Cheney was at Halliburton, the company merged with its biggest competitor, Dresser Industries, which at one time had ties with both Bush's father and grandfather.

Bush's national security advisor (2001–05) and then secretary of state (2005–09) was Condoleezza Rice. For almost ten years before joining Bush's cabinet, Rice sat on the board of directors of Chevron Corporation, one of the world's major oil companies. Chevron named one of its supertankers the *Condoleezza Rice* in 1993 to recognize her contributions to the company. The ship's name was changed when she was sworn into office, but she took staff from Chevron with her to her cabinet position.[160]

Bush's secretary of commerce from 2001 to 2005 was Donald Evans. Evans had spent his career with the large petroleum drilling and exploration company Tom Brown Inc., including more than a decade as its CEO. After he stepped down as secretary of commerce, Evans returned to the energy industry, taking senior positions in companies with interests in both petroleum production and coal-fired electrical generation. Meanwhile, Tom Brown Inc. was bought for $2.4 billion US in 2004 by Calgary-based EnCana, one of CAPP's biggest members. To add to the list, Secretary of Interior Gale Norton, who the *Los Angeles Times* called "the Bush administration's leading advocate for expanding oil and gas drilling . . . in the west"[161] joined Royal Dutch Shell as legal counsel after leaving public office.

It turns out that one of the petroleum industry's most important pipelines was to the American government, and it carried a slurry of the industry's concerns. The scale of that pipeline only became clear after disaster struck, and by then the Bush administration was history.

* * *

At 9:50 pm on April 20, 2010, the Deepwater Horizon drilling rig exploded in a fireball.[162] The rig, a semi-submersible floating platform, was drilling about fifty miles off the Louisiana coast in the Gulf of Mexico. It was working on an extraordinarily difficult hole. The water was 5,000 feet deep, and the crew had drilled into the seabed another two-and-a-half miles beneath the seafloor. The drilling had reached a zone rich in oil and lighter hydrocarbons, and the project was nearly complete. Then, because of a sequence of complications, equipment failures, and questionable decisions, the extreme pressures deep under the seabed were able to force lighter hydrocarbons into the wellbore, where they shot up the pipe toward the rig on the water's surface far above.

When the hydrocarbons reached the rig, they ignited in a series of explosions that merged into a single inferno burning at 1,600°C. After two days of this inferno, the Deepwater Horizon listed and sank, causing the drill pipe to shear off where it entered the seabed almost a mile below. Crude oil gushed out of the hole at rates of tens of thousands of barrels a day for eighty-seven days, until it was capped on July 15. Of the 126 crew members on the rig when it exploded, 115 survived. Eleven were never seen again despite search efforts, their bodies presumably consumed by the fire.

The Deepwater Horizon spill is the worst oil spill in American history and the worst accidental release of oil into ocean waters ever in the world. It spewed twenty times the volume of America's second largest spill, the 1989 *Exxon Valdez* disaster off the coast of Alaska.

The Deepwater Horizon rig was working for BP. BP had long been known as a company with a poor safety record. Just five years earlier, in 2005, fifteen people were killed and 170 injured in an explosion and fire at its Gulf coast refinery at Texas City. Badly outdated equipment was a major factor. BP was a large player in Alaska's North Slope oilfields, where its record was controversial. In 1967, the first-ever supertanker to wreck and sink, the *Torrey Canyon*, was chartered to BP and ran aground off the coast of Cornwall, England, while taking a shortcut to save time. Despite this decades-long trail of problems, American officials allowed BP to take on some of the riskiest projects in the Gulf, including that fateful final hole of the Deepwater Horizon.

That hole faced a cascade of problems. The special cement used deep down in the well to secure against leaks failed. The blowout preventer failed. Sensors failed. The general alarm on the rig that should have sounded automatically to warn of the blowout did not function. When the well blew and the inferno ignited, BP's emergency plan was woefully inadequate. Among other things, it called for the protection of walruses and sea lions, which don't live in the Gulf of Mexico, and it didn't address the risks of hurricanes and tropical storms, which are common there. The marine biologist named in the plan to guide a clean-up operation had died five years before. It turned out the same plan, provided by a small consulting firm, had been adopted by other oil giants for offshore Gulf drilling.[163]

The environmental impacts of the Deepwater Horizon spill were devastating. Towering underwater plumes of crude rose from the hole in the seafloor, broke free, and drifted through the blue waters of the Gulf like billowing storm clouds in an ocean sky. The crude fouled the coast of Louisiana and then spread to other states. Gulf coast fisheries were closed for extended periods, and the wildlife die-off included vast numbers of birds, fish, oysters, turtles, otters, and dolphins. BP began using a controversial chemical dispersant called Corexit, which dissolved the crude oil into tiny droplets. They used aircraft in a secretive night-time campaign to spray Corexit on oil slicks on the water's surface and released large quantities of it underwater near the blown-out hole. Corexit is known to be highly toxic, and clean-up workers were soon showing symptoms: nausea, headaches, cognitive problems, and internal bleeding.

As attempts to cap the blowout failed, one after another, and the seafloor geyser of crude spewed unabated for nearly three months, the question everyone asked was, "How was this allowed to happen?"

* * *

On the surface, the Deepwater Horizon disaster could hardly differ more from the legal case against Bruce Carson. The one had spectacular devastation and widespread tragedy, while the other was a seedy political controversy that ended with a sad whimper. But beneath the surface, where the public is rarely allowed to look, both cases exposed the ways the oil industry shapes public policy to meet its private goals. Scandals involving industries often raise the question "have the regulators been captured by the industries they were meant to regulate?" The Deepwater Horizon disaster and the Bruce Carson affair suggest it isn't just regulatory agencies that are prone to capture; it is the broader institutions of democracy. Parallel patterns emerged in both cases, with sophisticated and extremely well-funded campaigns aimed at regulators, the civil service, politicians at various levels, and universities.

There were at least ten investigations into the causes of the Deepwater Horizon blowout, often focusing on issues such as the quality of the equipment or the inadequacy of safety procedures. The National Commission into the BP Deepwater Horizon Spill and Offshore Drilling took a broader view.[164] Without letting the oil companies off the hook, the commission also turned its attention to the failures of government agencies. Its report provided important lessons in the relationship between the fossil fuel industry and the government. In effect, it found the boundaries between the industry and the government were breaking down.

The final report of the National Commission spent thirty pages analyzing why the American government failed to act on the evidence that offshore drilling in the Gulf of Mexico was facing a crisis in safety.[165] The failure to respond to the foreseeable risks of offshore drilling offers important clues about the failure to respond to the foreseeable risks of global warming.

The report described a series of disasters involving American oil companies that claimed hundreds of lives and caused untold environmental damage in the North Sea and off the coasts of Canada, Alaska, and the Gulf of Mexico, including the tragic sinking of the *Ocean Ranger* off the coast of Newfoundland in 1982, which killed eighty-four men, and the horrifying fire on the Piper Alpha rig in the North Sea in 1988, which killed 167 men. While the governments of Norway, Britain, and Canada responded to these disasters by overhauling their safety procedures for North Sea and North Atlantic drilling, the American government balked at action in its territory, so that in the words of the commission, "the only question had become not whether an accident would happen, but when."[166]

The National Commission found that the American Petroleum Institute (API) was essentially writing the government's regulations. API was producing safety and technical standards that "the US Department of the Interior has historically adopted . . . as formal agency regulations." The commission then bluntly concluded that API's standards had come to express "the lowest common denominator" rather than best industry practices: "Because . . . the Interior Department has in turn relied on API in developing its own regulatory safety standards, API's shortfalls have undermined the entire federal regulatory system."[167]

The commission found API persistently opposed safety improvements by the government branch that governed American offshore drilling, the Minerals Management Service (MMS). "Beginning early in the last decade [i.e., shortly after 2000], the trade organization API steadfastly resisted MMS's efforts to require all companies to demonstrate that they have a complete safety and environmental management system . . ." The commission drove home its point: "For years, API also led the effort to persuade the Minerals Management Service not to adopt a new regulatory approach . . . and instead has favored relying on voluntary, recommended safety standards."[168]

In the extreme conditions of a deep-sea well, the performance of the cement used to seal the wellbore is crucial. The report singled out Halliburton, one of two major contractors working on the well for BP, for providing cement that "repeatedly failed Halliburton's own laboratory tests."[169] How could this happen? The commission had an answer: "notwithstanding the enormously important role cementing plays in well construction . . . there were no meaningful regulations governing requirement for cementing a well and testing the cement used."[170]

The result of a regulatory system like this could be fatal. "From 2004 to 2009," the commission found that

> fatalities in the offshore oil and gas industry were more than
> four times higher per person hours worked in US waters
> than in European waters, even though many of the same
> companies work in both venues. This striking statistical
> discrepancy reinforces the view that the problem . . . depends
> on the differing cultures and regulatory systems under which
> members of the industry operate.[171]

The commission's report did not mince words. The efforts of the Minerals Management Service (MMS) to adopt a more rigorous regulatory regime "were repeatedly revisited, refined, delayed, and blocked alternatively by industry or skeptical agency political appointees."[172] Singling out the American Petroleum Institute, the commission wrote, "Industry served as an initial impediment to MMS reform efforts — and has largely remained so."[173] Another industry association, the Offshore Operators Committee, "vehemently objected" to increased requirements.[174] It wasn't just industry that resisted action: "In 2003, the White House stiffly opposed MMS's efforts to update its requirements for the reporting of key risk indicators."[175] In other words, the White House of George W. Bush and Dick Cheney, both former oil executives, was actively opposing the efforts of an agency within its own government to improve safety standards in the oil industry.

When the commission got to the bottom of the issues impeding action, they found it was neither incompetence nor bad luck. It was more insidious. "The root problem," wrote the commission, was that

> political leaders within both the Executive Branch [i.e. the White House] and Congress have failed to ensure that agency regulators have had the resources necessary to exercise authority, including personnel and technical expertise, and, no less important, the political autonomy needed to overcome the powerful commercial interests that have opposed more stringent safety regulation.

Starved of resources by politicians who were friendly to the oil industry and thwarted in its need for the autonomy to stand up to powerful commercial interests, the MMS never had a chance. It was an institution captured by the private interests of the industry it was meant to regulate.

The National Commission was careful to say the great majority of employees at MMS were ethical and committed, but the record of the MMS was stained years before the Deepwater blowout. In 2008, investigators at its Denver office reported "a culture of ethical failure" that included a key group of staff receiving gifts and gratuities from oil and gas companies, in two cases over 135 times; illicit drug use "in consort with industry"; and two staff who "had brief sexual relationships with industry contacts." The inspector-general who led the investigations wryly noted, "Sexual relations with prohibited sources cannot, by definition, be arm's length."[176]

A different investigation found that the MMS operation along the Gulf coast was also plagued with problems and conflicts of interest. "Of greatest concern to me," wrote the acting inspector-general on this file, "is the environment in which these MMS inspectors operate — particularly the ease with which they move between industry and government."[177] She went on to describe an organization rife with "fraternizing and gift exchange" between agency inspectors and the industry they inspected.

Within weeks of the Deepwater disaster, the Obama government concluded the MMS was an institution damaged beyond repair and disbanded it.

* * *

The reach of the fossil fuel industry extended far beyond the MMS and offshore drilling. From government agencies to political parties to universities, the industry held remarkable sway with public institutions, which it used to shape public understanding, influence laws and regulations, avoid accountability, and rearrange the use of language.

The White House Council on Environmental Quality

Shortly after coming into office, the government of George W. Bush appointed a fifteen-year veteran of the American Petroleum Institute (API) as chief of staff at the powerful White House Council on Environmental Quality, which had the longstanding job of coordinating the American government's environmental agencies and laws.[178] His name was Philip Cooney, and he worked with a wide range of top officials, including in Vice-President Cheney's office.

Cooney, an economist and lawyer but not a scientist, had been the "climate change leader" at API, which had worked for years to oppose limits on fossil fuel emissions. He continued his interest in climate change in his new job and began editing drafts of government reports on the topic.[179] Staff at government agencies soon realized that Cooney's edits were consistently aimed at sowing doubt about the science of global warming by removing references to the issue or adding words that amplified the unknowns. With Cooney's edits, "uncertainties" became "significant and fundamental uncertainties" and phrases such as "Earth is undergoing relatively rapid change" became "Earth may be undergoing relatively rapid change."[180] Government staff who were preparing a major report for Congress "were told to delete the pages that summarized the most recent Intergovernmental Panel on Climate Change report and the material about the National Assessment of climate change impacts that had just come out," as one staff member later recalled.[181]

In March 2005, Rick Piltz, a soft-spoken senior officer with a key government environmental agency, could take Cooney's interference no longer and resigned. He took his concerns to a non-profit legal team, and two months later blew the whistle on Cooney's activities, providing the story to the media, along with copies of documents with Cooney's handwritten edits on them.[182] Days after the story hit the media, Cooney stepped out of his position at the council and almost immediately into a position at Exxon. Cooney had spent four years shaping American climate change policy and political and public opinion.

Cooney's approach was to massage language so it would relax concern about fossil fuel emissions and global warming. Reworking the language of global warming became a kind of team sport, and it caught on in Canada, where CAPP and government officials began referring to fossil fuels as "clean energy," even when talking among themselves. Perhaps it was moral anesthetic, easing any discomfort they might feel: "If we don't say it, it won't hurt." By then, the gamesmanship of language in the global warming debates had taken a pivotal turn.

The Republican Party

In the lead up to the 2002 mid-term elections, polling showed that Bush and the Republicans were weak on environmental issues. One of their top advisors, Frank Luntz, wrote a long report providing strategies to change perceptions not by changing policies but by changing language. It is a classic piece of communications strategy worth reading to understand the more cunning machinations of some political campaigns.[183] The section on the environment is disturbingly cynical. It confirms that on issues of environmental protection, the Republicans were "viewed through the prism of suspicion," so the "first (and most important) step to . . . bringing people around to your point of view on environmental issues is to convince them of your *sincerity* and *concern*." "Sincerity" and "concern" are italicized in the report to emphasize their importance. When it came to "Winning the Global Warming Debate," the first recommendation was that "*The scientific debate remains open . . . you need to continue to make the lack of scientific certainty a primary issue in the debate . . .*" — all italicized. A bit later, the report delivers another message, again in italics: "*The most important principle in any discussion of global warming is your commitment to sound science.*" The report never mentions that the science was sound in 1965 when the president's science advisory committee published concerns, or that it was sound in 1978 when James F. Black warned Exxon executives about global warming, or in 1980 when Dr. Laurman told the API task force about the risk of "globally catastrophic effects," or in 1992 when the world signed the agreements at the Rio Earth Summit.

Here, though, is the awful twist. In the next paragraph, the report admits the truth, also in italics: "*The scientific debate is closing (against us) but not yet closed.*" The bracketed words "against us" are right there in the report. It is hard not to conclude that the team who worked on this report and those who read it knew they were on the wrong side of science, and chose nonetheless to convince the public that their position was right. So much for sincerity, concern, and a commitment to sound science.

One of the first outcomes of this report was a shift in terminology. The report's research showed the term *climate change* drew much less public concern than the term *global warming*. As one research respondent said, climate change "sounds like you're going from Pittsburgh to Fort Lauderdale." It is time, said the report, "*to start talking about 'climate change' instead of global warming,*" continuing its enthusiasm for italics. The Bush administration took the advice. The *New York Times* reported that President Bush, who had used the term *global warming* in speeches in 2001, began consistently using the term *climate change* after receiving the report.[184] It did not say if he used the term with sincerity and concern.

The American Government and Congress

Startling numbers of people moved through "revolving door" positions among the petroleum industry, lobbying firms, government, and Congress. Philip Cooney's career track from API to government to industry was an example, and he had a lot of company. Colonel Lawrence Wilkerson, chief of staff to Bush's Secretary of State Colin Powell, estimated that under Vice-President Cheney, 1,600 people were recruited from the petroleum industry to take positions in environmental and energy agencies that regulated fossil fuel industries.[185] It is unlikely they were champions of reducing fossil fuel use.

Spurred by interest in the Deepwater Horizon, the *Washington Post* reported in July 2010 that the oil and gas sector retained over 600 lobbyists in Washington, and three out of every four had held positions in the federal government, including eighteen former members of Congress.[186] Congress was a primary target for election financing and lobbying by the fossil fuel industry. In 2009, the year before the Deepwater disaster, oil and gas interests spent at least $154 million on lobbying, while the largest coal user in the United States, the electric utility industry, spent $134.7 million, according to work by the non-partisan Project on Government Oversight.[187]

The Government of Louisiana

Deepwater Horizon drew special attention to Louisiana, the state closest to the blowout. Like Alberta's government, Louisiana's government depends heavily on oil and gas royalties, which provide 15 to 40 per cent of state revenues, depending on the year.[188] Louisiana did not collect royalties on offshore wells, which were under federal jurisdiction, but that didn't stop the state governor from stepping up for offshore drilling. Despite the devastation to the fishing and tourism industries and the concerns for public health, just six weeks after the blowout and long before it was capped, Louisiana Governor Bobby Jindal urged President Obama to lift the six-month moratorium the federal government had placed on offshore drilling.[189] The moratorium was intended to halt further drilling in the Gulf until the cause of the Deepwater Horizon blowout was known. It was fought in court by oil companies and was lifted after five months.

In 2014, Governor Jindal signed a bill that killed a major lawsuit brought by a state agency against the oil and gas industry claiming damages for coastal destruction, including the Deepwater Horizon blowout. A consortium of environmental groups charged that Jindal was influenced by financial contributions by oil and gas companies to his political campaigns, and released a list of 231 contributions from 2003 to 2013 from oil and gas companies totalling $1,019,777.[190] The bill Jindal signed was sponsored by state Senator Robert Adley, who had held ownership and executive positions in the oil and gas industry since 1972, and continued as president of a gas management company while serving as senator. His position on the bill was clear:

> I think it is absurd to say that the oil and gas industry has damaged the coast. They did what they were told to do, and a lot of what they have done has helped us, not hurt us.[191, 192]

Universities
In the months after the Deepwater Horizon blowout, BP committed $35 million in grants to four major universities in the Gulf region, one each in Louisiana, Florida, Mississippi, and Alabama.[193] A scientist from Louisiana State University, Dr. Ed Overton, became a prominent media figure in the summer of 2010, saying the Gulf would recover surprisingly quickly from the spill. Five years later, BP was claiming the Gulf had recovered, yet still had workers cleaning hundreds of tar

balls and occasional tar mats from beaches. The Gulf state fisheries had completed a five-year disaster recovery plan with mixed success.[194] The Gulf had proven resilient, but as Executive Director of the Gulf Restoration Network Cynthia Sarthou said,

> Dolphin deaths continue, oil is still on the bottom of the ocean, tar balls keep coming up, and nobody really is able to say what we may find in five years, ten years . . . It's not publicly seen but it is out there . . . and so whether we see it or not the potential impacts of its presence may plague us for decades.[195]

Despite the reassurances from BP and selected university scientists, she was right to be concerned. When the Deepwater Horizon exploded, a reporter for the *Guardian* returned to the site of the 1967 wreck of the *Torrey Canyon* and found "crude from the *Torrey Canyon* is still killing wildlife on a daily basis"[196] — forty-three years after it broke apart on rocks off the Cornwall coast.

Chapter 5
The road to Trump

By 2010, the year Deepwater Horizon exploded and eighteen years after the nations of the world committed to action on global warming at the Rio Earth Summit, the money flowing in the United States to *defeat* action on global warming was almost beyond imagination. The effects of this money inevitably spilled into Canada through a tangled web of industry associations, corporations, political interests, and news media that carried the same information and misinformation in both countries.

As you will recall from Chapter 3, the atmosphere is a commons and protecting it from carbon emissions requires tough government regulations on fossil fuel use. These regulations need to curtail, and in the long run eliminate, the use of fossil fuels. Naturally, the fossil fuel industry — some of its members more than others — will fight back. They have a lot of money and welcome allies wherever they find them. They find a lot of them in the political far right.

A far-right stream has long flowed in American politics, with strong anti-government, anti-regulation, and anti-tax currents. Though this stream was not always dominant, it was often powerful. It worked to undermine Franklin D. Roosevelt during his presidency; built up behind Barry Goldwater in his failed 1964 campaign as Republican presidential candidate; and pulled Ronald Reagan to the right during his presidency in the 1980s.

The far right was an excellent fit with the fossil fuel industry's agenda on global warming; as an anti-government movement, it offered the perfect vehicle for blocking government action on global warming.

So it was not coincidence that the far-right stream in American politics gained strength in the decades after the Rio Earth Summit. In the late 1990s, it helped defeat the Kyoto Accord in the Senate, and in 2000 it supported the Bush-Cheney ticket in the controversial win over Gore. In 2009, one month less a day after President Obama's swearing in, the Tea Party was launched — spontaneous in appearance but, in reality, well organized and largely staged.[197] In 2016, the far right came to the fore as Tea Party Republicans won majority control of both houses of Congress and helped put Donald Trump in the White House. Canada was not immune to these trends: The long-established Progressive Conservative Party was effectively taken over in 2003 by the harder right Conservative Party of Canada (which itself was a merger of the Reform and Alliance parties), largely led by a power base in Calgary, the headquarters city of Canada's oil industry.

There was no way to tally all the money spent opposing action on global warming, but watchdog and environmental groups including the Union of Concerned Scientists and Greenpeace kept tabs on the spending that was publicly declared. It wasn't easy. One important accounting was conducted by Robert Brulle of Drexel University in Philadelphia.[198] Using previous studies, Brulle identified 118 organizations in the United States that had a "substantive focus" on opposing legislative action to reduce carbon emissions, including think tanks, trade associations, and advocacy groups. Of these 118 organizations, he was able to obtain reliable financial data on ninety-one of them published by the Internal Revenue Service.

Brulle's findings were astonishing: From 2003 to 2010, the combined income of these organizations averaged more than $900 million US a year, for a total income of more than $7 billion US during those eight years. Brulle was clear that most of these organizations had multiple focuses, so not all this income was spent opposing action on global warming; it was not possible to know that level of detail. The $900-million-a-year went to the larger "conservative movement," of which the "climate change denial movement" was a "subsidiary movement." But all these organizations had a substantive focus on opposing action on global warming, and Brulle's research missed many other organizations with the same agenda.

To put $900 million into a Canadian perspective, it is *nine times* greater than the total combined spending of the Conservative, Liberal, and New Democratic parties, plus all 923 of their candidates in the 2011 federal election campaign, paying for everything from staff to brochures, polls to television ads.[199] In the United States, that $900 million was flowing every year, not every four-year election cycle, and it represented only a subset of conservative and global warming denial groups.

Brulle traced the sources of the money pouring into the counter climate change movement as far as records allowed. The biggest source was membership dues paid by businesses into trade associations; another source was conservative foundations, which paid more than $500 million during this period. Laws in the United States enabled the identities of many donors to be concealed from public view. Among donors Brulle could identify, the largest included those affiliated with the Scaife family foundations, whose fortune originated with banks and Gulf Oil, and foundations affiliated with brothers Charles and David Koch.

Charles and David Koch were particularly notable in resisting action to reduce emissions. They were the owners of Koch Industries, the second largest privately held corporation in the United States, which made them two of the richest men in the world. Owning Koch Industries privately (i.e., owning it personally) offered some great advantages. They had no outside shareholders to hold them to account; they didn't have to disclose much information nor share decision-making power with others; and they didn't have to pay dividends, so they could plough the company's profits into growth or personal priorities.

Koch Industries was headquartered in Wichita, Kansas, and globally employed more than 100,000 people. The company started in the 1930s with the oil refining business of Fred Koch, father of Charles and David. Fred was an engineer who, in the 1920s, invented a better way to refine oil, but couldn't get American oil companies to invest. He got his big break building refineries for the Soviets under Stalin from 1930–32 and in Nazi Germany in 1934–35.[200]

Charles and David took over the company in the 1960s, and by 2015 the company had major holdings in forest products, fertilizers, chemicals, and electronics, producing everything from Lycra stretch fabric to plywood.[201] Its heart, though, remained petroleum, and its refineries, pipelines, and terminals were integral components of North America's petroleum system. Through a subsidiary called Flint Hill Resources, the Kochs were one of the largest purchasers, shippers, and exporters of Canadian oil, much of which went to their refinery at Pine Bend, Minnesota, which processed over 300,000 barrels of Alberta crude each day. The *Washington Post* reported in 2014 that the Kochs were the largest non-Canadian leaseholders in Alberta's oil sands and stood to benefit substantially if the Keystone XL pipeline were built.[202]

★ ★ ★

Fred Koch held extremely right-wing political views, and Charles and David took up the their father's banner. Charles Koch set up the right-wing Cato Institute in 1977, giving it $10 to $20 million in tax deductible donations in its first three years alone.[203] The following year, he wrote a revealing essay in the magazine *Libertarian Review*, which read like a manifesto. It revealed the anti-government spirit that a decade later was to begin merging into the movement opposing action on global warming. The headline on the magazine cover, in giant, bold capitals, was "Toward the Second American Revolution: Libertarian

Strategies for Today." Koch's article was titled "The Business Community: Resisting Regulation." He took American business leaders to task for seeking too much government support and regulation and drifting away from the principles of a free market. He did not mince words: "Strategically, the critical point is to fight to eliminate, rather than continue, all government interventions, even those that provide short-term profits" (p. 32). Koch's anti-tax message was blunt:

Morally, lowering taxes is simply defending property rights . . . Strategically, lowering taxes reduces government . . . There is no "fair" share of taxes. Our goal is not to reallocate the burden of government; our goal is to roll back government. We should consistently work to reduce all taxes . . .

Koch's article revealed a man who wasn't just discussing ideas; he was planning action. He urged the business community, "Do not cooperate voluntarily with governments ; instead, resist wherever and to whatever extent you legally can. And do so in the name of justice."[204] He continued:

We have accepted the fallacious concept that the corporation has a broad "social responsibility" beyond its duty to its shareholders. We have been . . . hoodwinked into characterizing government regulation as "virtuous" and in the "public interest." As a typical example, the Advertising Council, backed by most of the major U.S. corporations, goes so far as to describe regulation as, "the promotion of fair economic competition and the protection of public health and safety." What simple-minded nonsense!

Koch criticized universities and foundations of the day for being "philosophically dedicated to the destruction of our businesses and of what remains of the free market" and called for the "development of talent" that would have "the knowledge, skill, and sophistication to meet statist adversaries and their arguments head on, and to defeat them. They must have the desire and commitment to unceasingly advance the cause of liberty." True to his cause, he opposed foreign wars "as the single greatest force behind the growth of government."

Koch concluded his article with a call to action to which he himself would commit much of his life and fortune: "Businessmen should be involved in politics and political action — from local tax revolts to campaigns for Congress and the presidency." The key to success was to launch a movement. "Ideas do not spread themselves; they spread only through people. Which means we need a *movement.*" His purpose for the movement was absolute and clear: "our movement must destroy the prevalent statist paradigm." In the article's final sentences, Koch urged readers to support the Libertarian Party. Koch eventually gave up on the Libertarian Party, but he stayed with the other ideas in the article with conviction.

In her important book *Dark Money,* Jane Mayer examined the central role the Kochs have played in American politics in recent decades. David Koch ran for vice-president under the Libertarian banner in 1980 and was trounced by voters.[205] The Kochs concluded that political change would be wrought more effectively from behind the scenes. Despite setbacks, they steadily laid the groundwork in the 1980s for an anti-regulatory, anti-government "free market" social movement by establishing and funding advocacy, training, and lobbying groups across the country at the cost of millions of dollars. They were laying the groundwork for the movement Charles Koch had described in his *Libertarian Review* article. By the 1990s, after a series of worker safety and environmental failures at their businesses led to losses in courts and with regulators, the Kochs realized they needed mainstream political traction. They now faced a world with widespread calls for governments to reduce fossil fuel emissions through regulation and taxes.

They turned their focus to the Republican Party. Koch money and determination quickly gained attention, and David became vice-chair of Bob Dole's 1996 presidential run against Bill Clinton. The Kochs were the Dole campaign's third largest financial backers.[206] Through the final Clinton term (1996–2000) and the two terms of George W. Bush (2001–08), the Kochs broadened and deepened their political movement, reaching into state and local politics and recruiting extraordinarily wealthy allies who added hundreds of millions of dollars and much-needed organizational capacity to the movement. The Kochs' political machine had so many tentacles it became known as the "Kochtopus."

Mayer described some of the activities supported directly and indirectly by the Kochs and others in the far-right network:

• Two dozen privately funded academic centres typically housed on university campuses, that sustained a brain trust; conducted research; refined strategies; lobbied governments; and provided pedigreed commentators to appear on television, radio, print, and web programs.[207]

• Subsidies for pro-business, antiregulatory, and anti-tax programs at hundreds of colleges, universities, and higher education institutions. The Charles Koch Foundation alone was supporting such programs at 307 different institutions in 2015, with plans to expand.[208] (NBC News reported the Koch network funded 300 "university professor positions" across the country.[209])

• Hundreds — and at times thousands — of campaign workers to support chosen candidates in local, state, and federal elections.

• Computer centres with databases containing detailed profiles on millions of American voters.[210]

• A national network of agencies that drafted fossil fuel–
friendly legislation for elected officials to present as their own:
"In 2013 alone the American Legislative Exchange Council
produced some seventy bills aimed at impeding government
support for alternative, renewable energy programs."[211]

• Money and material for media personalities; lobbyists;
attack ads; newspaper columns; school curricula and church
gatherings; and lavish receptions to impress decision makers.[212]

• A campaign in evangelical Christian communities centred
on *Resisting the Green Dragon*, a film promoted by a flashy
website, ominous percussion, and a voice-over that began
with these words:

> In what has become one of the greatest deceptions
> of our day, radical environmentalism is striving to
> put America and the world under its destructive
> control. This so-called green dragon is seducing
> your children in our classrooms and popular
> culture. Its lust for political power now extends to
> the highest global levels . . .[213]

In the context of a strategy to build a social movement that would
destroy "the prevalent statist paradigm," this mix of activities made perfect sense. It fit together like gears in a machine. The academic centres
— the Mercatus Center; the American Enterprise Institute; the Heritage
Foundation; the Hoover Institution; the Cato Institute; and, in Canada,
the Fraser Institute[214] among them — functioned to build a public discourse that minimized or even denied the risks of global warming. These
centres gave an imprint of credibility to the counter–climate change
movement. The hundreds of college and university programs cultivated
young minds and provided a constant flow of recruits to the movement.

The campaign workers were foot soldiers of the movement, turning ideas into organization, and organization into political power. They were armed with the best possible voter profiles from the databases, telling them how individuals felt about issues and how their minds could be changed or their votes secured. The supply line of money and material kept the whole operation going, and the evangelical congregations who believed their children were being seduced by the "green dragon" provided a moral and righteous vanguard to quell doubt and justify faith above reason.

The Kochs counted among their largest allies a stellar list of fossil fuel billionaires.[215] Corbin Robertson, Jr., owned what were reportedly the second largest coal reserves in the United States, behind only those of the American government. Harold Hamm, head of Continental Resources, and Larry Nichols, chairman of Devon Energy, had both made billions from fracking in oil and gas formations around the United States. Nichols served on the board of the American Petroleum Institute for many years, including two years as its chairman, and his company, Devon Energy, had an important presence in Alberta's oil sands.[216] In full, the Kochs' network included oil, natural gas, and coal investors from producing regions across the continent.

One of their top priorities was to resist action on global warming. Inevitably this brought the network into direct opposition with President Obama, who was determined to address the threat of global warming. As Mayer wrote,

> If there was a single ultra-wealthy interest group that hoped
> to see Obama fail as he took office in January 2009, it was
> the fossil fuel industry. And if there was one test of its
> members' concentrated financial power over the machinery of
> American democracy, it was this minority's ability to stave off
> government action on climate change . . .[217]

The years of paralyzing standoff between the Obama White House and Congress were in no small part due to fossil fuel influence and money. The fossil fuel industry directed between 70 and 90 per cent of its donations to Republicans,[218] who consistently blocked action on global warming. By 2011, 156 members of Congress had signed a "No Climate Tax" pledge organized by the Koch network, and Republicans had pushed through a painful 16 per cent budget cut to the most important environmental organization in the United States, the federal Environmental Protection Agency (EPA).[219] Anti-tax, anti-regulation, and anti-government themes provided perfect frames to promote these initiatives to politicians and the public.

The Kochs and their allies had high hopes that the 2012 presidential election would see Obama replaced by Mitt Romney. Romney had respected global warming science for years, telling his campaign in 2011 that it was "important for us to reduce our emissions of pollutants and greenhouse gases that may well be significant contributors to the climate change and the global warming that we're seeing."[220] The following year, his position had reversed. He wanted support from the fossil fuel industry and the Koch network, and now his view was that "we don't know what's causing climate change on this planet . . . the idea of spending trillions and trillions of dollars to try to reduce CO2 emissions is not the right course for us."[221] He made other promises too, including income tax cuts, and in Mayer's words, "If these policy shifts were designed in part to win the Kochs' support, they succeeded. By July 2012, David Koch not only embraced Romney but threw a $75,000-per-couple fund-raiser for him at his Southampton estate."[222] Money didn't speak in American global warming politics; it shouted, and the shouting was about to get even louder.

* * *

Although Romney lost to Obama in 2012, the Kochs and their allies did not retreat. They were conducting a permanent campaign and had a powerful new tool to deploy, which had begun taking form four years prior. In the weeks before the 2008 primary vote, in which Hillary Clinton vied with Barack Obama for the presidential nomination for the Democratic Party, a conservative non-profit organization called Citizens United wanted to run television advertisements for a film that was critical of Clinton. The Federal Election Commission blocked the ads, ruling they violated campaign laws restricting corporate and union electioneering in the weeks before any primary or presidential vote. Citizens United took the election commission to court, arguing the laws restricted its right to free speech. In 2010, the US Supreme Court ruled in favour of Citizens United. This, combined with other rulings, had the effect of removing restrictions on political funding by corporations, unions, and non-profit groups.

The Citizens United ruling opened a flood of special interest money into American politics, and the biggest flows tended to come from those interests with the deepest pockets. The fossil fuel industry had very deep pockets, none deeper than those belonging to Charles and David Koch. Though the brothers had opposed the Obama government time and again, their personal fortunes more than doubled during its tenure: According to *Forbes* magazine, their wealth rose from $16 billion apiece in 2009 to $42 billion apiece in 2016.[223] As individuals they were tied with each other as the seventh richest persons in the US; taken together, their $84 billion would place them in top spot.

Romney's loss to Obama in 2012 drove division in the Republican Party between its traditional organization and the politically frustrated Koch network. The Koch network would not be denied. As Mayer's research revealed, they invested heavily in political databases, hiring a hundred staff to operate a new computerized system to assemble detailed portraits of more than 190 million active American voters and 250 million American consumers. Integrating consumer and political data could get the system deep into people's lives. It could blanket individuals with personalized communications, urging them to vote or to stay home. The databases were constantly updated by fieldworkers who used handheld electronic devices to collect information on voters in real time. Political databases of this sophistication were moving beyond the traditional function of keeping tabs on voters; now they were actively bringing individuals in line with pre-established political programs and norms, in this case those of the anti-government right. Population surveillance was evolving into mass discipline.

The Kochs' system out-performed the Republican Party's own, and "With little other choice, in 2014 the RNC [Republican National Committee] struck what it called a 'historic' deal to share data with the Kochs."[224] Managing and controlling voter data is a crucial function for any modern political party, and that data is guarded jealously. The traditional Republican organization was losing exclusive control of its data system. A key boundary defining the Republican Party was breached.

The 2014 mid-term elections, in which all members of the House of Representatives and one-third of senators faced re-election, delivered big wins for the Republicans, who got majority control of both houses and isolated Obama in the White House. These were the costliest mid-term elections in history with the largest ever flow of outsider money:

> ... the largest overall source fuelling this explosion of
> private and often secret spending was the Koch network. All
> told, it poured over $100 million into competitive House and
> Senate races and almost twice that amount into other kinds
> of activism.[225]

The group Americans for Prosperity, substantially funded and controlled by the Koch brothers and a central cog in their political machine, swelled to 550 paid staff during the 2014 elections, with as many as fifty assigned to a critical state such as Florida.[226]

One of the Kochs' favoured candidates was Mitch McConnell.[227] McConnell was a Republican from Kentucky, home to some of

America's largest coal mines, and he had a history of vigorously opposing action to reduce emissions.[228] After the 2014 elections, McConnell became the Senate majority leader in Congress and immediately began attacking Obama's efforts to reduce emissions. In an attempt to undermine the president's global warming campaign, McConnell wrote a letter to every state governor providing a legal blueprint for states to challenge federal requirements to reduce carbon emissions in court. He urged the states to refuse to comply with Environmental Protection Agency (EPA) regulations to reduce carbon emissions.[229]

Many states took McConnell's suggestion and sued the EPA. One of these states was Indiana under Governor Mike Pence,[230] and another was Oklahoma, where the attorney-general in charge of suing the EPA — more than a dozen times — was Scott Pruitt.[231] Pence and Pruitt would soon go on to top positions with President Trump.

By this point, the far-right movement had long depended on the fortunes, organization, and power of fossil fuel interests. If all the coal, oil, and gas money were to be withdrawn from far-right politics, its movement would be staggered and opposition to action on global warming would sag like an old balloon. The far-right movement was like a partially owned subsidiary of the fossil fuel business.

As long as the American president was determined to act on global warming, the EPA and the rest of the climate change community had their backs covered. That era ended on November 8, 2016, with the election of Donald Trump. Trump was a loud champion of fossil fuels and repeatedly dismissed global warming as a hoax:

> The concept of global warming was created by and
> for the Chinese in order to make U.S. manufacturing
> non-competitive;[232]

Global warming is a total, and very expensive, hoax!;

Give me clean, beautiful and healthy air — not the same
old climate change (global warming) bullshit! I am tired of
hearing this nonsense.

Trump ran for office as an outsider to the American political system
and seemed in open combat with the Republican establishment during
the campaign, with withering public denouncements flying in all direc-
tions. Charles Koch was publicly nervous about Trump's volatility and
distanced himself from Trump in August 2016,[233] directing the Koch
network's money to non-presidential races. The scale of money was
unprecedented. In 2012, the Koch network, fully backing Romney for
president and heavily involved in congressional and other races around
the country, spent $400 million.[234] In 2016, it spent $750 million without supporting any presidential candidate, and its political machine
had 1,600 paid staff working in thirty-five states.[235] When the 2016
election was over, the Republicans dominated America's political scene
with majorities in the Senate and the House of Representatives and a
president in the White House.

Within hours of Trump's inauguration on January 20, 2017, the
White House website had erased all references to climate change.[236] My
search for the term *climate change* on the website highlighted references
to changes in the "tax climate." The day after inauguration, January 21,
scientists began noticing a surge in defunct Internet links to American
government research on climate science. The Arctic is especially vulnerable to global warming, and researcher Victoria Hermann reported
the US National Strategy for the Arctic, plus its implementation plan
and all reports of progress were "gone within a matter of minutes . . .
as more and more links turned red." It must have been like watching
the heart and breathing monitors on a hospitalized patient flat-line.
January 21 marked "the beginning of a process that transformed into a
slow, incessant march of deleting datasets, webpages and policies about

the Arctic." Each defunct page, reported the researcher, was "an effort by the Trump administration to deliberately undermine our ability to make good policy decisions by limiting access to scientific evidence."[237]

Trump's cabinet choices tilted the American government sharply toward fossil fuels. Rex Tillerson stepped from the CEO's office at Exxon/Mobil into the office of secretary of state. Trump's energy secretary was former Texas Governor Rick Perry, an enthusiast for fracking (and, to his credit, for wind power). The new administrator of the Environmental Protection Agency was Scott Pruitt, the former attorney-general of Oklahoma who had spent previous years suing the very institution he now headed. Pruitt's 2013 election committee in Oklahoma had been chaired by oil billionaire Harold Hamm,[238] an important figure in the Koch network. Hamm was delighted to see Pruitt put in charge of the EPA. In fact, Hamm was delighted with the whole picture, saying Trump "continues to pick awfully good candidates for all the cabinet posts."[239]

Despite Trump's victory, the Kochs remained uneasy with his immigration restrictions, spending plans, and unpredictable personality.[240] The story spread that the Kochs were not on side with Donald Trump, but alumni of the Koch network were strewn about the Trump administration like chunks of coal at a mine face.

Vice-President Mike Pence had been a favourite of the Koch network for many years, and his campaigns for Indiana governor received $300,000 from David Koch.[241] Pence's senior advisor for managing Trump's transition to power, Marc Short, came from a position running the Kochs' donor organization, Freedom Partners.[242] Mike Pompeo, Republican congressman from Koch Industries' home state of Kansas, became Trump's director of the CIA. The Kochs had been investors and partners in Pompeo's business ventures before he went into politics, and "Pompeo was the single largest recipient of Koch campaign funds in Congress," wrote Jane Mayer.[243]

Another key player on the Trump team was Michael Catanzaro, a one-time lobbyist for the Kochs and a global warming skeptic with strong ties to the fossil fuel industry. His role was to advise the president on energy policy. There was also Myron Ebell, who worked at a Washington think tank partly funded by fossil fuel money, including that of the Kochs.[244] Ebell was a strident global warming skeptic who declared, "The environmental movement is, in my view, the greatest threat to freedom and prosperity in the modern world."[245] He led Trump's transition team in taking over the EPA.

Trump and his cabinet worked quickly to reverse plans to reduce fossil fuel use put in place by President Obama. By the end of his second month in office, Trump had signed a presidential permit allowing the Keystone XL pipeline to proceed[246] and introduced a budget to Congress that proposed cutting the EPA's budget by 31 per cent.[247] He promised, to a cheering crowd of autoworkers, that his government would ease up on regulations demanding higher standards for vehicle fuel efficiency[248] and released plans to roll back the phase-out of coal-fired power plants.[249] Whether or not he could steer his agenda past his opponents remained to be seen, but his pro-fossil fuel direction was clear.

The fossil fuel industry had captured an impressive array of institutions. The White House delivered to the industry the EPA, the energy department, the Department of Interior (which managed drilling and mines on federal lands and waters), and a host of other agencies. There were fossil fuel majorities in the Senate and the House of Representatives and in about half of the country's state legislatures, and the industry could count on support from an important portion of the media and a sizable number of think tanks and university programs. Twenty-five years after the Rio Earth Summit, the fossil fuel industry still stalked the corridors of power, the carbon load in the atmosphere was climbing fast, and average global temperatures were the highest ever recorded.

PART TWO
CAPTURE

Chapter 6
The dynamics of democracy

This book started with the question, "Why have democratic governments failed to act to reduce carbon emissions despite dire warnings and compelling evidence of a profound and growing threat of global warming?" The five chapters of Part One presented detailed evidence from police investigations, courtrooms, government commissions, scientific reports, and media stories that begin to answer this question. The purpose of the three chapters in Part Two is to step back from these details to make sense of this evidence from a broader perspective. Chapter Six discusses how democracy functions, and the following chapter builds upon this to present a theory of the deep state. The final chapter in Part Two examines the factors that engender a particular type of deep state — oil's deep state. Together, these chapters begin to show the connections among global warming, the fossil fuel industry, and modern democracy.

* * *

Democracy is much more than people voting for their governments through elections. Democracy is an assemblage of institutions.

Institutions are where democracy becomes real, where its principles and ideas are turned into actions, its conflicts fought and resolved, its rules made and enforced.

The word *institution* has many meanings reflected in a large literature across the social sciences.[250] Here, we're not using it in a broad sense such as "the institution of marriage," nor in the physical sense of a place ("my cousin just escaped from an institution"). We're focused on one kind of institution: formal organizations with important roles in the democratic function of society. Such institutions exist for long periods (sometimes centuries), have written rules to be followed and enforced, and employ people who occupy defined positions that exist independently of any individual. Police forces, for example, are formally organized and have positions of chief, deputy chief, and officers that continue even while different people come and go through those positions, so police forces are institutions, whereas mobs are not. An institution is, essentially, a set of interlocking rules of behaviour supported by rewards and punishments: Your job is to do x and y, but not z; you take direction from this person and give direction to that person; you can allocate this amount of money and no more, and only for these purposes.

In a modern democracy, every government department fits the criteria of a formal institution. Natural Resources Canada (NRCan), in which Bruce Carson, EPIC, and CAPP were so interested, is organized under the *Department of Natural Resources Act*, and its mandate under the *Act* includes "the sustainable development of Canada's natural resources," "the responsible development and use of Canada's natural resources," and "cooperation with the governments of the provinces and with non-governmental organizations in Canada."[251] Environment Canada is organized along the same lines as NRCan. Its mandate under the *Department of Environment Act* is to address matters concerning "the preservation and enhancement of the quality of the natural environment."[252] It is easy to see why the oil industry paid such close attention to these departments.

Democratic institutions exist far beyond the government. The courts, universities, schools, regulators, police, political parties, and the news media are all democratic institutions with their own mandates and rules that allow them to do their jobs and not somebody else's. The education, science, economy, intellectual development, and cultural life of a democracy all require institutions.

One other point to remember: Institutions, even formal ones, are not made of only rules and procedures. They are made of human beings, so they function at two levels: the formal procedural level and the informal level of human personalities and relationships. The people who occupy positions in a formal institution use their judgment, experience, and personal priorities to shape how their institution operates. When Scott Pruitt was appointed to lead the Environmental Protection Agency, he brought his personal skepticism about global warming to that position, even while the position sat atop an institution with a mandate that included addressing global warming.

Sometimes the rules defining the boundaries of an institution are broken. When this happens, the offender can lose his position and end up in court, as Bruce Carson found out; in effect, he was breaking down the boundaries that separated industry, the Canada School of Energy and Environment, and the federal government. In more extreme cases, where boundaries have turned into sieves, an entire organization can be dissolved, which was the fate of the US Minerals Management Service.

★ ★ ★

In his seminal 1968 book, *Political Order in Changing Societies*, Samuel P. Huntington stressed the importance of autonomy if institutions are to serve public rather than private interests. For democracy to develop and flourish, he wrote, political organizations and procedures cannot "simply be expressions of the interests of particular social groups. A political organization that is the instrument of a social group —

family, clan, class — lacks autonomy." A key premise for Huntington was that autonomy "was measured by the extent to which institutions have their own interests and values distinguishable from those of other institutions and social forces."[253] Years later, the finding of the National Commission on the Deepwater Horizon that the US Minerals Management Service failed because it lacked autonomy was an apt illustration of Huntington's point.

This leads to a core point of this book, one long understood by close observers of politics and government: For modern democracy to endure, its institutions must have clear boundaries; they must be substantially autonomous. They need to have purposes and resources of their own, their own sense of identity, and they need to be self-directed. This does not mean they have freewheeling unaccountability, for they are part of a system, but it does mean they should serve their own mandate and maintain their integrity. With its autonomous institutions, a democracy contrasts to, say, a theocracy, where parliaments, police, armies, schools, and the courts defer to religious leaders; or to dictatorships, where lines of accountability across institutions lead to a military leader or some other type of strong-man. In Iran, for example, the constitution requires all candidates in presidential elections be approved in advance by the supreme Islamic council, while in Russia under President Vladimir Putin, opposition leaders can face forbidding adversity from the police, courts, and state-owned media dominated by his interests.

Like moss grows in the spaces between paving stones, democracy takes root in the spaces between autonomous institutions. Autonomous institutions stand apart from one another, providing choices and creating room for new ideas and actions. When there are many strong and autonomous institutions, there are many spaces for democracy to root. Correspondingly, weak institutions and a loss of autonomy mean a decline of democracy.

With autonomous institutions, modern democracy expresses itself as an unending flow of contests among people with differing political, social, and economic priorities, within a set of procedures that are understood and generally accepted as legitimate by all participants. We can watch these contests in any municipal council, regulatory agency, courtroom, or election. They fill the news and add spice to dinnertime conversations. In the words of Valerie Bunce, a leading scholar on democracy,

> we need to think of democracy as a two-part proposition, having uncertain results (or competition) but also having certain procedures. Indeed, it is precisely this combination of competition bounded by rules that makes democracy both responsive and effective . . .[254]

This "competition bounded by rules" is largely established, managed, and enforced through institutions.

An inseparable part of the rise of autonomous institutions was the rise of "the individual," brought on by centuries of philosophical, scientific, and technological change; by widespread literacy; and by the emergence of capitalism. The human being, once thought of as property in the form of the slave, serf, or subject, gradually became the citizen — the autonomous individual. As political scientist David Held writes, autonomy for the individual "connotes the capacity of human beings to reason self-consciously, to be self-reflective and self-determining. It involves the ability to deliberate, judge, choose and act upon different possible courses of action . . ."[255]

A key to democracy, then, is freedom of expression and thought, because the ability of people to think and speak freely provides the tension and energy needed to prevent institutions from converging into conformity. Modern democracy is a system that expects there to be differences among people and conflicts among institutions. A judge challenges the decision of a public servant, a public health officer questions a government policy, a voter argues with a politician, a university scientist calls to account a corporate executive. Contained conflict is the energy that drives democracy.

David Held, who has spent his career studying democracy, points out that democracy does not presuppose agreement on issues and values. Rather, it provides ways of resolving differences on values and issues that are open to participants and public, managed, and legitimate. Democracy, says Held, lays down

> good grounds for the defence of a public dialogue and
> decision-making process about matters of general concern,
> and suggests institutional paths for its development . . .
> democracy can be seen to lay down a programme of change
> in and through which pressing, substantive issues will receive
> a better opportunity for deliberation, debate and resolution
> than they would under alternative regimes.[256]

The most profound offence to democracy by the fossil fuel industry may be the way it uses misinformation to debase public dialogue and decision making on global warming. Left to its free devices, a healthy democracy will respond to a pressing and substantive issue such as global warming with deliberation, debate, and resolution. This is exactly why some interests in the fossil fuel business have worked so hard to spread misinformation and distortion. During the 1980s and through to the Rio Earth Summit in 1992, democracies such as Canada and the United States were on track to respond wisely to global warming; since then, the prolonged efforts and vast expenditures of the fossil fuel industry have corrupted the shape and form of the democratic process itself.

Chapter 7
A theory of the deep state

Things go wrong for modern democracy when public institutions are captured by private interests. A democratic institution is "captured" when its decisions, actions, or resources are consistently directed away from the public interest toward a private interest, through the intentions and actions of that interest.[257] Capture is rarely an all-or-nothing affair; rather, it happens by degrees, but it always involves a breakdown of the autonomy of the institution. Many institutions fundamental to modern democracy only gained their autonomy after lengthy struggles, and those struggles must continue if democracy is to be preserved.

The concept of capture has evolved and broadened over many decades. Initially, it focused on public agencies established by governments to regulate industries in the public interest that ended up acting in the interests of those same industries. A famous early example arose in 1910 with the US Interstate Commerce Commission, which was meant to defend the public from the predatory practices of railway companies but soon became their ally. The US Supreme Court eventually weighed in on the matter, making clear in its ruling that the commission's responsibility was to the public, not the railroads: "The outlook of the Commission and its powers must be greater than the interest of the railroads or of that which may affect those interests. It must be as comprehensive as the interest of the whole country."[258]

Attention to institutional capture intensified in the 1980s and 1990s as Eastern European countries faced the challenges of political and economic transformation in a post-Soviet world, and by the turn of the 21st century, "capture" was part of the lexicon of organizations such as the International Anti-Corruption Convention and the World Bank. The concept broadened to include policy making by governments. "Capture," said one paper cited by the World Bank, "concerns the loss of independence on the part of the regulatory or policy making organ to the industry over which it has regulatory authority."[259] While capture may involve illegal activities, it also can be perfectly legal.[260] Very few of the activities described in this book broke any laws.

Capture can happen when the rules of an institution are weak, for example, when the rules of a public regulator allow its staff to move easily between itself and the industry that it regulates, permitting the interests of the industry to sit at the desks of the regulator. Capture can also happen when good rules are ignored, which happened in the case of Bruce Carson. One of the documents presented at his trial is a letter from federal Conflict of Interest and Ethics Commissioner Mary Dawson, granting permission for Carson to become head of the Canada School of Energy and Environment, but only on several conditions.[261] Dawson's letter takes several paragraphs to spell out these conditions, telling him the exact section of law that would be violated if a condition wasn't met. Carson, choosing to ignore the rules, seemed to violate them all.

Capture can happen before an institution even begins functioning, if a private interest is able to control the way the institution's purpose or structure is established. For example, when Alberta's royalty system for its publicly owned oil and gas resources was overhauled in 2009–10, its very purpose was rewritten. In 2007, its purpose had been to "secure the highest price for the resource owners [i.e., the government of Alberta] over the long term while allowing a fair share to industry."[262] By 2011, after an intense campaign by the oil and gas industry, the purpose of the royalty system was transformed: "Alberta will have a combined royalty and tax rate that is in the top quartile of investment opportunities compared to similar jurisdictions."[263] In short, the purpose of Alberta's royalty system had gone from serving the public to serving investors. This wasn't merely changing the rules; it was capture of the royalty system's reason for being.

Yet another form of capture is what scholars call "social or cultural capture," which arises from "repeated interaction with the regulated industry . . . such that the regulator begins to think like the regulated and cannot easily conceive another way of approaching its problems."[264] Senior staff at NRCan moved into this form of capture when they started calling the oil sands "clean energy," even in their internal emails. By 2017, Alberta Deputy Premier Sarah Hoffman was falling into this kind of capture when she said of the Trans Mountain pipeline: ". . . *our* pipeline is moving forward," even though the pipeline is owned by Kinder Morgan Inc of Texas. Her government had become such agents of the corporation that the distinction between the government and the corporation seemed to be blurred.[265]

The basic dynamics of capture, although sometimes difficult to see, are straightforward in principle.[266]

> First, there needs to be a "public interest." To adopt the language of the American Petroleum Institute's own scientists in 1982, the public interest in the case of global warming is to avoid "globally catastrophic effects" by eliminating carbon emissions. This is clear, crucial, and urgent.

> Second, there needs to be an institution with responsibility for the public interest. Given the scale of global warming, responsibility lies with whole families of institutions. Of these,

some are crucial because they are in lead positions, including elected governments; various government departments and agencies; political parties; universities; and courts.

Third, capture requires an organization to do the capturing, a hunter on the prowl. This is a private interest intent on directing institutional decisions away from the public interest, toward its own. As the historian William Novak says, "There must, somewhere, be an attempt to lobby, an attempt to offer an implicit bribe or implicit contract, an attempt to stack the deck of an institutional process, or . . . an attempt to influence frames, assumptions, and worldviews of regulators or professionals involved in regulation."[267] Capture is distinguished from mere organizational drift because capture is driven by private intent.

Finally, there must be an indication the hunter has caught its quarry. It is not enough just to point at the growth in emissions in Canada and the United States. We need to show that public institutions have directed their decisions, actions, and resources away from the public interest of eliminating carbon emissions and toward the interest of the fossil fuel industry.

In Canada's case, one indication of capture is the federal government's stark reversal on emission goals. Canada's government enthusiastically supported the 1992 Rio Earth Summit and signed the initial treaty committing to lowering emissions. It then went further, signing the Kyoto Protocol, with its goal of lowering emissions 6 per cent below 1990 levels by 2012. Parliament ratified the Kyoto Protocol in 2002, and in line with that Ontario, Quebec, and British Columbia took steps to reduce emissions. Even so, the federal government let Canada's total emissions climb because of oil sands developments in Alberta. This double standard turned to outright reversal with the 2006 election of Stephen Harper's government, with its attacks on climate science and its strong commitment to developing oil and natural gas resources. The Harper government withdrew Canada from the Kyoto Protocol in 2012 and allowed emissions, which were already climbing, to jump. By 2014, they were 20 per cent higher nationally than in 1990.[268] Alberta's emissions shot to the highest of all provinces, and the federal government stated exactly why in one of its publications: "primarily because of the increase in the oil and gas industry for export markets."[269]

The reversal on global warming was no ordinary adjustment to public policy. It was done in defiance of compelling science in order to support the fossil fuel industry; it required widespread distortion of public institutions, as previous and subsequent chapters show; and it entailed withdrawing from a major international treaty, the Kyoto Protocol. As of 2016, Canada was the only country to have signed and ratified the Kyoto Protocol, to then withdraw from it.

* * *

Capture may sound like politics as usual. While bribery is illegal in developed democracies, lobbying is normal and legitimate, and private interests of all kinds constantly use public relations to influence the frames of reference under which public officials operate. EPIC's Canada-wide tour of consultations on a national energy strategy was a fine example.

Drawing the line between healthy autonomy and capture lies less with the actions of private interests than with the responses of democratic institutions, which must rigorously impose and enforce standards of democratic conduct, turning those standards into cultural norms. A useful example is the rules governing judges in Canada, which are encoded in practice, training, legislation, and the constitution. The Canadian Judicial Council's *Ethical Principles for Judges* is unequivocal:

"Judges . . . must be and be seen to be free to decide honestly and impartially on the basis of the law and the evidence, without external pressure or influence and without fear of interference from anyone."[270] Judges may hear exhaustive verbal arguments on cases, listen to expert testimony and eyewitness accounts, and receive volumes of printed submissions arguing both pro and con. Judges may search widely to conduct their own research and consult with colleagues. But judges must not work to align their priorities with one of the parties to a case, and they won't spend hours in the offices of one interested party or ignore the case of the other. The autonomy of judges is sacrosanct, the boundaries around their work clearly drawn and almost obsessively respected. Not all democratic institutions need the same rules as judges, but they all need clearly drawn and well-respected boundaries. The rules for judges offer a good benchmark.

Previous chapters showcased tawdry examples of broken institutional boundaries, like the shared drug use, sexual relations, and torrent of gifts from industry to regulators at the Minerals Management Service office in Denver. Those types of stories grabbed headlines, but previous chapters also included clearer examples of capture, many of which were perfectly legal. In Canada, top civil servants "fully aligned" their departments' priorities with the oil industry; government scientists were muzzled; and leaders of university institutes (some on the payroll of industry) redirected institutional focus to the priorities of the oil industry. In the United States, the fossil fuel–friendly White House of George W. Bush appointed a former API official to serve as chief of staff for the White House Council on Environmental Quality, where he consistently revised government documents to undermine the science of global warming. In both countries, industry associations wrote government regulations for themselves. "Revolving doors" moved people from industry into the civil service and politics, then back to industry.

In the turbulent and relentless currents of politics, institutions are constantly falling into capture and are just as constantly being pulled out of it by other institutions. When one institution is compromised, other institutions take corrective action. When a governing party becomes too autocratic, the courts, an opposition party, or voters can draw a line; when an industry produces distorted science, a university can provide unbiased information; when the civil service stops being non-partisan, an auditor-general or an ethics commissioner can investigate. It is almost unending. Modern democracy has remarkable resilience because of its system of interacting autonomous institutions.

But this raises a key question: What happens when a whole series of institutions falls under the sway of one outside interest? What happens when the governing party, the opposition party, universities, regulators, key parts of the civil service, and maybe even the courts are all partially or substantially captured by the fossil fuel industry? What is the fate of democracy at that point?

We've covered a lot of ground quickly, so let's pause for a brief review before we take the next step. Modern democracy depends on an extensive system of institutions developed over many centuries. These institutions must be focused on public rather than private interests, and they need their own purposes and resources along with clear rules that separate them from other interests. Sometimes an institution is captured by a private interest, in which case it becomes an instrument of that inter-est. When that happens in a healthy democracy, the many autonomous institutions eventually restore the few that are captured, or disband them. A strong democracy usually heals itself and moves on.

But not always. This is where two streams of political analysis con-verge: work on institutional capture and work in the emerging field of deep states. My argument is that if several key institutions of democ-racy are captured and held long enough by the *same* private interest, then the ability of the system to restore democracy is impaired. The state continues, of course, but its commitment to the public interest declines while its commitment to the private interest grows. The appearance of democracy is maintained, but its substance is diminished. Democracy "hollows out." Disgruntled citizens sense the change and start speaking of "unelected power," "the state within a state," and increasingly, "the deep state."

The term *deep state* was coined in 1974 by Turkish Prime Minister Bulent Ecevit to describe a covert system of military, security, business, and other interests that undermined the rise of democratic institutions in Turkey.[271] Concepts of deep state and state capture spread to other countries and garnered academic interest, rising in step with broader discussions about threats to democracy. For example, the World Bank's anti-corruption campaigns began raising concerns about "captive states" in the late 1990s, focusing largely on governments and states that fell under the illicit influence of private businesses.[272] Under President Jacob Zuma in the 2010s, South Africa appeared to many as a captive state, serving the interests of the extremely wealthy Gupta family.[273]

Other analysts were concerned that some democratic states were being captured through processes that were perfectly legal. In his best-selling book *Captive State*, published in 2000, George Monbiot drew on examples from a host of government programs to argue that corporations in Britain were "seizing powers previously invested in government, and using them to distort public life to suit their own ends,"[274] which led to "the corporate control of the means of government." Monbiot observed that "enterprising companies will always seek to maximize their opportunities. But a government which allows them to do so at public expense is a government that has surely lost its way."

In 2008, the global financial crisis intensified concern with capture because of the failure of financial regulators to control the rapaciousness of banks, and the willingness of governments to bail out the banks, no matter how disgraceful their actions. In the United States, subsequent popular movements on both the right (e.g., the Tea Party, Donald Trump) and the left (e.g., Occupy Wall Street, Bernie Sanders) concluded that the state was slipping its democratic moorings, and analysis of regulatory capture and deep states quickened. Books by diplomat and academic Peter Dale Scott, social anthropologist Janine Wedel, and moderate Republican Michael Lofgren emphasized the threat posed to democracy by private interests that used legal means to undermine the autonomy of institutions.

Peter Dale Scott, in his book *The American Deep State*,[275] described the deep state as a system "which habitually resorts to decision-making and enforcement procedures outside as well as inside those publicly sanctioned by law and society." Drawing on decades of examples, he cautioned that the political dynamics required for the United States to engage in permanent international interventions such as "the war on drugs" and "the war on terror" created a culture of force and subversion that rebounded back into American politics, undermining its domestic democratic institutions.

Janine Wedel's book *Unaccountable*[276] argues that the capture of government and public institutions has

> reconfigured what constitutes government. In the old world, government meetings were mainly made up of government officials. In the new world, a very real question is: Who is the government? Today, contractors, consulting firms, think tankers, and quasi-official bodies daily stand in for it, in the process composing a new and more dispersed and fragmented governing system.

After serving as a Republican staffer in the US Congress for more than twenty years, Mike Lofgren, in his 2016 book *The Deep State*,[277] concentrated on the power dynamics in Washington D.C. His experience inside the political system led to this conclusion:

> While the public is now aware of the disproportionate influence of powerful corporations over Washington . . . few

fully appreciate that the United States has in the last several decades gradually undergone a process . . . that the journalist Edward Peter Garrett described in the 1930s as a "revolution within the form." Our venerable institutions of government have outwardly remained the same, but they have grown more and more resistant to the popular will as they have become hardwired into a corporate and private influence network with almost unlimited cash to enforce its will.

Lofgren defined the deep state as "the hybrid association of key elements of government and parts of top-level finance and industry that is effectively able to govern the United States with only limited reference to the consent of the governed as normally expressed through elections."

★ ★ ★

A Theory of the Deep State

There is frustratingly little theory to take the reader beyond a series of alarming examples, in order to illuminate the underlying effects of a deep state on democracy. By linking the concepts of "institutional capture" and "deep state" and placing them in a framework that regards democracy as an unending contest of competing interests within a system of autonomous institutions, I hope to add structure and analytical power to the notion of the deep state. The result will be a better understanding of how democracy gets undermined, and some indication of how it can be fortified, especially in the face of the global warming crisis.

Here is a theory of the deep state:

1. A deep state can be defined as the unofficial system of government that arises separately from, but is closely connected to, the official system, when several key

democratic institutions are captured and held by the same
private interest in order to advance its private agenda
over the public interest. The captured institutions become
accountable to the dominating private interest, and
serving that interest becomes the standard of institutional
success. The cluster of captured institutions reinforces the
captivity of each individual institution in the cluster, and
draws others into it. Captivity becomes normal. When
this happens, the ability of a democracy to respond to
a changing world and meet the needs and aspirations
of a majority of its citizens will suffer and decline.
Public dialogue and decision making based on the best
information becomes systematically corrupted.

2. A deep state typically comprises leading owners and
executives of major private interests; together with a
selection of politicians and bureaucrats inordinately
committed to the success of those private interests; and
third-party supporters (trade associations, interest groups,
etc.) with a stake in or commitment to the success of
those interests. A deep state has its own rules, norms, and
hierarchies of varying degrees of formality. A successful deep
state is parasitic, capturing and harnessing the organs of
democracy for its own use, but not killing them, at least not
in the short term.

3. Deep states need to span several institutions; a key
difference between a captured institution and a deep state is
the reach of the deep state across a range of institutions.

4. Deep states prefer to avoid democratic accountability and
are, therefore, a threat to the foundations of democracy.
They need to be largely submerged beneath the political

surface so they can assume their influence over institutions outside the view of voters and competing interests. We saw an excellent example of this secrecy earlier, in Justice Kehoe's ruling on the Bruce Carson case:

> It is especially egregious in the case of EPIC where Mr. Carson was representing a non-profit corporation set up to represent numerous major private Oil and Gas Energy Companies whose sole purpose was to develop energy policy for Canada for the commercial benefit of the companies *while the public including other interested companies, environmentalists, etc. had no knowledge of what was transpiring behind the scene with Ministers, Deputy Ministers, and other very senior officials in government, both federal and provincial.*[278] [italics added]

5. Sooner or later, a deep state will need to distort the flow of information that informs public dialogue and deliberation, in order to protect its interests. Once a deep state begins distorting public information, it cannot stop without running a serious risk of exposure and collapse.

6. A deep state is richly resourced and enduring, far outlasting election cycles. Therefore, it needs to be politically non-partisan or opportunistically partisan, working with whichever political forces are most useful at the time.

7. A successful deep state becomes an institution itself, existing independently of any individuals and enduring for long periods, operating with rules of behaviour enforced

with rewards and punishments. If a deep state survives long enough, it becomes part of the enduring political culture of its society.

Very few private interests have either the resources or the motivation to capture and hold several key democratic institutions for extended periods, but one that does is the fossil fuel industry, particularly the oil industry. Not only is it among the wealthiest and most powerful industries,[279] it is in a fight for survival that puts it in direct conflict with democratic institutions working to address global warming. It is time to look at the particular case of oil's deep state.

Chapter 8
Oil and the deep state

Deep states do not arise in economic and historical vacuums; rather, they reflect their societies' economies and histories. Most deep state analysis comes out of the United States and Turkey and concentrates on military and security interests joining with corporate, technological, and financial interests to form deep states.

But military and security interests are not essential to a deep state. Canada has an oil deep state that built strength in the 1990s and gained ascendancy during the time of Prime Minister Harper, which it substantially maintained under Prime Minister Justin Trudeau. The United States, with a much larger and more diverse economy, saw its oil deep state reach ascendancy with the presidency of George W. Bush, lose ground in the period of President Obama, and convincingly regain its position with the 2016 presidential and congressional elections. By spring 2017, it had a grip on a remarkable range of institutions.

An oil deep state has particular characteristics. One of these, of course, is that its business is contributing to globally catastrophic effects. While many people in the industry deny the implication of this, it means the fossil fuel industry is a sunset industry: Its end is foreseeable, and it is fighting for its life with guile and determination. Every economic sector produces CO_2 emissions, including transportation, buildings, and cement production, to name three of the largest. There is, however, a fundamental difference for the fossil fuel industry: It is possible to imagine vehicles, buildings, and construction materials without fossil fuels, but it is not possible to imagine a fossil fuel industry without fossil fuels. Coal and oil will always be used for plastics, lubricants, and other products, but these are not fuels and the amounts needed for these uses are comparatively small. When the world stops using fossil fuels, as it must, the fossil fuel industry will cease to exist.

Another trait of a fossil fuel deep state is less obvious but fundamental, and a special concern in Canada. Economists and scholars have long known that economies based on extracting minerals have particular political patterns, and that Canada and its provinces, especially Alberta, have mineral economies.[280] Canada depends on mineral production much more than any other wealthy country, with the exception of Australia. For Canada, the value of all resource production is 10 per cent of gross domestic product (GDP). While this may sound small, it is double the proportion of the American economy, and triple or more the proportions of Japan, Germany, France, and Britain.[281] Oil, natural gas, and other minerals account for about 30 per cent of Canada's merchandise exports[282] while the Toronto Stock Exchange claims to be the largest exchange in the world for both oil and gas companies and mining companies.[283]

In Alberta, the proportions are far higher, with petroleum production accounting for 38.7 per cent of GDP[284] in 2011 and over 70 per cent of merchandise exports.[285] Royalties from petroleum were the largest component of government revenues in Alberta until the price collapse of 2015, historically accounting for over 30 per cent of the total.[286] Mineral production in Alberta is ten, and in some cases twenty, times the portion of the economy compared to Europe, Japan, and the United States, and this inevitably shapes politics and democracy. The World Bank's threshold for a mineral economy is at least 10 per cent of a jurisdiction's GDP and 40 per cent of total merchandise exports.[287] Alberta soars far beyond these markers because of its petroleum production, which sets the stage for a special kind of deep state.

Mineral economies are breeding grounds for deep-state politics for specific reasons. Mineral extraction is bound to a particular piece of land in a way seldom seen with manufacturing, services, or even agriculture. Cars can be assembled in Ontario or Mexico and a call centre can be in Manila or New Brunswick, but a mine or an oilwell must be exactly where the ore or crude is located and, because that location is ultimately under the control of a particular state, the nature of the state becomes a prime concern for the mining or oil company. If regulations or tax increases make a factory insufficiently profitable, a manufacturer can invest in a factory somewhere else; in contrast, if regulations or royalties make mineral extraction insufficiently profitable, the company needs to invest in changing the state. Mining and oil companies have an existential imperative to influence the state that manufacturers and other industries do not have.

This dynamic is compounded because the state plays a double role in mineral development. In its first role, it establishes the laws and context for labour, environment, security, infrastructure, and so on, and collects taxes, as it does for all other economic activities. In a narrow sense, the state is like a referee who collects a fee — taxes — for setting and enforcing the rules of the game.

With mineral development, the state also plays another role. In most of the world minerals in the ground are owned by the state until they are mined or extracted, so the state determines the conditions and price of sale of the raw material. This is the case in most of Canada and for American federal lands and offshore resources. In effect, the state is now a player as well as the referee, with all the attendant complications. The state has an incentive to develop the resource, and at the same time becomes a target for capture by interests who want the state to set the price below full value. Business has a compelling reason to meddle in the state, and the officials running the state are often tempted to welcome such meddling.

For corporations, the return on investment from influencing governments can be far better than the return on investment from new equipment, research, or development. In Canada, the $5 million price tag of one large truck to haul bitumen is more than the cost of a comprehensive campaign of political lobbying.[288] The incentives go the other direction too. Political leaders can be tempted to pursue mineral interests in return for economic and even personal benefits. For governments with mineral economies, royalties can be a politically addictive way to cut taxes and subsidize services. As a result, state leaders can become more devoted to mineral exploitation than to social and economic development or environmental protection. Mineral exploitation can trump all other priorities.[289]

The National Commission on the Deepwater Horizon spill confirmed the dangers of a conflicted mandate for regulator and owner.[290] The US Mineral Management Service was formed, in the words of the commission, as a "political compromise" under the Reagan administration and made responsible for both regulating offshore drilling and maximizing royalties. It soon became clear which of these responsibilities was number one. "Revenue generation — enjoyed both by industry and government — became the dominant objective."[291] There was a "built-in incentive" to promote drilling that was "in sharp tension" with safety and environmental protection. The MMS and industry collaborated in exploiting the offshore resources of the Gulf of Mexico in a deal that was worth billions of dollars a year to both parties; in its peak year of 2008, offshore mineral revenues for the American government were $18 billion, mostly from drilling in the Gulf. But as the commission found, "there was a hidden price to be paid for those increased revenues" in the form of escalating risks to environmental and human safety.[292] The state became as committed to oil development as the industry; they behaved like joint shareholders in a partnership that sacrificed the environment and public safety for increased revenue until it quite literally exploded.

Fossil fuels take the political hazards of mineral economies and jack them up with dizzying exorbitance. Three factors in particular separate fossil fuels, and especially oil, from other minerals. First, demand for them is inelastic, barely budging even when their prices swing. Businesses pay the price demanded, and consumers line up for hours when supply is short. It takes significant, long-term price changes to alter demand. Second, oil has often been controlled by cartels that keep prices artificially high. The Organization of Petroleum Exporting Countries (OPEC), for example, manipulated the international price of oil for substantial periods from the early 1970s to the global gluts of 2015, generating decades of disproportionately fat profits and royalties for oil producers that stoked investment in the Athabasca oil sands and offshore rigs like the Deepwater Horizon. By defying the laws of supply and demand, OPEC's cartel generated "rewards in excess of effort" easily appropriated by the state and corporations.[293]

Third, fossil fuels are strategically pivotal in geopolitics and war. Russia could bring Europe to crisis in a matter of days by cutting its umbilical pipelines of oil and natural gas. Coal fuelled the foundries of war for two centuries, while the flow of oil was a prevail-at-all-costs priority in both world wars. Nations under duress will do anything for fossil fuels.

Terry Lynn Karl's 1997 book *The Paradox of Plenty* delivered a benchmark analysis of the political effects of oil and confirmed 'petrostate' as a scholarly term. At various times in the twentieth century, petroleum brought staggering flows of wealth to Venezuela and other countries outside the industrialized West, including Saudi Arabia, Iran, Iraq, and eventually Nigeria and other African countries.

Economists and others expected this wealth to spur democracy and industrial prosperity. Instead, many of these countries struggled with political oppression, war, corruption, gross inequalities, and weak civil society. This paradox was made more intriguing because many under-developed countries that did *not* have petroleum flourished, including South Korea, Taiwan, and several others.

Karl, a Stanford historian, preceded her analysis of petrostates by describing the effects of gold and silver imports from the New World on Imperial Spain. Spain soared with the discovery of gold and silver in its Central and South American colonies in the 16th century. For many decades, these resources provided an enormous boost for government coffers and economic prosperity for the Spanish empire. Sustaining and increasing the shiploads of treasure became the government's top economic concern, overshadowing domestic industry and agriculture. By the 18th century, however, Spain's preeminence was surpassed by European rivals who grew their domestic industries, science, agriculture, and statecraft. The Spanish government had to borrow against future shipments of ore to sustain its vast military and other expenses, miring itself in debt while obsessing over the viability of its New World mines and trans-Atlantic supply lines (perhaps an equivalent of Canada's pipelines today). Spain gradually slid into long-term economic backwardness and political oppression, while its plight spawned a phrase common to this day: "Waiting for your ship to come in."[294]

Karl then turned her attention to Venezuela's experience as an oil producer. As in northeastern Alberta, bitumen in parts of Venezuela was so abundant it oozed from the ground, where indigenous peoples used it for medicine and to caulk canoes. Early Europeans adopted these uses and the state laid claim to the resource, as states are wont to do. Spain's "Mining Ordinances for New Spain," issued in 1783, claimed as crown property "perfect or semi-perfect minerals, bitumens, or juices of the earth,"[295] and not long after Venezuela won its war of independence, its new congress legislated state ownership of all minerals in 1832. After independence from Spain, Venezuela fell into eight decades of civil war and anarchy that decimated its population and left control of the country in the hands of chronically warring local militias. By the first decade of the 1900s, these conflicts had drawn in the British, German, Italian, and Dutch governments, concerned for their neighbouring Caribbean colonies and West Indies trade. By 1909, the United States had asserted its dominance in Venezuelan affairs. By then, Venezuela's rich oil resources were attracting international interest, which was soon magnified by the thirst for oil navies and armies displayed during World War One.

Venezuela's 20th-century history illustrates a process by which a state and its institutions are conceived around the central fact of oil production.[296] At its birth, modern Venezuela was utterly lacking in modern institutions. When the first oil boom hit Venezuela during and after World War One, for example, it had no modern police, court, or education systems; no modern civil service or regulators; no modern royalty or tax systems; and very little physical infrastructure. Petroleum companies needed these, so of necessity they and their home governments, largely in the United States and Britain, helped develop them, working with whichever locals were most sympathetic or powerful and against those who were not.

Karl expanded her analysis from Venezuela to major petroleum-producing countries in the Middle East, Africa, and Asia. Time and again, traditional societies were overwhelmed by the demands of the petroleum business and its allies, the floods of money, and the pressures of international markets and politics. The origins and characters of these states became entangled with and defined by the production of petroleum and the fights over its spoils. Democracy, state building, and good government were secondary priorities.

Her conclusions lead right back to the importance of institutions: "dependence on a particular export commodity [i.e., oil] shapes not only social classes and regime types . . . but also the very institutions of the state, the framework for decision-making, and the decision calculus of policy-makers."[297] In other words, said Karl, "The manner in which a state earns its living influences its own patterns of institutionalization." If a state earned a disproportionate amount of its revenue from minerals, then the policy environment of officials, the goals of the state, the types of public institutions, and the locus of authority — the matter of who actually runs the country — were all altered. In the particular case of petrostates, "oil-provoked changes in state capacity are *the* intervening variable," regardless of geography, religion, culture, or history.[298] This effect helped explain why, by the 1990s, countries as diverse as Venezuela, Nigeria, and Iran ended up with similar anti-democratic political and economic profiles: They were configured by their reliance on petroleum. They were petrostates.

As a contrast to petrostates, Karl presented the case of Norway. When North Sea oil was discovered in the 1960s, Norway was a cohesive and deeply entrenched state that had government, political parties, public service, courts, tax systems, universities, and other institutions needed to successfully manage the petroleum companies and the surge of wealth. It was the opposite of Venezuela, with an unusually effective state, rule of law, and strong democratic accountability. Even then, managing its oil production while maintaining rigorous democratic accountability and autonomous institutions was a nearly overwhelming challenge. "If there is one clear lesson from the experience of oil exporters," writes Karl, "it is that developmental outcomes depend on the character of state institutions."[299] This same lesson applies to any state that becomes overly dependent for its prosperity on mineral extraction. This leads us to Canada's defining example: Alberta.

PART THREE
POSSESSION

Chapter 9
The origins of oil's deep state in Canada

Now we take our theory of democracy and the deep state and return to the boardrooms, backrooms, and courtrooms where we spent the first five chapters. This chapter and the next seven present a case study of Alberta, a place where the oil industry has captured such a wide swath of institutions for so long that democracy itself has become fossilized. Rather than counter-balancing each other, key institutions line up to reinforce the interests of the oil industry. Alberta's deep state deflects and denies information about its changing environment, so its ability to adapt to an evolving world is diminished. Public debate stagnates, and the status quo is strengthened. It is a hollowed-out democracy, a relatively pure form of deep state that provides a model for studying this condition — and a warning about the dominance the fossil fuel industry is capable of achieving elsewhere in Canada and beyond.

* * *

From the earliest days of Alberta's petroleum industry, the conditions were right for the eventual development of a deep state. The relations between the state and the industry were intimate from the start, involving the most powerful of politicians and business leaders.

The first commercially viable petroleum well in Alberta was drilled in 1914 at Turner Valley, near Calgary, by a two-year-old company called Calgary Petroleum Products.[300] In 1921, the owners of Calgary Petroleum Products sold it to Imperial Oil. Imperial Oil, based in Ontario, was majority owned by Standard Oil of New Jersey (which eventually became Exxon), and it reorganized Calgary Petroleum Products under the brand Royalite.[301] Production at Turner Valley increased under Royalite and other companies, and soon Alberta's oil and gas production surpassed all other provinces combined, though by international standards production was still relatively small.[302] In 1947, Imperial hit a much bigger play at Leduc No. 1, and the transformation of Alberta from an agricultural economy to a mineral one was underway.

Calgary Petroleum Products was backed by a handful of business leaders from Calgary. One was a lawyer named Richard B. Bennett. Bennett, raised in a once-prosperous New Brunswick family fallen on hard times, was interested in law, business, and politics. As a young lawyer looking for opportunity, he moved to Calgary in 1897 and joined the law firm of James Lougheed, grandfather of Peter Lougheed, Alberta's premier from 1971 to 1985. In 1898, Bennett won a seat in the Legislative Assembly of the Northwest Territories (Alberta and Saskatchewan were not provinces until 1905).

Bennett built a fortune through real estate and business interests, all the while advancing his political career. When Calgary Petroleum Products discovered oil in Turner Valley, Bennett was a Conservative member of parliament in Ottawa. He moved in and out of parliament from 1911 to 1939, served as a government MP through part of World War One, held a clutch of cabinet posts, and served as prime minister of Canada from 1930 to 1935, then as opposition leader until 1938. Along the way, Bennett added to his very substantial wealth. His major business interests, several of which involved his law partner Lougheed, included some of Canada's largest grain, lumber, industrial, and utility companies, and by the 1920s, he sat on the boards of the Royal Bank of Canada and Metropolitan Life Insurance of New York. In 1939, he moved to England and quickly entered a circle of prominence that included lifelong friend and fellow New Brunswicker Max Aitken, known by then as Lord Beaverbrook of Fleet Street, and Sir Winston Churchill, who helped Bennett obtain the title "Viscount" in 1941. Viscount Bennett died in England in 1947.

Bennett seemed to perfectly integrate the world of immense corporate power with the height of political office, and his senior partner in law, James Lougheed, was much the same. If anything, Lougheed and his wife, Belle Clarke Hardisty, more fully represented the early days of Alberta's thick network of corporate and political interests.

James Lougheed, born and raised in a carpenter's family in Ontario and trained as a lawyer, arrived with little more than a travel bag and a winning attitude in the hamlet of Fort Calgary in 1883, weeks shy of his thirtieth birthday and just before the tracks of the Canadian Pacific Railway reached the settlement.[303] Bright, ambitious, and charming, he set up his law practice and the following year married Isabella (Belle) Clarke Hardisty, whom he met in Calgary. The Lougheeds immediately flourished. The CPR was an important client of his firm, and by 1887, he was investing actively in Calgary real estate. Lougheed was known in some circles as a sharp operator who likely used his inside knowledge of the CPR's development plans for Calgary to benefit his own fast and aggressive real estate deals.

Lougheed was an enthusiastic supporter of the federal Conservative Party and Prime Minister John A. Macdonald, and in 1889, he was appointed by Macdonald to the Senate at the unusually young age of thirty-five. Two years later, and just eight years after James had arrived in the West, the Lougheeds began construction on the finest mansion in Calgary, which they named "Beaulieu" — known today as Lougheed House National Historic Site. The Lougheeds were one of the wealthiest families in town, with investments in office buildings, a theatre, the *Calgary Herald* newspaper, and ventures that eventually included

Calgary Petroleum Products. When Lougheed sold his share of Calgary Petroleum Products to Imperial Oil in 1921, the deal provided him with two thousand shares in Imperial's new company, Royalite, the value of which multiplied twelvefold by 1925.[304] In 1915 and for several years after, Lougheed's real estate holdings were so large that he was assessed over half the City of Calgary's property taxes.[305] His legal clients included the top business leaders of southern Alberta, and his family's mansion was the social hub of establishment Calgary. The prestige and wealth of the Lougheeds can be judged by the guests who visited and sometimes stayed at Beaulieu, including two governors-general; Prince George of Britain, who would become King George VI; Prince Erik of Denmark; future conservative prime minister of Britain Stanley Baldwin; and the Prince of Wales, the future King Edward VIII, who visited three separate times.[306, 307]

Lougheed and Bennett were at the centre of an alliance of business owners, investors, ranchers, and professionals who developed Calgary's water, electricity, and telephone utilities and streetcar service; the natural gas utilities of Calgary and Edmonton; coal mines in Lethbridge and the foothills; and companies that formed the backbone of the Turner Valley oil and gas fields.[308] Unlike manufacturing or agriculture, these businesses — utilities, coal mining, and oil and gas — all required close relations with the politicians, civil servants, and regulators who were responsible for governing utility markets and natural resources. This alliance and its assets developed into cornerstones of Alberta's corporate world, including companies such as ATCO, TransAlta, and Imperial Oil, and influenced a corporate culture that had a central focus on shaping public policy.

Lougheed worked hard as a senator and split his time between Calgary and Ottawa, which was why he recruited the young Richard B. Bennett to his firm in 1897. Lougheed became Conservative Party leader in the Senate in 1906, adding substantially to his influence, and when the Conservatives formed the federal government, Lougheed became government leader in the Senate and a member of cabinet from

1911 to 1921, holding several positions. He was a strong voice for the interests of Western Canada and undertook important work to support the resettlement of returning World War One veterans. A Conservative political associate of Lougheed and Bennett from Manitoba, Harold Daly, recalled "Lougheed and Bennett had a lot of dealings with the Department of the Interior, and made a lot of money out of government lands, which I suppose they had a right to do, but they were not very popular with Government officials."[309]

There is no denying the ability, hard work, and ambition of James Lougheed, but there is a further explanation for his rise from near penniless rookie lawyer in a frontier hamlet in 1883 to a solicitor for the CPR in 1885; real estate developer in 1887; senator in 1889; millionaire owner of a mansion by 1892; business mogul, repeat host of royalty, cabinet minister, and petroleum investor. Almost certainly this astonishing ascent owed much to the woman he married, Isabella (Belle) Clarke Hardisty, and her family.

Belle was born in 1861 in the tiny trading post of Fort Resolution on the shores of Great Slave Lake in the Northwest Territories, to parents who were both of mixed European and First Nations ancestry.[310] She spent her earliest years in isolated trading posts in northern Canada, especially at Fort Simpson in the sub-Arctic. Sent by her parents to the Red River Settlement for schooling at age six, she spent her early teen years at Wesleyan Ladies College in Hamilton, Ontario, and then with her grandparents in the Montreal area. She returned to the Northwest Territories in 1875.

Hardisty came from the wealthiest and most powerful family in the Hudson's Bay Company (HBC).[311] Established by a royal charter from the king of England in 1670, which gave it a monopoly on trade and colonization, HBC is the oldest incorporated joint-stock company in the English-speaking world. The fur trade in North America was flourishing at the same time a declining Spain was desperately trying to maintain the diminishing flow of silver and gold from South and Central America. By the early 1800s, HBC's trading territory, named

Rupert's Land after Prince Rupert who was one of the original investors, covered half of North America and beyond, an area larger than
Europe. It was a fur-trading enterprise, and its business model was
like that of Spain's New World mines or much of Canada's petroleum
industry: Extract a raw material under government licence and ship it
to a market where it could be sold for processing by others, profiting
from the difference between the cost of collecting the raw material and
the price of selling it.

HBC divided its territory into regions and appointed chief factors to
govern each region, giving them a share of profits. There were almost
no Europeans in these regions before 1840 and the role of government,
such as it was, was largely filled by the chief factor. Except for issues
relating to the fur trade, the First Nations and Métis were largely left
to their own devices. In those years, HBC was both the dominating
business interest and the governing institution for a sizable portion of
North America. Belle's grandfather had been a senior trader for HBC
and her father, William Hardisty, spent his career with the company,
finishing with a ten-year term as chief factor of MacKenzie District.
Her uncle Richard Hardisty also spent his career with HBC, culminating as chief factor for the Upper Saskatchewan District, headquartered
at Fort Edmonton.[312] He was reported to be the richest man in the
Northwest Territories.[313] Prime Minister Macdonald named Richard
Hardisty to the Senate in 1888, and when he died in 1889, Macdonald named Hardisty's nephew by marriage, thirty-five-year-old James
Lougheed, to take his place.

Belle's family ties were even more impressive. Belle's aunt Isabella
Sophia Hardisty was married to Donald Smith,[314] making him "Uncle
Donald" to Belle and James. Smith is better known to Canadians as
Lord Strathcona, perhaps most famous for the archival photo of him
driving the last spike into the transcontinental line of the CPR in 1885.
During her youth, Belle spent time at her aunt and uncle's grand mansion in Montreal, no doubt acquiring skills and experience she would
use to run Beaulieu later.

Donald Smith rose from the lower ranks of HBC to become its chief commissioner in the 1870s, when it was shifting its role from fur trade to land development, and by the time Lougheed married into the family, Smith was on his way to owning most of the company. He was also a major industrialist and railway owner, with his holdings including a substantial share of the CPR. He backed the CPR with a large chunk of his fortune to the immense gratitude of its political architect, Prime Minister Macdonald. Smith also spent many years as a member of parliament, sometimes as a Conservative and sometimes as an independent.

Smith's business interests included dozens of major companies in Canada, the United States, and Britain. He was a substantial shareholder in several railways, Dominion Coal, various newspapers, several manufacturers, and a number of financial businesses. He was a major shareholder in, and served a stint as president of, the Bank of Montreal, which was a key bank for the CPR, HBC, *and* the Government of Canada.[315] The Canadian government appointed him high commissioner to Britain, and he was granted the title Lord Strathcona. He personally financed a regiment of mounted soldiers from Western Canada in 1900 to fight in the South African War (Boer War), known as "Lord Strathcona's Horse." Realizing the importance of oil in fuelling the Royal Navy, Smith invested in companies exploring for oil in the Middle East and, in 1909, became the largest shareholder and chairman of the board of the Anglo-Persian Oil Company, which evolved into British Petroleum (BP), infamous a century later for the Deepwater Horizon disaster. Isabella Smith died in November 1913, and Donald Smith died in January 1914, at age ninety-four.

With major holdings in HBC and the CPR, Smith had created a spectacular synergy for land and mineral development. In 1870, HBC negotiated with Prime Minister Macdonald to transfer the massive Rupert's Land territory to the Canadian government in return for a large sum of cash and 4.5 million acres of land in Western Canada, including land around HBC trading settlements, three of which became provincial capitals: Edmonton, Winnipeg, and Victoria. Ten years later, the Macdonald government granted the CPR 25 million acres in Western Canada to help it finance railway construction, an area 20 per cent larger than the Republic of Ireland and Northern Ireland combined. Both grants included mineral rights and allowed each company to choose specific areas of land strategically over a period of decades. The CPR made its final choice in 1903, selecting three million acres east of Calgary. Donald Smith and his fellow shareholders in HBC and the CPR had a firm grip on much of Western Canada's urban lands, farmlands, minerals, and the railway that served them.

The mineral rights became core assets of each company and cornerstones of Canada's petroleum industry. In 1926, HBC set up Hudson's Bay Oil and Gas based on the land grants of 1870. In 1982, Hudson's Bay Oil and Gas was sold to Dome Petroleum, and in 1988 Dome Petroleum was sold to the American oil company Amoco for $5.5 billion. Amoco merged with British Petroleum in 1998 in what was then the largest corporate merger in world history. British Petroleum was the direct corporate descendant of the Anglo-Persian Oil Company that Donald Smith helped establish in 1909, and he likely would have smiled to see it merged with a descendant of his Hudson's Bay Company.

The CPR spun off its mineral rights into a separate company that eventually operated as Pan-Canadian Petroleum. In 2002, Pan-Canadian merged with the Alberta Energy Company to form EnCana, one of the largest companies in Canada's petroleum sector.

The predilection for a deep state was etched into Alberta's politics and economy before the province was even formed. The integration of interests in land, resources, petroleum, money, corporate power, government policy, and political office created a political and economic order in Alberta that was at times so concentrated it was embodied in one family or even one person. For Donald Smith, James Lougheed, and R. B. Bennett — three generations of immensely powerful men tightly connected through businesses, politics, and family, if not always friendship — there was very little space between the institutions of democracy and the interests of business. From the early 1870s to the mid-1930s, these men were dominating figures in both province and country, and their approach of integrating business with government became an enduring part of the political and economic culture of Alberta that long outlived them.

* * *

James Lougheed died in 1925. Without his leadership, his personal business empire weakened, and the collapse of Calgary's real estate market in the Great Depression of the 1930s wiped out the Lougheed family fortune. Tenants couldn't pay rent and vacated their premises, yet expenses continued. In 1934, Beaulieu was repossessed by the City of Calgary for unpaid taxes, though in an act of compassion Calgary city council allowed Belle to stay in the mansion until her death in 1936. In August 1938, the contents of the mansion went up for public auction, many of the items hauled out and displayed in the yards. Over the two-day auction, a crowd of 2,600 curiosity seekers and bargain hunters picked through fine furnishings, oriental rugs, oil paintings, and anything else that could be stripped from the house and sold. Most items went for pennies on the dollar; the entire library of several hundred leather-bound books sold for $22.[316]

Among those watching and wandering through the objects and the crowds was one of James and Belle's grandsons, ten-year-old Peter. He had not been in the mansion since he was too young to remember, and the day before the auction, he snuck into the vacant building and wandered its echoing halls and rooms, impressed by its silent grandeur.

He returned on the first day of auction, and, dismayed at the low prices for even the finest items, predicted the second day would see higher bids. His prediction was wrong, and his grandparents' estate was quickly sold off and scattered. The memory of the estate and the auction stayed with him for life.

During his boyhood, Peter Lougheed's family lived in a variety of rental accommodations around Calgary, but they were never destitute and his parents made sure he knew of his family's achievements.[317] After completing high school in 1947, he moved to Edmonton to get a law degree at the University of Alberta. By the time he graduated, Alberta's economy was roaring from a series of oil strikes far larger than Turner Valley, which launched the mineral economy and would transform the province. In 1952, Peter and his new wife, Jeanne, moved to Boston, where he obtained an MBA from Harvard. Like his grandparents, Peter Lougheed was keenly interested in business, law, and politics, and when he returned to Calgary from Harvard, he worked for a law firm, then became in-house lawyer for a major construction company, and in the early 1960s established his own law firm.

His next move was to provincial politics. The Conservative Party of his grandparents had changed its named to the Progressive Conservative (PC) Party in 1942 when it merged with remnants of the badly fractured Progressive Party, and in 1965, Lougheed won the leadership of the Alberta PCs. In 1966, he and five of his colleagues won seats in the Alberta legislature in Edmonton, forming the Official Opposition, and in August 1971, Peter Lougheed became premier of Alberta, defeating the long-governing Social Credit Party. The 1971 election was the only election from 1935 until 2015 in which the governing party changed in Alberta, and Peter Lougheed would prove to be one of the few powerful voices to stand up to the oil industry.

Chapter 10
Peter Lougheed and the rise of the oil sands

In Alberta, the Progressive Conservative Party governed uninterrupted for forty-four years, winning twelve consecutive general elections from 1971 until a surprise defeat toppled them in 2015. Eventually there came to be an easy flow of people between the oil industry and the PC Party; like tributary rivers joining to create one great waterway, the oil industry and the PCs streamed together to form the Government of Alberta.

It did not begin that way. When the PC Party won its first election in 1971, only one of its twenty-two cabinet ministers, Don Getty, came from the industry, and during the government's first term, relations with the oil and gas industry were often strained. When their political careers ended at various intervals over the next two decades, only two of the original cabinet ministers went into the oil industry. Both had been premiers: Peter Lougheed and Don Getty.

Though Lougheed came from Calgary's business community, he was not prepared to give private corporations free rein over Alberta's petroleum resources. With his family's deep political roots in Western Canada, he was acutely aware that the federal government had refused to transfer its ownership of natural resources to the prairie provinces, something it automatically did for all other provinces. Only in 1930, after long and difficult political battles, was resource ownership finally granted to Alberta, Saskatchewan, and Manitoba. James Lougheed had been one of many combatants on behalf of the prairie provinces[318] and Peter Lougheed was not going to betray their victory. In his first major speech in Ottawa, three months after taking office, Lougheed reminded his audience that under the constitution, Alberta owned its oil and gas, and he demanded observer status for Alberta at any energy discussions between Canada and the United States: "If Alberta poker chips are involved at the poker table, we will be at that table."[319] He never wavered from the principle of ownership.[320] His mantra to the people and Government of Alberta for developing its resources, and especially the oil sands, was to "think like owners."

In an interview about the oil sands with the Glenbow Museum in Calgary in 2011, the year before he died, Lougheed drove home this message of ownership with almost obsessive frequency:

Well, it was obvious that the oil sands were owned by the people of Alberta, hence it was a major responsibility of the Government of Alberta for the development of the oil sands. So we were, as owner, we consistently and constantly made sure that the industry understood that the Government of Alberta was the owner and we weren't just there in a supervisory or regulatory way. We were there as owner and that was the constant stress of our time in government, that we were the owner of the resource, so clearly we were very extensively involved, because we were the owners.[321]

★ ★ ★

The Alberta government and the University of Alberta had long been committed to unlocking the immense wealth of the oil sands. The original predecessor of the 1,000-plus oil sands researchers who worked at the U of A in 2015 was Dr. Karl Clark, an Ontario-born chemist recruited in 1920 by the university's president. Clark and a graduate student worked in a laboratory of boiling cauldrons and steaming drums in the basement of the university's old brick power plant on the south side of Edmonton,[322] struggling to separate oil sand bitumen, which is 80 per cent carbon, from the grains of quartzite sand it coated.[323] Clark learned that by cooking and stirring oil sand in a broth of extremely hot water and chemicals, the sand separated from the bitumen and sank to the bottom; the water, frothy with contaminants, rose to the top; and the bitumen, heavier than water but lighter than sand, formed a layer in the middle that could be extracted. It was a hot bitumen parfait.

When bitumen is separated from sand, it is much like asphalt, and in Clark's time it was tested as road pavement. Converting bitumen into crude oil requires a specialized refinery called an "upgrader" that uses heat, pressure, and chemicals to break the large bitumen molecules into smaller molecules. One output is a high-quality "synthetic crude oil" that matches the best conventional crude oil obtained from standard oil wells. Synthetic and conventional crude oils are major feedstocks for refineries, where they are made into gasoline, diesel, jet fuel, and other products. Producing synthetic crude on a large scale requires advanced technology, skilled workers, and far more water and energy than producing conventional crude. None of this deterred the Alberta government, because the oil sands deposits were large enough that, if successfully tapped, they could propel the economy of Alberta and rearrange the economic and political nature of Canada.

In 1921, the Alberta government formed the first provincial research and development agency in Canada, the Alberta Research Council,[324] with priority on converting oil sands into marketable oil. Year by year and decade by decade, the research gradually paid off. In 1951, the

Alberta government sponsored a conference on the oil sands that stirred private sector interest, and by the 1960s the forerunners of Suncor and Syncrude were coming on stream.[325] Both ventures were largely money-losing pilot projects meant to solve problems that included working with sand so abrasive it wore through hardened steel; winters so cold that equipment turned brittle and cracked; and such large volumes of wastewater that it created lakes of toxic fluid. The work was exceedingly slow, tough, and expensive, but the size of the potential pay-off kept the bets coming from governments and private investors. The commitment to develop the oil sands spanned every government in Alberta's history: Liberal, United Farmers, Social Credit, and Progressive Conservative, and it would continue under the New Democrats a hundred years after Karl Clark was first hired. Without the oil sands, Alberta's oil deep state would likely have withered.

There was no doubt in Peter Lougheed's mind about who should be in charge of Alberta's resources, and he had no tolerance for capture. Private investors were expected to take a major role because Lougheed was a pro-business leader, but they were required to work within a framework actively managed by public regulators, civil servants, the governing party, and the legislative assembly. As for the federal and other governments, the message was a forceful "hands off."

This meant tough political and legal fights with a range of business interests and with both the federal and Ontario governments. At the time, oil and natural gas markets in Canada and the United States were highly regulated by national governments working closely with a handful of giant multinational oil companies. Their combined agendas were to safeguard national security during the height of the Cold War; stabilize wild swings in the market that could hurt both consumers and oil companies; generate healthy oil company profits; and, in Canada, to encourage the growth of Alberta's relatively small and remote production so it could feed Ontario's industry.[326] Alberta's interests were often lost in the tangle.

From its first year in office, the Lougheed government worked to assert autonomy over the resources it owned. Crude oil was trading in the range of $3 per barrel and the Social Credit government had a longstanding ceiling on oil royalties of 16.7 per cent, no matter how lucrative production became. In its first legislative sitting, the Lougheed government raised royalty rates on newly drilled oil wells to 25 per cent. When prices spiked to $12 per barrel after the 1973 OPEC crisis, the government tore up the agreements on old oil wells as well, and royalties rose to a range of 35 to 65 per cent across the board.[327]

In 1972, Lougheed's PCs blocked a set of apparently routine applications by pipeline companies to ship Alberta natural gas out of province. They then commissioned an independent review of the price collected for those shipments, and when the review found the gas was being sold 40 per cent below market value, the government refused to approve the permits until higher prices were obtained. This immediately drew the ire of Ontario, where much of the gas was to be consumed.[328]

The Lougheed government also established the Alberta Energy Company, gave it some attractive oil and gas properties, and sold shares to the public so Albertans could invest directly in their own resources, an extraordinarily popular move. In order to develop a petrochemical industry in Alberta, the government challenged federal policies that encouraged Alberta's raw natural gas to be shipped to Ontario for processing, and it created policies that supported the establishment of a large petrochemical complex in central Alberta.

The Lougheed team took the same determination to developing the oil sands. They dramatically bolstered oil sands research; directly invested in oil sands mega-projects and upgraders; built roads, bridges, airports, schools, and hospitals to serve the oil sands workforce; and assembled the laws, regulations, and tax arrangements designed to make it all happen. They wanted to squeeze the most value from oil sands projects by approving one project at a time and negotiating separate royalty and regulatory schemes for each of them,[329] and they used this process to grow related industries such as upgrading, petrochemicals, and manufacturing.

Peter Lougheed was working to break the old pattern of Alberta's economy that shipped raw materials such as fur, grain, coal, crude oil, natural gas, and bitumen for processing elsewhere. He had lived the hard lessons of that kind of economy. He knew every resource boom would eventually collapse, and his view was that governments had responsibility to offset the risks.

There was reason for concern. Alberta's conventional oil production peaked in 1973 and immediately began to decline.[330] The ace in hand was the oil sands. Oil price increases, together with improved technologies, finally offered a realistic chance the oil sands would be commercially viable. The Syncrude project on the Athabasca oil sands near Fort McMurray had been mired in planning and feasibility tests for years, and the Alberta government was determined to get it going. In August 1973, it sat down to finalize a deal with Syncrude's backers.

These negotiations show how fiercely the government of the day asserted control over resources. The 1973 negotiations on Syncrude were much more than a dramatic few days of high stakes bargaining. They provided a benchmark by which to measure the sorry collapse of later governments and the triumphant capture of the oil sands by private interests twenty years later.

The Syncrude negotiations were held in Edmonton. Syncrude's team was led by the Syncrude project manager, supported by a number of vice presidents. In the wings, but out of sight, were the CEOs of the four large oil companies behind Syncrude: Imperial Oil, Gulf, Cities Services, and Atlantic Richfield. The government team was led by Alberta energy minister Don Getty, supported by the Resource Development Committee, a special cabinet committee of five other ministers. A number of top civil servants had prepared briefing notes. Lougheed followed every move but waited off-stage until the final round.

One of the closest observers of the negotiations was the head of communications for the Alberta government, David G. Wood. He was on standby should the government need to announce negotiations had failed, in which case the premier planned to explain the situation to Albertans through a direct television broadcast. Wood provided a detailed account of the negotiations in a book published at the end of Lougheed's time as premier,[331] and his description is worth quoting at length.

> The government really wanted the Syncrude oil sands plant to go ahead . . . In spite of this, they had to be prepared to let the project die. Don Getty explained, "The key to our whole negotiation was to let them know that much as we wanted an oil sands plant, we were prepared to let the project drop. But how could we do it in such a way that they'd know that we meant it?" The method and opportunity came about when Syncrude wrote a letter saying, in effect, "These are our terms, and if these terms aren't generally what we get, then we're not interested."

> . . . The government had a very definite plan and a well thought out bargaining strategy. Getty took the letter down to Lougheed's office where they discussed it. Getty said, "I'm convinced that now we have to prove to them that we don't have to have this deal. It may be a great risk, but I think we're at the stage in negotiations where we're stalled unless we do."

> The premier agreed and the next meeting was set.

> On one side of the table sat Frank Spraggins [project manager of Syncrude] and a vanguard of vice presidents.

On the other side sat Getty and the Resource Development Committee . . . Syncrude began by saying they had a presentation they wished to make, but Getty pulled the Syncrude letter from his folder and said, "Before we get into that, let me be sure that I understand the contents of this letter correctly. In it, are you saying it has to be on these terms, or you're not going to go ahead?"

The Syncrude spokesman said, "Yes. You understand it correctly."

"Gentlemen," said former quarterback Don Getty, standing and looking as if he'd just spotted a receiver clear in the end zone, "I don't mean to be abrupt, and I really do appreciate your coming, but gentlemen, I guess it's time to say goodbye. If that is your stand there will be no Syncrude project, and this meeting is over." Getty then slammed shut his thick book of negotiation briefings and headed for the door.

Before he could make it, one of the Syncrude people grabbed him by his coat sleeve, "You can't go, Mr. Minister. If you walk out of here there won't be a Syncrude."

Getty said, "I'm sorry, but that's your fault, not mine." The fellow still clung to his coat, but Don Getty had an edge in the experience of breaking tackles. He tore his arm away and strode towards the door, where he turned and said to the rest of his committee, "Come on, fellows, the meeting's over."

They all left with the exception of Minister of Mines and Minerals Bill Dickie, who was deliberately lingering behind. He went over to Frank Spraggins and said, "Frank, if we've overlooked anything, or if there's something you've missed telling us, you can start negotiations again simply by calling. But meanwhile, as far as we're concerned, it's all over." Then he, too, left the room.

The strategy forced Syncrude's backers to retreat from their positions. Negotiations resumed the following day, and when they broke for the night, the companies had agreed to pay the government a 50 per cent royalty of net profits, starting from first production. The following day, a Friday, Lougheed and one of the CEOs joined directly in the bargaining. When all was said and done, the agreement included Alberta owning a 5 per cent portion of Syncrude in return for buying shares, with an option to buy more; an ownership position in the pipeline from the oil sands to Edmonton; partial ownership of the plant that supplied power to the Syncrude site; and a 50 per cent royalty on net profits. The following year, the deal had to be renegotiated because Atlantic Richfield pulled out to concentrate on its Alaska properties, and Alberta ended up investing $200 million for a 10 per cent ownership position, with a long-term option on 40 per cent of the entire venture.[332] The Alberta government had established that it was master in its own house.

Chapter 11
Pulling the levers of power: From Lougheed to Klein

In his first two terms as premier from 1971 to 1979, Peter Lougheed made it clear the Alberta government was not subservient to the oil industry or anyone else. His government professionalized the civil service and expanded the province's universities. It enhanced the legislative assembly itself, producing a daily verbatim record of legislature debates for the public and providing full-time pay for all members of the assembly, including opposition members. Ironically, by his third term, Lougheed was so personally powerful he began running the risk of becoming a kind of monarch himself and was sometimes called "King Peter" or "the blue-eyed Sheik." His success was aided by surging oil prices, but Alberta was on the brink of entering a classic crisis for a mineral economy: price collapse. World oil prices reached a historic high in March 1980, selling for $117 per barrel (adjusted to 2016 dollars), then began a prolonged decline.[333] They fell below $23 a barrel (adjusted to 2016 dollars) in March 1986 and wouldn't reach the 1980 level again until 2008.

The 1980s plunge in oil prices brought an extended economic crisis to Alberta that put Lougheed's political order in danger. The flow of oil money was too small to cover the industry's costs or fill the government treasury with royalties. New investment dried up, and the province's economy entered a severe stall. Before the price plunge, Alberta's unemployment rate hovered around 4 per cent; in 1984, it hit 12 per cent.[334] Five-year mortgage rates — driven by American monetary policy — ranged between 15 and 20 per cent,[335] and real estate values in Alberta had fallen so far that many houses were not worth the mortgages financing them. Some people sold their homes for a dollar, just to escape the mortgage payments.

The public was getting desperate for new political options. A movement to separate the four Western provinces from the rest of Canada gained momentum and the separatist Western Canada Concept Party elected a member to the Alberta legislature in a 1982 by-election, although he was soon defeated in a general election. Public desperation also showed up in recurring political protests and labour disruptions. Workers at Suncor struck for six months in 1986;[336] there were two strikes at Zeidler Forest Products, one lasting from 1988 to 1993;[337] Alberta Liquor Control Board workers struck for almost two months in 1986; and there was a series of strikes at meatpacking plants, including the notorious and violent walkout at Gainers Meats in Edmonton for six months in 1986.[338]

The economy and politics of the province were in upheaval, and voters and the oil industry began looking for change. Peter Lougheed, still popular, retired from politics in 1985, and Don Getty took his place as premier. Getty's PC government steered a moderate political course, making modest cuts to spending, running large deficits, keeping taxes low, helping the oil industry with various programs, and trying to diversify the economy with a range of contentious and often failed investments. The first powerful wave of political opposition came from the New Democratic Party on the left, which won sixteen seats in general elections in both 1986 and 1989.

By 1992, the economy was still flat, provincial deficits were still high, and Getty's government had been caught in a number of damaging controversies. A new wave of opposition was building under the Alberta Liberals, who were running from the right on a campaign of dramatic spending cuts. (I had no involvement in Alberta politics at this time.) Getty and the PCs were trailing badly in public opinion polls. Late in 1992, Getty, having been premier for six difficult years, resigned and turned the premier's office over to the new leader of the PCs, Ralph Klein. Though far behind in public support when he took office, Klein and his advisors managed an impressive political recovery for the PCs and in the 1993 general election pulled off a convincing victory. Klein would remain premier until he retired in 2006.

Ralph Klein's arrival as premier corresponded with an internal over-haul of the PCs and a marked opening of the party and the government to the fossil fuel industry, which led to the ascent of the deep state. Capturing and holding a governing party is as close as it gets to seizing the command centre of a modern democracy. From the top positions of a governing party, the levers of power pull directly or indirectly on all other institutions. And pull they did. The Klein government sliced dramatically into the budgets, capacities, and the autonomies of the civil service, local governments, universities, school boards, health authorities, and regulators. It sold the government's interests in the Alberta Energy Company (1993), the massive Husky upgrader (1994), and Syncrude (1995).[339] This remaking of government and state was billed as "the Klein revolution" and operated under a series of slogans, including "get government out of the business of business." What went unstated was that business was getting into the governing of government.

From Premier Getty's last term in 1989 to the post-Klein era, at least seven people who served as ministers of energy or finance either came from the fossil fuel industry into politics, or stepped out of cabinet into senior positions in the industry.[340] Three did a full circle, from the industry into cabinet and back to industry. In total, these people served with more than twenty fossil fuel companies, often as directors.

These cabinet ministers sat on and often chaired the most powerful committees in the government. They had key input into royalty and environmental policies. Those who were ministers of energy were responsible for the public agencies that regulated Alberta's oil, gas, and coal industries. The seamless blend of political position with oil interest was epitomized when, in 1996, three PC cabinet ministers joined with four other PC members of the legislature to form a numbered company to invest in oil and gas drilling in Alberta. They ran the company, nicknamed "Tory Oil," while sitting in public office, and operated it with the full knowledge of the premier and cabinet.[341] This largely unhindered integration of public and private interests was squarely in the tradition of Donald Smith, James Lougheed, and R. B. Bennett, as if the boundaries distinguishing government and business were as porous at the end of the 20th century as they had been at its beginning. The old ways of Alberta's oil industry had returned.

The period from 1992 to 2007 coincided with shifts in government policy that sliced royalties and taxes. These changes helped launch a dramatic rise in the overall rate of profits earned by Alberta corporations, which was duly noted by TD Bank in a high-profile 2005 research report: "Corporate profits grew 44 percent in Alberta . . in 2003 and a further 19 percent in 2004. This growth brings corporate profits to 22 percent of Alberta's nominal GDP, roughly twice the share posted in the rest of Canada."[342] The point was sustained in TD Bank's 2007 report, with the profit levels even higher.[343] During the same period, spending on most public services hovered near the Canadian average.[344] A massive transfer of public wealth into private bank accounts was occurring as Alberta's publicly owned resources were sold on generous terms to private investors. Voters were delighted with the economic quick fix after years of economic stall, and popular support for the Klein Conservatives was solid.

Alberta cabinet ministers who took positions with the oil industry after leaving politics and serving a six-month cooling off period were often paid well. Former Deputy Premier Shirley McClellan, for example, sat on the board of PennWest Energy from 2007, the year she resigned from the legislature, until 2014. PennWest's corporate filings indicate she was paid $150,612 in 2013 alone.[345] Former Minister of Energy Greg Melchin sat on the board of Baytex Energy from 2008, the year he resigned from the legislature, until 2014. Filings for Baytex indicate he had $1,571,254 in "Director Equity Ownership" on March 3, 2014, and in 2013 had been paid $154,892 in fees and share-based awards by Baytex.[346]

One of the casualties of the Klein years was Alberta's global warming policy. In September 1990, two years before the Rio Earth Summit and seven years before the Kyoto Accord, the Alberta Department of Energy published a discussion paper on ways to reduce carbon dioxide emissions in Alberta.[347] At the time, it was part of normal government policy work. The discussion paper acknowledged the science of global warming and showed how carbon emissions in Alberta could be reduced. The report predicted emissions could be cut 7.3 per cent by 2005 even with a growing economy, as long as there was strong government leadership.

Government leadership was strong all right, but in the opposite direction. Within three years, the office that produced this plan was disbanded. The PC government actively opposed the 1997 Kyoto Accord, which committed Canada and other countries to reduce carbon emissions and would hinder the growth of the fossil fuel industry. This reached a grim vacuousness in 2002 when Premier Klein joked that he didn't know much about global warming, but perhaps in the past it had been caused by "dinosaur farts."[348] Emissions in Alberta, instead of declining from 1990 to 2005, rose dramatically.[349]

Chapter 12
Industry captures the oil sands

Canada as a whole had a fighting chance of meeting the goals of the 1992 Rio Earth Summit and the 1997 Kyoto Accord when it signed the treaties endorsing them. The Kyoto goal was more ambitious than the Rio goal, calling for total emissions in 2012 to be 6 per cent below their 1990 level.[350] By 2014, five provinces representing two-thirds of Canada's population met or surpassed that goal.[351] Two other provinces failed but were reasonably close. The three that completely missed the goals — Alberta, Saskatchewan, and B.C. — were the country's largest producers of fossil fuels,[352] and of these, Alberta stood out as the worst offender by far, allowing emissions to rise from 175 million tonnes in 1990 to 274 million tonnes in 2014. How far offside was Alberta? Its 99 million–tonne increase in emissions was more than the *total* emissions of any province except Ontario, which had more than three times Alberta's population. More than 80 per cent of the increase in Canada's emissions from 1990 to 2014 came from Alberta, which was home to just 11 per cent of Canada's population. That increase came from oil and natural gas production, primarily the immense energy required for the province's ballooning oil sands production, most of which was exported,[353] and it put the whole country offside of Kyoto.

It was as though a gate at the entrance to two paths for Canada had swung 180 degrees, closing off the route to success against a warming climate and directing the country down a different path, toward ever-steepening climbs of fossil fuel emissions. That gate was anchored in Alberta's oil sands, but it affected all Canadians, and among the people swinging the gate was Alberta's energy minister from late 1992 to early 1997, Patricia Black (Patricia Nelson after she remarried in 1998). She was the most important energy minister Alberta would have for decades, guiding decisions on oil sands development that had impacts across Canada and around the world. Under Black, Peter Lougheed's approach to the oil sands was turned on its head.

Black described herself as "a ticked off taxpayer" and "a very, very right-wing conservative" who felt Alberta was "over taxed and over regulated."[354] Her father, Raymond Ballard, had been an accountant who served four years on Calgary city council and then one term as a Conservative member of parliament from 1965 to 1968 for Calgary South. Ballard owned a small oil and gas drilling company, and when Patricia completed her commerce degree at the University of Calgary, she followed in her father's line, immediately joining Sun Oil.[355]

Sun Oil was a pioneering investor in the oil sands, and Black worked on the team that transformed it into the oil sands giant Suncor. She openly loved the oil sands: "My first love, right from the beginning when I came out of university, was the oil sands. To me, it was the ninth wonder of the world, and the jewel of Alberta . . ."[356] By the time she won a seat in the legislature for the Alberta PCs in 1989, she had worked fifteen years in the oil and gas industry with three different companies. Premier Klein appointed her to his first cabinet as energy minister in late 1992, the year of the Rio Earth Summit, and she stayed in that position until early 1997,[357] the year the Kyoto Protocol was signed. Black then served in several other cabinet positions, including finance, but it was her work as energy minister that enlarged the carbon footprint of Canada so dramatically.

When Black became energy minister in 1992, a lifetime had passed since Karl Clark first heated drums of bitumen in his basement laboratory in Edmonton. Under the framework of the Lougheed and Getty governments, production from Syncrude, Suncor, and smaller operations had reached 350,000 barrels of synthetic crude a day.[358] Syncrude alone was meeting 10 per cent of Canada's oil needs.[359] Even so, Alberta's total oil production was small when ranked on a global scale, providing about 3 per cent of world supply.[360] World oil prices had begun to recover from their depths in the 1980s, and after relentless cost cutting, oil sands producers were once again profitable. There was no sign, though, of major new projects that would tap the still largely untouched resource. Syncrude and Suncor were chafing under the agreements they had signed with the Lougheed team, and potential investors were uncertain about negotiating new agreements with the government. The oil sands industry wanted a change that would open up their opportunities and reduce their risks. Across the table, the Klein government, committed to balancing its budget and boosting the province's economy was, as it often said, open for business. Pat Black would do their deals.

Change for the oil sands industry began in 1993 with a unique political convergence. A federal Liberal Party candidate named Anne McLellan, a respected law professor at the University of Alberta, squeaked out an election win in Edmonton by the slimmest possible margin: one vote. On recount a few days later, she won by twelve votes and was thereafter nicknamed Landslide Annie. Liberal Prime Minister Jean Chrétien, glad to have a political toehold in Conservative Alberta, promptly appointed McLellan as Minister of Natural Resources Canada (NRCan).[361] Suddenly, both the federal and provincial ministers responsible for oil sands development were from Alberta.

The leading industry association in those days was the Alberta Chamber of Resources, and seeing the political opportunity, it ramped up its "National Task Force on Oil Sands Strategies."[362] Though the oil sands were publicly owned, the task force was structured so that all senior positions were held by powerful industry leaders, while sub-teams had a majority of officials from private interests and a minority from governments, regulators, and public research agencies.[363] It was a classic manoeuvre of capture, and the interests of the industry prevailed. Syncrude was the unofficial leader, and its agenda was to end the system put into place in the 1970s by Peter Lougheed and his team.

As one of the Alberta government representatives on the task force said years later, "Peter Lougheed had negotiated a pretty good deal for the Alberta Government I think it's fair to say. In the early years, especially, they got a lot of royalty dollars out of Syncrude. And Syncrude were very motivated to try to get a royalty treatment that would be less onerous . . ."[364] Syncrude and others on the task force wanted more than lower royalties; they also wanted simplified approvals with fewer strings attached and improved tax treatments. For two years, the task force worked without relent to open up government policies that would accelerate oil sands expansion, travelling across the country on speaking tours and endlessly pursuing federal and provincial politicians and civil servants.[365] Task force members turned up at so many political events in so many different places that NRCan minister Anne McLellan began making good-natured jokes about them.[366] Political donations had a place in this process; seven of the fourteen largest donors to the Alberta PC Party during this period were petroleum companies.[367]

In 1995, the task force produced an impressive twenty-five-year plan for the oil sands that covered everything from research to royalties, production to pipelines, capital investment to capital write-off. One thing it did *not* cover was the impact of oil sands expansion on global warming. In sixty-two pages, the plan spent three sentences on CO_2 emissions.[368] This absence confirmed the unspoken truth that expanding oil sands production while reducing total carbon dioxide emissions was not possible.

The task force couldn't plead ignorance of global warming. The Rio Earth Summit had boosted public awareness of the dangers of CO_2 emissions, and Canada was now actively negotiating the Kyoto Protocol to reduce emissions. Perhaps the task force was too committed to its own mission to see the broader implications, or too aroused by the financial payoff to think beyond it. Perhaps its members were influenced by the American Petroleum Institute's propaganda. Some members bluntly denied the science of global warming, and others were inclined to turn a blind eye to the issue.[369] When Howard Dingle, Imperial Oil's top representative on the task force, was questioned on environmental issues at the oil sands, his reply was telling:[370]

> Interviewer : And, the environmental questions with the oil sands always come up. What can you say about that?
>
> Dingle: I spend a lot of time worrying about the environment. But, as far as I was concerned we did as good a job as anyone could do. You cannot drill holes in the ground and you cannot produce oil without making some disruption. But, I think we did as fine a job as possible.
>
> Interviewer : And, the carbon, the CO2 issue?
>
> Dingle: Well, I'm not going to go into that.

Unfortunately, avoiding the CO2 issue does not make it go away.

★ ★ ★

Black and McLellan set aside their political differences and worked to enact the task force recommendations in their respective governments. They were both looking for an economic boost for Alberta, because much of the province was still in the economic doldrums. Of the two ministers, Black, representing the government that owned the oil sands, was the lead. Howard Dingle of Imperial Oil described Black's involvement:

The key individual from the Alberta Government when
we dealt with it was the former Energy Minister, Pat Black.
And, she was the principal person that saw the need to
change the existing agreements particularly for Syncrude
to enable Syncrude to grow. So, it was really the agreement
with the Alberta Government that drove everything behind
this Task Force. So, Pat was the front-runner in the Alberta
Government that led the charge.[371]

The charge that Black led replaced the Lougheed era system of oil
sands regulations with a system that cleared the way for industry. Eric
Newell, a crucial figure in the task force and for many years CEO of
Syncrude, said,

. . . part of the task force work was to identify the key
barriers. And once we got everybody excited about what the
potential was, it was amazing how easy it was, relatively easy
it was to figure out how to knock down those barriers or
modify them . . .

There was a reason it was easy: The key government minister, Pat
Black, pretty much turned the process over to the industry. The outcome was the "Generic Oil Sands Royalty Regime," enacted on July 1,
1997. In 2011, Black, now known as Patricia Nelson (she had changed
her surname after remarriage in 1998) spoke at length to the Glenbow
Museum about her approach to developing this regime:[372]

Interviewer: What would you consider to be some of the main
achievements or highlights of your involvement with the oil
sands, particularly during your time in government?

Nelson/Black: The number one thing was the generic royalty
scheme, the structure to attract investment. That brought

people into Alberta. That was the number one thing . . .

Interviewer : And this was all about making Alberta more industry friendly?

Nelson/Black: Well, you needed somebody to do the work, and it had to be the industry. There's no point in making an enemy out of the people you're depending upon to do the work. So, to me, bring them to the table right away. And they were very good, the industry. I took the view that no one could expect me to know everything about the industry. So, I created a kitchen cabinet that I relied on heavily. I had people from pipelines, I had people who were contract drillers, I had people that were water haulers, I had people in conventional play. Every aspect of the industry: I had land people I would bring in and they would be part of this kitchen cabinet, and we would meet every Saturday morning.

And, they would sometimes just beat me up fiercely, and at other times I could go to them and say, "What do you think of this?" and they'd either say, "Perfect!" or "Oh, my word. You better have a look at this, this and this." I was very lucky to have key people . . . all of these people were fundamentally key to helping with the change that we went through. And, I've always been eternally grateful to them, to be honest with you, because I couldn't have done it on my own.

Black didn't see this merging of government and the oil industry as a problem. To her it was a good thing — after all, she had come from the industry and would return to it. Her priorities and the industry's converged, and concerns like overheating the economy, giving away a public resource too cheaply, and global warming were not going to get in the way. (Anne McLellan did not come from the corporate sector before she entered politics, but six months after her electoral defeat in 2006, she was appointed to the board of Nexen, one of Canada's largest independent petroleum companies.)[373]

The industry was thrilled with the new approach to oil sands development, and why not? From then on, oil sands projects would have fewer standards of accountability to democratic institutions and more accountability to investors. The system of governing and managing the publicly owned oil sands had been captured by private interests, and the government itself had become, to adapt the phrase of political scientist Samuel P. Huntington, an instrument of the oil industry.

Chief among the system's appeals was the royalty rate, which collected only 1 per cent of the gross revenues of oil sands producers until the investors had recovered the full capital cost of their investment, at which point it climbed to 25 per cent of net revenues. A 1 per cent royalty is virtually a gift to the industry. One of Black's successors as energy minister, Murray Smith (who also came from and returned to the industry), described the system this way at a presentation he gave in Austin, Texas:

> The model that has worked so well for us is that the royalty
> structure for oil sands is we "give it away" at a 1 percent
> royalty structure and share in the risk of these great ventures
> and great investments. As soon as they reach payout, the
> royalty take goes to 25 percent of net.[374]

Oil sands growth exploded. The 1995 oil sands task force report predicted production might reach at most 1.2 million barrels a day by 2020.[375] It reached that level in 2005; doubled it by 2014;[376] and was expected to pass three million barrels a day by 2020.[377] The task force predicted up to $25 billion in capital investment over twenty-five years; $27.2 billion were invested in the year 2012 alone.[378] That was fifty-three times greater than the annual spending at the largest construction project underway in Toronto.[379]

By summer 2006, Mayor Melissa Blake of Fort McMurray/Wood Buffalo, the municipality where most of the oil sands are found, made a formal submission to Alberta's Energy and Utilities Board pleading to slow down mega-project approvals because her community couldn't provide the housing or services that were needed. The region's head of medical staff told regulators the community had only half the number of doctors it needed, and Aboriginal groups raised concerns about water use by the oil sands, which would cause their fisheries to collapse.[380] The Energy and Utilities Board, operating under legislation brought in by Patricia Black and Ralph Klein, said it did not have the mandate to address "socio-economic" issues, so the pleas from Fort McMurray were to no avail. The pace of expansion accelerated.

To do the work, thousands of "fly-in/fly-out" workers from across Canada and around the world were rotated through the projects, many of them arriving at airports designed for commercial jetliners built right at the work sites. The 2012 census in Fort McMurray/Wood Buffalo counted 40,000 mobile workers in nearly 100 work camps, but that count was taken during low season and the real number was likely 60,000 or more; the capacity of work camps was 92,000 beds.[381] The permanent population of Fort McMurray was only 73,000.

Meanwhile, Alberta's oil sands were being sold at fire-sale prices. Many high-paying, short-term jobs were created for workers, and many fortunes were made for investors. But tens of thousands of those workers weren't from Alberta, and many of the investors were from the United States, Europe, and Asia. The industry gorged itself until it grew so big, it began to trip on its own tentacles. Companies competed with each other for workers, housing, supplies, water, pipelines, and railcars. Yet the government did nothing to slow it down, because it had neither the policy tools nor the political autonomy to do so; it was servant to the oil sands master.

The financial weight of oil sands growth bent the Canadian economy into a new shape. Unprocessed bitumen and crude oil became Canada's largest exports, and the value of the Canadian dollar rose and fell with world prices of oil.[382] For several years, bitumen royalties gushed into the Alberta government treasury, peaking at $5.2 billion in 2013–14,[383] but the PC government kept tax and royalty rates so low that it was often running deficits.

The skyrocketing investments to produce raw bitumen overwhelmed Alberta's capacity to upgrade the raw bitumen into higher value synthetic crude. Workers simply weren't available to build upgraders in such an overheated economy, so upgrading, refining, and related manufacturing were driven elsewhere, where regulations were lower and labour was cheaper. By 2014, over half the production from the oil sands was shipped as unprocessed bitumen,[384] diluted with solvents so it would flow through pipelines or into rail cars. It was mineral economics on steroids: Strip the resource from the land and sell it abroad for others to process. In the vernacular, the approach was called "rip and strip."

Inevitably, the economic, social, and environmental repercussions caught up with the frenzied scheme. Alberta's oil sands boom was part of an international surge in petroleum production that, by 2014, had the world awash in oil. Prices dropped by more than half from 2014 to 2016,[385] and capital investment in the oil sands fell by 60 per cent.[386] Royalty and tax revenue to the Alberta government collapsed, driving up the provincial debt at breakneck speed. By 2016, Calgary's unemployment rate was the highest of any major city in Canada,[387] and in downtown Calgary, the headquarters of Canada's petroleum sector, office vacancy rates approached 25 per cent.[388]

Even before the 2014 price crash, two other problems loomed over the oil sands. The first was the shortage of pipeline capacity to deliver bitumen to markets. The increase in production was far greater than existing pipelines could carry, but there was no easy way to build new ones. From Vancouver to Montreal, North Dakota to Nebraska, people did not want pipelines carrying diluted bitumen running through their territory and into ships in their ports. The political opposition to pipelines spread and hardened like molten lava.

The other problem was the burgeoning scale of CO_2 emissions from bitumen production, which made it almost impossible for Canada to achieve its international commitments to reduce emissions, no matter what the rest of the country did. Canada was offside with the world on emissions, and the Alberta government, as an instrument of oil's deep state, was happy to do the tough political work this required. Even in the months before the Rio Earth Summit in 1992, Ralph Klein, then Alberta's environment minister, was opposing limits on emissions that would curtail Alberta's fossil fuel industry.[389] After he became premier in 1993, the rhetoric from his government was unrelenting. In 1994, he said a carbon tax would kill the oil and gas sector and "would go against everything we stand for in this province."[390] In the months prior to the 1997 Kyoto Protocol, he spoke out against limiting emissions, and when the Kyoto Protocol was settled, he and various members of his cabinet threatened a constitutional challenge against the federal government, describing the process as a betrayal.[391] At every step, the Klein government's positions followed the lead of the industry in a lop-sided dance that would continue as one premier was exchanged for the next.

★ ★ ★

Peter Lougheed kept his views on the generic oil sands royalty regime to himself until Ralph Klein's time as premier was winding up. Then he began to speak. In September 2006, Lougheed delivered a public interview that laid out his concerns with the royalty scheme. The publisher titled the interview "Sounding an Alarm for Alberta."[392] Lougheed said oil sands development was going too fast and the royalty regime was too generous. "What is the hurry?" he asked. "Why not build one oil sands plant at a time?" He had just returned from a visit to the oil sands:

> It is just a moonscape. It is wrong in my judgement, a major
> wrong, and I keep trying to see who the beneficiaries are . . . It
> is not the people of the province, because they are not getting

the royalty return that they should be getting. So it is a major, major federal and provincial issue.

Unbridled oil sands development, said Lougheed, pushed up inflation, caused labour shortages, overwhelmed infrastructure, and "you also have the risk if it turns down, a lot of people get badly hurt." A carefully staged approach to oil sands development would reduce the risk of overheating the economy and help contain environmental liabilities. Lougheed was speaking in 2006. The oil sands boom didn't peak for another eight years, and, as Lougheed predicted, when it turned down, a lot of people did get badly hurt.

Lougheed's comments were echoed by Allan Warrack, a minister in Lougheed's cabinet and a member of the Resource Development Committee that walked out during the 1972 negotiations with Syncrude. Oil sands development had become "reckless" and "disorderly," he said, and added, "orderly development, pacing of the plants . . . went out the window. And, if it's far enough out the window, it's beyond salvage. And, unfortunately, I think that's where it stands now."[393]

The government of Alberta, firmly in the grip of oil's deep state, had abandoned Peter Lougheed's command to think like an owner, and he acknowledged as much: "...a lot of people in this town," he said, referring to Calgary, the headquarters city of Canada's oil industry, "... have a hard time with the word "ownership." But the ownership is with the people of Alberta."[394] Lougheed's notion, though legally correct, was getting swamped. By 2017, the CEO of Suncor, Steve Williams, would come out of an annual shareholders' meeting to tell reporters, "Now what we have is a Canadian resource, increasingly owned by Canadian corporations, working with Canadian provincial and federal governments to try and get the proper access with absolutely the right environmental standards to market."[395] There was "alignment," said Williams, among the federal and provincial governments; Canada's big oil companies; the resource to which they claimed ownership; and environmental standards, and that was, he concluded, "a good thing."

* * *

Lougheed's and Black's approaches to oil sands development could hardly be more different. Lougheed assembled a powerful cabinet committee and built expertise in the civil service, which provided detailed briefing binders for negotiations. He and his team were tough negotiators with careful strategies who challenged the industry and walked out of bargaining sessions. They got 50 per cent royalty starting with the first barrel of Syncrude's production, partial ownership, and control of the pace of development.

All that changed under the Klein government. Alberta's civil service went through tumultuous cuts and reorganizations. Black's department was no different.[396] Her most senior civil servant, Deputy Minister Myron Kanik, who had been with the department in various positions for almost twenty years, was replaced shortly after Black arrived. His replacement, David Manning, had spent the previous five years as Alberta's trade counsel in New York City. He stayed only two years as deputy minister with Alberta Energy. Next up was Richard Hyndman, who lasted less than three years.

Deputy ministers from Alberta Energy tended to land on their feet in industry. Kanik became president of the Canadian Energy Pipeline Association and went on to serve as a director with several oil companies and organizations.[397] Manning left Alberta Energy in 1995 to become president of CAPP, where one of his first roles was to lead CAPP's delegation to the Kyoto Protocol negotiations.[398] Hyndman, respected for his intellect, moved from deputy minister at Alberta Energy to become senior policy analyst for climate change at CAPP, taught as an adjunct professor at the University of Alberta Business School, and was parachuted in to run CSEE when Bruce Carson resigned.[399]

Most senior government managers, especially deputy ministers, are bright, well informed, connected, and have years of experience on tough files, so of course industry wants to hire them. Even so, the ease with which people like Kanik, Manning, Hyndman, and others circulated among the provincial government, industry, universities, and regulators spoke to the weak boundaries separating these institutions. Who was going to hold whom to account? This segment of Alberta began to look like a village where everyone had met everyone else, where pasts were known and futures were managed, and everyone was a booster for the same team — a village where the laws would never have tripped up Bruce Carson.

Presumably, Black had briefings from staff, though in her long interview with the Glenbow Museum she mentions neither briefings nor staff. She preferred to rely on industry for advice. She assembled her "kitchen cabinet" of people from industry that met with her every Saturday, to whom she would ask "What do you think of this?", to which they would reply either "Perfect" or "You'd better look at this, this and this." She was "eternally grateful" for industry's help with the changes she enacted. Under Black's approach, the 50 per cent royalty plummeted to 25 per cent, and that was only paid after the company had recovered all construction costs. Partial public ownership fell to zero, and public control of the pace of development was abdicated. Black and the Klein government had locked in place the economic forces that led to Canada's vaulting levels of CO_2 emissions and put oil's deep state in high gear.

Did the changes wrought by the National Oil Sands Task Force, Pat Black, and the Klein government amount to institutional capture? Or was it just politics as usual?

A quick review of the dynamics of capture is in order. First, there were public interests. The public owned the oil sands and had an interest in getting the most benefit from their development while minimizing environmental problems, including emissions. Second, there were public institutions responsible for the public interest, most notably the Government of Alberta as represented by Minister of Energy Pat Black and Premier Ralph Klein. Third, there was a party intent on asserting its own control of the oil sands, the oil industry as represented by the Alberta Chamber of Resources and a host of corporations. Finally, there is glaring evidence that the Alberta government (with support from the federal government) redirected itself to meet the desires of the oil sands industry, indeed to make it "perfect" for them.

So "yes," the oil sands were captured by the oil industry. That doesn't mean this wasn't politics as usual. In a mineral economy like Alberta's, capture *is* politics as usual. The *un*usual politics happened during the first two terms of the Lougheed government, when the Alberta government worked to escape capture by taking control of the resources it owned. Pat Black utterly defeated that effort. In the process, she surrendered the possibility that Alberta — and Canada — could effectively fulfill responsibilities to address global warming.

Chapter 13
Pushing the bar higher

Although the rapport between the oil industry and the PC government in Alberta was strong, it was not without strain. For a brief time, the industry felt its hold on the governing party slip. When Ralph Klein retired in 2006, the PCs held a leadership race in which some of the candidates mused that Alberta had gone too far in unleashing oil sands development. Front-runner Jim Dinning said, "It concerns me when I hear companies planning to ship more of our raw resources for refining in the United States. I believe if you mine it here, you upgrade it here." Another candidate, Ed Stelmach, used an old Prairie metaphor to describe the problem: "Shipping raw bitumen was like scraping off the topsoil, selling it and then passing the farm on to the next generation. What value does it have?"[400]

Stelmach went on to win the race and become leader of the PCs and premier of Alberta. He was a farmer without close ties to the oil industry who defeated the industry's preferred candidate. His campaign benefited from targeting specific ethnic and geographic groups and a preferential voting process that favoured the most popular second choice on each ballot. His win was unexpected, and he soon put his relationship with the industry through a series of tests that would prove fatal to his political career. The Stelmach government introduced a $15-per-tonne levy on the largest emitters of carbon dioxide and proposed to raise royalties, particularly on oil sands producers. Indeed, during Alberta's 2008 general election, which Stelmach's PCs won, all major parties, including the Alberta Liberals (which I led), called for royalty increases and stricter environmental accountability.

For the first time in many years, oil industry leaders felt alienated from Alberta politics. I was pressed hard in meetings and phone calls with many industry executives to soften our party's stance on increasing oil and gas royalties, and I still remember the cold stares I received from them during a Calgary luncheon speech when I reiterated our position. Corporate donations immediately tightened, and with less than $500,000 in revenues, we could only run a sparse and ultimately doomed campaign. Donations to the PCs, who had been giants of fundraising for decades, were clobbered, falling from almost $2.1 million in the previous election to $580,000. To run their $3-million campaign they had to drain their substantial bank accounts.[401] Corporate Alberta, dominated by oil companies and behaving as if it were a single organization, spoke with one voice in what was both an astonishing display of corporate conformity and a telling manifestation of the narrow foundation upon which Alberta's political and economic life was built. The thick network of oil barons was letting the state know who was important.

* * *

In Canada, including Alberta, the controls on political donations and election spending are much stricter than in the United States, which immediately gives Canadian democracy an advantage. A person running for a seat in the Alberta legislature can mount a credible campaign for $30,000, sometimes much less.

Despite these controls and limits[402] on political donations, the reality in Alberta was that oil interests financed a good portion of the province's political activity. Elections Alberta reported that in the 2012 Alberta general election, for example, EPIC member Canadian Natural Resources Ltd. (CNRL) contributed $5,000 to each of the PC and Wildrose parties.[403] That's not the full story though. Allan Markin, the chairman of CNRL until 2012,[404] made a personal donation of $6,000 to the PCs. Murray Edwards, the most powerful investor in CNRL, made personal donations of $3,000 to a PC candidate and $5,000 to the PC Party. On top of that, EDCO Financial Holdings Limited contributed $12,500 to the PC Party, as did EDCO Capital Corporation. Both of these companies were closely tied to Edwards, and a June 2009 email from NRCan Deputy Minister Cassie Doyle to other federal officials identifies "Murray Edwards of EDCO Financial" as attending meetings as part of the EPIC/CSEE process.[405] This totals $49,000, and there may have been other companies or individuals with ties to CNRL who also made political donations. There certainly were other members of EPIC that did.

Party leadership campaigns were more of a free-for-all because the legislation that controlled party and election finances did not cover leadership races. The 2011 campaign that chose Alison Redford as PC leader and premier of Alberta burned up more than $6 million, $1.3 million more than the cost of the PC's entire general election campaign the following spring. Choosing a premier was expensive business. The political newsletter *Insight into Government* tallied contributions from some of the "major business players":

> Some names still stood out. Allan Markin, past chair of Canadian Natural Resources Ltd. and one of the owners of the Calgary Flames hockey club, gave a total of $90,000 to four candidates. Another $15,000 is shown . . . from an "Alan Markin" . . . A total of $62,500 came from Calgary financier Murray Edwards or from his Edco Financial Holdings Ltd. and Edco Capital Corp. to four candidates. . . . MEG Energy

Corp. gave $65,000 to five candidates . Wild Buffalo Ranching,
owned by Ian MacGregor, a principal in the North West
bitumen upgrader project, gave $50,000 to five candidates. . . .
Transalta Corp., $45,000 . . . Cenovus Energy Inc., $50,000.[406]

One major candidate, Rick Orman, who had held senior positions
with several different fossil fuel companies, didn't even disclose
his contributors.

Political historian Francis Fukuyama describes political donations
as a form of gift and says, "In a gift exchange the receiver incurs a
moral obligation to the other party, and is then inclined at another
time or place to return the favor . . . A human being in any culture
who receives a gift from another member of the community will feel
a moral obligation to reciprocate."[407] In Alberta, the oil industry used
donations to create an obligation on political parties, and especially
on individuals seeking the leadership of the governing PCs, to pay
attention to them.

★ ★ ★

After the 2008 Alberta general election, a group in the industry decided
they could no longer rely on the PCs, and that the Alberta Liberal opposition would never be to their liking. They formed an organization to
build a political party in which the interests of the petroleum industry
would be paramount. The group was called "Protect the Patch," referring to the "oilpatch," and the political party was the Wildrose Party,
named after Alberta's provincial flower. Until that time, this party had
been on the political margins since it was founded in 2002.

An early indicator of the direction of Protect the Patch was found
in a letter dating from April 2009, raising funds and support for the
Wildrose Party.[408] Seven names were listed at the bottom of the letter,
including David Yager, a prominent industry figure who eventually
became president of the Wildrose. The letter, directed to "members of

Alberta's oil and gas industry," was exactly the kind of statement to be expected in a mineral economy: "the ultimate success of our industry is now political. Only when the government of Alberta supports and trusts its most important industry — oil and gas — will Alberta's future be truly secure." The letter sketched out a plan to help the Wildrose form a government, and concluded by saying, "Our oil and gas industry must continue to lead the way. Please help us to help Alberta to a new political future."

Members of Protect the Patch were among the biggest fundraisers for the Wildrose Party, shaped many of its policies, provided organizational capacity, sat on the party executive, and provided thirteen candidates for it in the following election, which was in 2012. In that election, Wildrose became the Official Opposition in the legislature.

The Wildrose Party was constructed from a mix of social conservatives who favoured traditional laws on marriage, crime, and gay rights, and libertarians who felt governments should stay out of people's personal lives. These odd bedfellows found common ground in their right-wing economic positions, the kind typical of the Koch network in the United States. What largely brought them together, in more ways than most of them may have realized, were the interests of the fossil fuel industry. Their platform reflected this: Corporate taxes should be kept rock bottom, royalties should be as low as possible, and global warming caused by CO_2 emissions was doubtful science best ignored.

The party's position on global warming might have come straight out of the American Petroleum Institute's anti-Kyoto communications plan of 1998 and Frank Luntz's strategy for the Bush Republicans in 2002 (as discussed in Chapters Three and Four). Luntz had advised the Bush Republicans to fuel public doubt about global warming by claiming the science was unsettled, though Luntz himself admitted the scientific debate was closing. Ten years later, the Wildrose Party was still following the Luntz line: "The science isn't settled and we need to monitor the debate . . . there are a lot of scientists with a variety of different views," Wildrose leader Danielle Smith said as she explained the policy in an election debate in April 2012.[409] That election did not go as well as hoped for the Wildrose, but they easily held their status as official opposition. At a party convention late the following year, members passed motions that cautiously acknowledged global warming but offered no serious plan to reduce emissions. When the time came in 2016, they sharply fought a carbon tax.

Having captured both the government and the opposition parties, the voices for lowering CO_2 emissions came from the much smaller Alberta Liberal and New Democratic Parties. In healthy democracies, the main opposition party is often the single most important counterbalance to the government, and the differences between them generate the ideas and energies that fuel elections and drive accountability and change. Not in Alberta. True to the dynamics of a deep state, both the governing party and the opposition party were captured and lined up in homage to fossil fuels.

While the Wildrose Party was getting built up by some industry groups, others were putting intense pressure on the PC Party to cut down Premier Ed Stelmach. From my seat in the Alberta Legislature, I was repeatedly astonished when members of Stelmach's own caucus would stealthily heckle him when he rose to speak. He was driven to resign in 2011 by a campaign of constant subversion,[410] his fate showing how closely the success or failure of executive power in the Alberta government had become linked to the interests of oil and gas. His successor as premier, Alison Redford, returned the PC government to its place as a loyal ally of deep state Alberta.

Redford took her seat at the head of the Alberta government in October 2011, and by January 2012, was positioned as chief spokesperson and apparent architect of the national energy strategy propounded by EPIC, Bruce Carson, and leaders in the fossil fuel industry. When *Alberta Oil* magazine opened its coverage of the issue on February 1, 2012, it made it sound like Redford herself had thought up the notion: "Alberta Premier Alison Redford has a big idea. She calls it a national energy strategy . . . Alberta and Canada need more people like Redford bringing forth new ideas that could be game-changers . . ."[411] The first person the magazine quoted, though, wasn't Redford, but the premier of a distant province: "Quebec recently voiced support for the concept. 'It makes immense sense,' Quebec Premier Jean Charest told reporters last month after meeting with Redford in Quebec City." The strategy may have gained weight with Charest because one of EPIC's founding members, Daniel Gagnier, had been Charest's chief of staff from 2007 to 2009, and would return to that role for several months in May 2012.[412]

Redford was a steadfast agent for deep state Alberta, constantly glossing over the contradiction between addressing global warming and expanding oil sands production. In step with Prime Minister Harper, she travelled to New York and Washington, DC, to promote the proposed Keystone XL pipeline linking Alberta to upgraders and refineries in the United States. Aware that environmental concerns with the oil sands weighed against the pipeline's approval in the United States, she seemed to claim that expanding oil sands production would help address the problem of global warming. In an editorial in *USA Today* intended to ease the way for more oil sands production, she wrote,

> I'm proud to say Alberta applauds and shares [President Obama's] strong desire to address climate change . . . The president's comments during his recent State of the Union address are fully in synch with Alberta's commitment to strong environmental policy . . . we are prepared to work with our federal government [of Stephen Harper] and our American friends to push the bar higher in addressing climate change.[413]

This was a classic example of saying one thing while meaning another: If any bar was being pushed higher, it was the bar marking the scale of global warming that future generations would need to deal with. The truth behind Redford's words was that CO2 emissions from Alberta were climbing fast and her government's plans would see them rise much more.

Premier Redford displayed her loyalty to Alberta's fossil fuel industry in word and deed. She advocated for a national energy strategy at the conference of Canada's premiers in 2012; she told an economic summit in 2013 that "supporting our energy industry is fundamental to our future economic success";[414] and she even had a private debate with global warming advocate Al Gore at the World Economic Forum in January 2014, although reports said it did not end well for her.[415] She made "an ardent pitch" to American executives "in a gilded room atop a Manhattan hotel" to support the Keystone XL pipeline, and threw in good words for the Northern Gateway pipeline across British Columbia and the Energy East pipeline to Quebec and New Brunswick as well. Those who opposed these pipelines, she explained to her guests, did not understand the issues.[416] Redford couldn't be faulted for her efforts on behalf of the fossil fuel industry, but she was faulted for other things. Her tenure as premier was cut short when she fell into expense account scandals and other controversies, and her public approval plummeted. In March 2014, she stepped down.

Next up as premier for deep state Alberta: Jim Prentice. Prentice had left Stephen Harper's federal cabinet, resigned his Calgary seat in parliament in late 2010, and stepped into the position of vice-chairman of the Canadian Imperial Bank of Commerce (CIBC). When his chance arose to run for leader of the Alberta PCs, the *Financial Post* reported that Prentice was earning a "seven-figure" pay package at CIBC, $160,000 annually in director's fees from BCE Inc., about $200,000 a year for serving on the board of CP Rail (Donald Smith's old company), and director's fees from Calgary-based Coril Holdings Ltd.[417] As with Harper and Redford, pipelines were a priority for Prentice, who was hired by Enbridge (an EPIC supporter) in March 2014 to help the company in its negotiations for the Northern Gateway pipeline, which would cut through First Nations territories in British Columbia.[418] Prentice stepped down from these positions or took unpaid leaves during his leadership campaign, and resigned from all when he won.

Members of the fossil fuel industry backed Prentice's leadership campaign hard. They knew him well from his days as federal environment minister and his interest in the Harper government's federal–provincial–industry working group. His campaign raised about $1.8 million from over 560 contributors, including between $10,000 and $30,000 each from senior executives of Suncor, Cenovus Energy, and Talisman Energy.[419] He swamped his party leadership rivals on the first ballot, and in September 2014 became leader of the PCs and premier of Alberta.

The PCs had been losing public favour to the Wildrose Party for years, but Prentice moved from success to success, rebuilding confidence in his party and sweeping four by-elections, knocking the opposition Wildrose on its heels. Then, in a move that stunned observers, most of the Wildrose members of the legislature, including its leader Danielle Smith, left their party to join the government. The PC policies under Jim Prentice, they explained, were perfectly acceptable. "If you're going to be the official Opposition leader, you have to really want to take down the government and really want to take down the premier," Smith announced from the steps of Government House in Edmonton. "I want to be part and parcel of helping him succeed . . . we have a premier that shares the same conservative values that we do." A smiling Prentice told reporters, "It was a good day for those working to make Alberta better."[420] Eleven Wildrose members of the legislature joined the PC government, leaving only five in opposition. Then Prentice called a snap election for April, 2015, a year earlier than normal. As Alberta launched into the campaign, it seemed the notion of political opposition, so central to democracy, lay dying on the floor of the Alberta Legislature.

But in an unprecedented moment of collective will, the voters, dis-gusted by the cynical moves of Prentice and Smith, shocked deep state Alberta by choosing a new government for the first time in forty-four years. The gap between the ideals of democratic accountability, in which the government is accountable to its citizens, and the self-serving maneouvres of political leaders, had become a chasm too large to con-ceal. Voters sensed a profound insult to democratic propriety and, like bystanders fed up with a bully, they decided to stand up and be counted. Danielle Smith lost her nomination; a humiliated Jim Prentice resigned on election night; Rachel Notley, leader of the New Democratic Party, was sworn in as premier; and members of the Wildrose Party, which had quickly re-grouped under new leader Brian Jean, once again took their seats as the Official Opposition, outnumbering a small rump of PCs and one member from each of the Alberta Liberals and the Alberta Party. Democracy was not fully dormant in Alberta.

Chapter 14
The NDP in a world made for oil

The nature of deep states is to work across the broad governing system rather than to commit fully to one political party. All political parties are eventually driven from power, and that is not a risk members of a deep state want to run. Canada's oil industry is global, and it does business with hard conservatives in Texas, social democrats in Norway, and a long list of colonels, generals, presidents, and sheiks. Having a grip on both the opposition party and the governing party in Alberta was just prudent, and if an unexpected twist of fate put a third party in office, there were other resources to employ. Deep states are opportunistically partisan in order to endure. It took less than twelve hours after the election for deep state Alberta to begin asserting itself with the New Democratic government of Rachel Notley.

The New Democratic Party was based on a complicated mixture of public and private sector unions, social justice advocates, intellectuals, progressives, and environmentalists. Though a respected opposition party, they had never come close to forming government in Alberta, and when the campaign began in April 2015, no one expected them to win, including their own candidates and organizers. Behind their well-spoken and appealing leader, Rachel Notley, they ran a smooth and smart campaign, and mistakes by the PCs and Wildrose added to the voter appetite for change, which had grown strong since the political nuptials of Jim Prentice and Danielle Smith. The NDP won a solid majority that made front pages across the country. The scale of the surprise and the bloody-mindedness of the voters can be judged by campaign budgets. The NDP swept every seat in Edmonton and carried several smaller cities. They won fifteen of Calgary's twenty-five seats, and in eleven of those, their candidates spent less than $1,000. In one constituency, the NDP candidate spent $350 to defeat the PC incumbent; the record went to Brandy Payne, who overcame the $85,000 campaign of an incumbent PC cabinet minister by spending $240, the price of a cheap suit marked down for clearance.[421] The NDP victor in Medicine Hat, Robert Wanner, had to be coaxed into the race three weeks before election day to replace a candidate who withdrew after facing assault charges; Wanner ended up as Speaker of the Alberta Legislature.[422]

The Notley government had to overcome its inexperience while dealing with a collapse of world oil prices and a sharply slowing Alberta economy. The provincial treasury they inherited had run deficits every year since 2008, despite record exports of oil and gas, a sign of how little the PCs were collecting from the resource. Alberta, with a population smaller than metropolitan Phoenix, Arizona, was selling more oil to the United States than Saudi Arabia or anyone else, yet was still sliding into debt. Despite controversies, the Notley government implemented several progressive policies the previous government would not have considered: raising minimum wages, ending the flat tax, and increasing corporate taxes. Its first bill was an important step to reduce the sway of big donors in Alberta politics by banning union and corporate donations to political parties. It even appointed a prominent environmental activist and former co-director of Greenpeace to co-chair the government's Oil Sands Advisory Group.[423]

Did that mean the oil deep state was defeated in Alberta? Not for a moment. In her speech on election night and again in her news conference the next morning, Notley emphasized her government's openness to its "partners in the energy industry." She told reporters, "I'm going to be reaching out to industry and they can count on us to work collaboratively with them." In response to a reporter's question, she reiterated her message to the energy industry: "things are going to be just A-OK over here in Alberta." She promised many phone calls and conversations with corporate leaders, and in her first Question Period as premier said, "Just to be clear, I'm very committed to ensuring that our energy industry is supported."[424] These were understandable messages from a new government in an economy dominated by one industry, but as the NDP's first year in office passed, the partnership began to look like a merger.

In late November 2015, Premier Notley presented the work of her Climate Leadership Panel, which formed the basis of her government's plan to help address global warming. "Our goal," explained the premier, "is to become one of the world's most progressive and forward-looking energy producers."[425] Two of the plan's biggest components were bold and really could reduce emissions: a carbon tax and an accelerated phase-out of coal-fired power plants. But any gains from these were going to be lost to the staggering increase the plan allowed for oil sands and other oil and gas expansion; emissions would be 55 per cent higher in 2030 than they were in 2005.[426] The premier was joined on stage by the heads of some of the biggest oil sands producers, including Steve Williams, CEO of Suncor, who said, "This plan will make one of the world's largest oil-producing regions a leader in addressing the climate change challenge." This statement was a blatant contradiction. It is not possible to address climate change with such a big jump in CO2 emissions.

Ten weeks later, at the end of January 2016, the premier announced the results of the government's royalty review. There were some minor adjustments, but the royalty rates remained essentially as they were. The industry quietly supported the government's position, a complete reversal of its prolonged rage over the 2007 royalty review commissioned by PC Premier Ed Stelmach, which concluded royalties had been far too low for far too long — a stance the NDP of the day had supported. In that case, extraordinary pressure from the industry meant royalties never really rose, and Stelmach was driven from office.

A much louder signal that Alberta's NDP government was now aligned with the oil industry came that April, when the federal NDP held its convention in Edmonton. A debate arose in the convention about a document called the "Leap Manifesto," which national party delegates agreed should be considered through a long process leading up to its 2018 convention. The Leap Manifesto was supported by a group of outspoken advocates for reducing emissions, including Naomi Klein, Avi Lewis, and David Suzuki. Barely two pages long, the document used occasionally flamboyant language to speed through several issues, including the rights of Indigenous peoples, the need to invest in public infrastructure, and calls to end trade deals and provide a universal annual income for Canadians. It might have disappeared from view except that it also took a stand on global warming, opposing any new pipelines and calling for the phasing out of fossil fuel use in Canada by 2050, thirty-four years into the future[427] and fifty-eight years after the Rio Earth Summit.

Alberta's oil industry barely had to say a word in opposition — members of the Notley government did it for them, with vehemence. The premier called the document "ill-informed, naïve, and . . . tone deaf," and said its ideas on energy infrastructure would "never form any part of our policy."[428] Shannon Philips, environment minister in the Notley government, fired a long string of attacks at the document that included calling it "ungenerous, short-sighted and . . . fundamentally a betrayal."[429] Gil McGowan, the president of the Alberta Federation of Labour and a pillar of the Alberta NDP, said they "had nothing to do with this nonsense" and took a swing at some of the document's backers: "These downtown Toronto political dilettantes come to Alberta and track their garbage across our front lawn,"[430] ignoring the support the document had across the country.

As if to drive home her pro-oil message, less than two weeks later, Notley indicated the NDP might be willing to reverse its longstanding opposition to the Northern Gateway pipeline to the west coast of B.C. "I'm not completely closed on it," she told reporters, "and I will say my opinion on this has evolved and changed a little bit over time."[431] The leaders of both the Official Opposition Wildrose Party and the third party PCs were pleased with the premier's stance. Fifteen days later, Enbridge, the backer of Northern Gateway, asked the National Energy Board for a three-year extension to the pipeline's approval permit.[432] The once-dead project seemed to be breathing in its grave.

Historically, the NDP had been effective critics of the oil industry, pushing for higher royalties, opposing the Keystone XL and Northern Gateway pipelines, and demanding serious action to address global warming. Times changed. The response to the Leap Manifesto was more than just strong words. Strong words register with those who speak them, as well as with those who hear them. In speaking those words the NDP were not just re-defining themselves to others, they were re-defining themselves to themselves. They were establishing rules of political discourse that framed both language and thought, and under these rules, it was now off limits for NDP members to think or speak about phasing out oil and gas. They were now wholly in the corner of the petroleum industry, fighting for oil sands production and working hard to outdo Jim Prentice, Stephen Harper, and their opponents in the Alberta legislature as pipeline and oil sands champions.

By the first anniversary of their surprise election victory, it seemed no one was left in the Alberta legislature to speak truth to power, to question the wisdom of adding another pipeline, or to point out the glaring fact that increasing oil sands production was not going to reduce greenhouse gas emissions.

* * *

The Notley government had entered a world made by and for the production of oil. The oil deep state guided them down the same path as the previous government, toward developing the oil sands, defusing opposition from environmentalists and First Nations, and building pipelines. Even the new government's Climate Leadership Panel,[433] the one that recommended a form of carbon tax and the phasing out of coal-burning power plants, accepted emission levels for Alberta more than 60 per cent higher than the 1990 levels, never noting that 1990 levels were so high they had been the maximum standard recommended by the Rio Earth Summit. In fact, the panel's levels were so high they made it virtually impossible for Canada to meet its international commitments,[434] but no one fussed — it was a silent and perfect victory for the deep state. There was no voice to ask what the offsetting costs of global warming would be. No voice to say that if the world followed Alberta's self-aggrandizing "leadership," there would be a shocking upward spike in global CO2 levels. In the legislature, the Wildrose and PCs thought these levels were punitive for the industry, with several members of the Wildrose caucus drawing bizarre parallels between the proposed carbon tax and the Soviet-era genocide of six million Ukrainians.[435] Elsewhere — in universities, the media, research agencies — there was little criticism. Debates on the minor points of the oil agenda were unavoidable, but debates about its general direction were barely tolerated. The harsh response to the Leap Manifesto was one sign of this — it was shouted down. Public institutions in Alberta had lost the ability to hold a serious discussion on global warming and the use of oil.

This was part of a larger picture. The 1 per cent royalty system set up in the 1990s under energy minister Patricia Black reached peak impact in the years before the NDP government was elected, creating the oil sands equivalent of a gold rush. The oil sands were so big that even a meagre portion of the wealth they generated could go a long way among Alberta's relatively small population. Average incomes and retail sales in Alberta had easily topped those in other provinces. Jobs were plentiful, taxes were low, and immigrants from other provinces and countries poured in.[436] Most Albertans had never had it so good and saw the oil industry — especially the oil sands — as the key to the province's future. A threat to the industry was now a threat to Albertans. Not many people wanted to face the fact that Alberta's situation was economically and environmentally unsustainable.

Chapter 15
Oil's deep state at work

Deep states need to hold more than politicians and parties; they need to grip the unelected officials who operate the institutions of state. These are the people who, more than any other, make a state effective. The documents exposed through the Carson investigation gave a glimpse of the network that was advancing the oil agenda from within the public sector. Alberta's public institutions were populated by supporters of the oil industry, and they were conducting business as if nothing fundamental were changing in the global environment. It was a classic example of the conservative bent of a deep state, clinging to the past and resisting change.

Cassie Doyle, the deputy minister of Natural Resources Canada (2006–10) who worked so hard to align the federal government with the petroleum industry, had come from a position as associate deputy minister of Environment Canada (2003–06) and, upon leaving the federal government, took a part-time position as a board director with the Alberta Energy Regulator (AER),[437] the provincial agency which, in its own words, "is responsible for managing Alberta's energy resources," including oil and oil sands, natural gas, coal, and 421,000 kilometres of pipelines.[438]

Faces around the AER board table would have been familiar to Doyle. Its chair was Gerry Protti, a founding director of EPIC, former assistant deputy minister of Alberta Energy, former executive of energy giant EnCana, and founding president of CAPP.

The CEO of AER was Jim Ellis, a former deputy minister of Alberta Energy who had been the "lead [Alberta] provincial official for the Canadian Energy Strategy."[439] Before that, he had been deputy minister of Alberta Environment. Jumping from the government to the regulator had its benefits. In 2016, the NDP government made the salaries of public employees and officials public, revealing that Ellis was Alberta's third highest paid public employee, earning $721,680,[440] more than double what people were paid in the positions he had left.[441] AER defended Ellis's pay by saying it was "benchmarked . . . against oil and gas firms rather than the public sector because that is the competing talent pool."[442]

One of Ellis's Alberta government colleagues had been Roxanna Benoit, who along with Ellis attended the March 2010 meeting in CAPP's head office that laid the groundwork for the federal–provincial–industry working group; this was when Doyle noted how closely the industry and governments were working together.[443] At the time, Benoit was deputy chief for the Alberta government cabinet. She had a long history with Stephen Harper's Conservative Party,[444] and in 2006, she had co-authored a paper titled "Significant Developments in the Canadian Energy Industry"[445] with Douglas Black, who would go on to chair the board of governors of the University of Calgary and become a founding director of EPIC. She left the Alberta government in 2013 to join Enbridge (backer of the Northern Gateway pipeline) as a vice-president.

The March 2010 meeting at CAPP was also attended by Peter Watson, who was deputy minister of Alberta Energy. In October that year, Bruce Carson noted in an email to EPIC committee members (including Black and Protti) that he had "met with Peter Watson and Alberta Energy Minister Leipert as the Minister will co-chair the meeting in Kananaskis —

both are enthusiastic and on side."[446] Watson had previously served as deputy minister of Alberta Environment and went on to become deputy minister of Alberta's cabinet, the top position in the Alberta civil service. He had been a key figure in the development of Alberta's climate change and energy strategies under the PCs.[447] Watson left the Alberta government in 2014 to become chair and CEO of the powerful National Energy Board, a federal agency whose website says, "We regulate pipelines, energy development and trade in the Canadian public interest."[448]

A prominent successor to Watson as deputy minister of Alberta Energy was Grant Sprague, who served from July 2013 to May 2016. Sprague had been deputy chief for the Alberta cabinet and had been director of the Alberta government's environmental law section for five years, until February 2009.[449] Sprague was deputy minister of energy during Rachel Notley's first year as premier and guided the NDP government as it adopted its industry-friendly positions on royalties, emissions, and climate change through its Royalty Review Advisory Panel and its Climate Leadership Panel.

Before Sprague even left his government position, Deborah Yedlin, a senior columnist on the energy business at the *Calgary Herald*, wrote an article lamenting his departure.[450] She tended to be a supportive voice for the interests of the oil industry. The timing of Sprague's departure "following completion of the province's climate change strategy and royalty review process" made sense, said Yedlin. She keenly praised Sprague, quoting an unnamed "industry insider" who said Sprague was "one of the most approachable, even-keeled individuals in the bureaucracy . . . he is collegial, wants to work with the sector . . . one of the best." (Relations between industry and government had certainly changed since the early years of Premier Peter Lougheed, to industry's warm satisfaction.) Sprague helped "ensure continuity" when the new NDP government took over. She also quoted praise for Sprague from Dave Collyer, whom she identified as a "former industry executive and current chairman of Bow Valley College." A more complete description would have noted Collyer had been president of Shell Canada and then president of CAPP for six years,[451] where he worked closely with Bruce Carson at EPIC, Cassie Doyle at NRCan, and various other federal and provincial officials such as Sprague.

Though it was undeclared in her column, Yedlin had close personal ties to the energy industry. Her husband was Martin Molyneaux, who had worked his way up the ranks to vice-chair of FirstEnergy Capital Corporation before stepping down in 2013. FirstEnergy Capital, a privately held merchant bank specializing in energy companies, was founded in 1993 and rapidly grew to a dominant position in the Canadian petroleum industry, claiming that "50% of all financings in the Canadian Oil & Gas sector are underwritten by FirstEnergy."[452] FirstEnergy also played a significant role internationally in oil and gas financing.

Among FirstEnergy's founders was Murray Edwards, who also had a key role in building the huge petroleum producer CNRL and ended up as its chair. CNRL backed EPIC and worked closely on the federal–provincial–industry working group with Bruce Carson, and Edwards stood with Premier Rachel Notley when the plan of the Climate Leadership Panel was unveiled in November 2015. "We appreciate the strong leadership demonstrated by Premier Notley and her government," he said in a government news release. "In this way, we will do our part to address climate change while protecting jobs and industry competitiveness in Alberta."[453] As Yedlin said in her column on Sprague, getting this plan completed had been an important task for the Government of Alberta.

Because institutions function on two levels — the level of the formal organization itself and the level of the individuals who hold positions within that organization — the interlinking of individuals facilitates an interlinking of institutions. Government environment departments were linked to government energy departments; federal governments were linked to provincial governments; national regulators were linked with provincial regulators; and they were all linked to the oil industry. It's no wonder that Alberta and Canada were global laggards in reducing emissions.

★ ★ ★

This kind of interlinking is a form of capture, and it has consequences for the public institutions it ensnares. The rise of the Alberta Energy Regulator (AER) provides an example. The Alberta government established its first regulator for the petroleum industry in 1938, after years of bitter resistance from petroleum producers that included inflammatory advertising and political campaigns and a legal challenge in the Supreme Court of Canada.[454] The government's right to regulate in the public interest was hard-won, and the regulator, eventually known as the Energy Resources Conservation Board, built itself a respected reputation for its competence and its quasi-judicial independence decade by decade. It was replaced in 2013 by AER.

Conceived in the period when EPIC was busily promoting a national energy strategy, AER was established to take over the Alberta government's responsibilities for environmental protection, water, and public lands as they related to energy development. AER's governing legislation was passed in late 2012, and it opened its doors the following summer with Gerry Protti as its chair and Jim Ellis as its CEO.

The legislation establishing AER removed previous references to protecting the public interest and weakened the quasi-judicial arm's-length nature of the regulator, making it more vulnerable to direct influence by the minister of energy. In addition, the entire cost of running the new regulator was turned over to the industry.[455] Then, in a move justified by government as improving efficiency, 150 environmental officers were transferred out of the government into AER.[456] If an oil company broke pollution laws, the government wouldn't lay charges; the regulator would. When it came to environmental enforcement, the Alberta government had eviscerated itself.

The end result was that the primary regulator of the petroleum industry in Alberta also had primary responsibility for administering the province's *Environmental Protection and Enhancement Act, Water Act,* and *Public Lands Act,* and simultaneously was granted reduced responsibility to protect the public interest; was completely funded by industry; was chaired by a strong industry ally; and had been handed a large number of the government's environmental protection staff.

A 2013 court case, when AER was gearing up, gave an inside view into the way environmental laws could be selectively applied when it came to the oil industry, exposing an erosion in the rule of law to favour oil development. The case involved the Alberta Department of Environment, which at that time was responsible for administering and enforcing the *Environmental Protection and Enhancement Act* and the *Water Act*. An oil sands company named Southern Pacific Resources wanted to expand production at its site, which would require more water. The company applied to Alberta Environment for permits under these acts to increase the amount of water it drew from the MacKay River, arguing that the impact on the mean seasonal flow of the river would be negligible.

Various groups were worried about this application. There was evidence the amount of water requested might dry up the river completely during low-flow periods. As Justice R. P. Marceau, the judge in the case, noted in his ruling, "Approving an application that could lead to the elimination of all flow in a river the size of the MacKay River would be precedent setting."[457] Some of these groups applied to Alberta Environment to file their concerns and potentially appeal the application, which legislation allowed. When Alberta Environment denied the groups their right to file concerns, two of them took the government to court, arguing Alberta Environment was improperly administering the law.

Justice Marceau's decision was a sharp rebuke of Alberta Environment.[458] The trial uncovered an internal government briefing note so important to the case that Marceau reproduced it entirely in his ruling. The briefing note was written for the deputy minister of Alberta Environment and recommended the two complainants in the case not be allowed to file their appeals because, among other things, they "are now less inclined to work cooperatively" with industry and government, and one of the groups had published "negative media on the oil sands."

Drawing on the briefing note, Justice Marceau found the department had denied the two plaintiffs — the Pembina Institute and the Fort McMurray Environmental Association — their rights to intervene not on the basis of law, but because the groups were known critics of oil sands development. In effect, they lost their right to appeal because the government did not agree with them.

The briefing note that Alberta Environment used to bar groups was written almost three years *before* Southern Pacific applied for water and, in Marceau's words, had been used repeatedly as a kind of "template" for keeping uncooperative groups out of the process. The environmental groups did not know the briefing note existed, which the judge said "clearly violated the principle that one has the right to be heard, and in this case, to answer allegations made against it in secret." The reasons given by Alberta Environment were "sparse" and "fatally flawed . . . because the entire process was tainted by the Briefing Note which I interpret as a formula for rejection of future submissions." The judge quoted at length from the *Environmental Protection and Enhancement Act* and found the Department of Environment's process violated the very legislation it was meant to uphold. As he came to his decision, he did not mince words:

> In my opinion a well-informed member of the public . . .
> would perceive that the valid object of the *Environmental
> Protection and Enhancement Act* to give the citizens of Alberta
> as much input as reasonable into environmental concerns that
> arise from industrial development is hijacked by the Briefing
> Note . . . It is difficult to envision a more direct apprehension
> of bias . . . Accordingly the Director's decision breaches all
> four of the principles of natural justice and must be quashed.

By reproducing the briefing note, the ruling revealed that the note was written for Deputy Minister Jim Ellis, who had since been named CEO of the Alberta Energy Regulator.

Chapter 16
The long reach of oil's deep state

The power of the deep state in Alberta reaches well beyond political parties, the legislature, government departments, and regulators. Carbon emissions and global warming are health issues as much as they are environmental and economic issues. The Intergovernmental Panel on Climate Change (IPCC) assessment reports typically spend several pages just summarizing the health impacts of global warming, all of which worsen as serious action to reduce and eliminate emissions is delayed. They predict increased death and injury from flooding and fires; reduced food security because of more severe droughts; more deaths due to heat waves; and the spread of diseases "due to the extension of the infection area and season" (think Lyme disease and West Nile virus), though here they offer a twisted form of good news: Some areas will become so hot that disease carriers like mosquitoes won't survive.[459] The World Health Organization, taking into account "only a subset of the possible health impacts" of global warming, estimates it will cause "250,000 additional deaths per year between 2030 and 2050."[460] In Canada and the United States, this includes 10,000 more deaths annually from increased heat stress among seniors.[461] After 2050, global warming will only intensify.

These major and foreseeable threats would normally be the business of public health institutions, especially medical health officers. Medical health officers are responsible for public health. They don't treat individual patients; they care for communities, cities, and countries. They can force the closure of water systems (as in Walkerton, Ontario) and block the sale of drugs (as with thalidomide in the United States, averting the tragic birth defects that struck Canada and Europe). Society grants them immense authority to speak freely and act forcefully because, at times, they must call to account powerful interests. They are a textbook example of the value of autonomous institutions.

It's easy to imagine a public health campaign addressing CO_2 emissions and global warming. Campaigns are undertaken all the time for health threats: Wash your hands, don't smoke, cover your mouth when you cough, get vaccinated, practise safe sex, eat fresh fruits and vegetables, wear sunscreen. Most adults in a developed country could fill a page with their basic knowledge of infectious diseases and how to prevent and treat them, because they are taught and reminded constantly about the information.

What is rarely seen are widespread public health campaigns explaining the basics of global warming. Most car drivers have no idea that burning one tank of gas emits the weight of a sumo wrestler of CO_2 into the air, most of which will linger for centuries. Few people are systematically taught that the way they use energy will affect the health of the planet and the wellbeing of their children and grandchildren. The opportunities for public health education about global warming and CO_2 emissions are endless, but in deep state Alberta, it seems medical officers can't even muse about the risks of global warming.

In September 2002, medical officers in Alberta held a regular meeting of their association. One item on their agenda was the long-term health threat posed by global warming, and they quietly passed a motion urging the Alberta government to meet the emission targets in the Kyoto Accord. One of their members who worked for a small provincial health region, Dr. David Swann, told one reporter from the local *Medicine Hat News* about their concerns, and the newspaper ran a story under the title "Health Officials Call for Kyoto Ratification."[462] The article opened by saying, "Cutting greenhouse-gas emissions is a health issue, said the Palliser Health Authority's chief medical officer for health," and in the fourth paragraph quoted Swann: "The bottom line is that the connection between human health and fossil-fuel burning is so strong we all have to put that together with Kyoto." The article used supporting references from the Ontario Medical Association, the Canadian Public Health Association, the federal government, and the David Suzuki Foundation.

Within days, Swann was fired by the regional health board. "Terminating jobs in the oil and gas industry is no healthier for the region than ratifying Kyoto," declared the board chairman.[463]

The chain of events that led to the firing soon became public. One of the PC members of the legislature for the region where Swann worked was environment minister Lorne Taylor. Upset that a medical officer had publicly raised concerns about global warming, even if only to one reporter at a small city newspaper, he phoned the chairman of the health board that employed Swann, a man named Len Mitzel. Mitzel, who was appointed by the PC government, also served as president of Taylor's local PC constituency association. Soon after that phone call, Dr. Swann was fired.

In this case, there was a counterbalancing reaction. The opposition in the Alberta legislature raised the alarm and corrective pressure came from institutions outside the province. The national media took an interest, as did the Canadian Medical Association, the federal government, and many others.[464] Embarrassed at being caught, the health board invited Dr. Swann to return to his job. After a long meeting, he declined.

Although Taylor was the minister responsible for the environment, he had been opposing the Kyoto agreement for months on the grounds it would hurt Alberta's economy, the same argument CAPP had been using for years.[465] Taylor even followed Canada's national environment minister, David Anderson, to a climate conference in Russia to oppose the federal government's efforts to support the agreement.[466] Just weeks before Swann was fired, Taylor had launched a $1.5 million Alberta government campaign opposing the Kyoto agreement that included newspaper, radio, and television advertising, plus national and international speaking engagements.[467] It worked. In May 2002, 72 per cent of Albertans supported the Kyoto Accord, a fact the *Globe and Mail* said "would appear to undermine the Alberta government's staunch opposition to the deal."[468] Rather than respecting this public consensus and standing up to the industry, the government chose to defend the industry and attack the public consensus. Six months later, after the Alberta government's campaign delivered the industry-friendly message to the people at taxpayer expense, public support for Kyoto had collapsed to 27 per cent of Albertans, while 60 per cent were opposed.[469]

The institutions that should have been protecting the environment and public health had fallen to the interests of fossil fuels, with the active support of the environment minister and the chair of a health authority. The message to the medical community, civil servants, and the public was loud and clear: Even if you were concerned about global warming, you'd better be quiet. And, mostly, they were.

The political vortex holding these three men continued spinning for years. Swann became politically active after his firing and won a seat in the Alberta legislature as a member of the opposition Alberta Liberals in 2004. In the same election, the board chair who fired him, Len Mitzel, won a seat for the governing PCs. That seat had been vacated by Taylor, who retired after three terms in office. In 2014, Taylor was appointed to chair the Alberta Environmental Monitoring Agency by the PC government. That agency was disbanded in 2016 by the Notley government. By then, Mitzel had lost his seat to the Wildrose, and Swann was serving a second round as leader of the Alberta Liberal Party and was its sole member left in the legislature.

Ten years after Swann was terminated, a detailed study of the impacts of climate change predicted that in one lifetime or less southeastern

Alberta, the region of Swann's health board, was likely to become a sagebrush steppe like the driest parts of Wyoming, dominated by plants adapted to "extreme aridity," with many lakes dried up and areas of active sand dunes.[470] Given the physics of global warming, the deterioration will continue for many lifetimes after that.

* * *

Oil's deep state also reached into universities. Universities are generally regarded as autonomous institutions, free from outside interference, which paradoxically makes them particularly tempting targets for capture — if the university is with you, your credibility increases. It is not coincidence that BP directed millions of dollars to Gulf coast universities immediately after the Deepwater Horizon disaster and then relied heavily on a university scientist to counter public concerns, or that the American Petroleum Institute's campaigns against global warming worked to recruit university scientists and academics.

The natural draw of the conservative movement toward universities got underway in the United States in the 1970s. Charles Koch and his political allies were already strategizing about the best approaches. Traditional gifts and endowments didn't give enough ideological control to the donor. In her book, *Dark Money,* Jane Mayer describes how Koch's political lieutenant of the time "advocated funding private institutes within prestigious universities, where influence over hiring decisions and other forms of control could be exerted by donors while hiding the radicalism of their aims."[471]

A leader in conservative funding to universities was the Olin Foundation, which distributed an average of about $10 million a year to American universities from 1985 to 2005 to establish what its executive director James Piereson called "beachheads."[472] Beachheads were formed around a tenured professor who was willing to mount an appropriate program. The professor must be chosen by the donor; "it is always dangerous," warned Piereson, "to allow university administration to choose this person," because other expectations come into play. The donor should start with a modest grant and then allow the professor to grow the program, bringing in more grants, more faculty, and more students, and soon lectures, courses, conferences, and credibility will follow. Through this process, the fringe becomes the mainstream.

The money was targeted at fields where conservatives wanted to gain the most influence, especially law, public policy, economics, business, and history. As was sometimes said, the idea was to take the "liberal" out of liberal arts programs. Year by year, the conservative movement made its mark. In the 1980s, it was difficult to find academics sympathetic to their cause, but by 2015 the vice-president of the Koch Foundation could boast of a "robust, freedom-advancing network" of almost 5,000 scholars in 400 colleges and universities.[473] The American experience is worth keeping in mind while reading about Canada's universities.

Universities in Alberta had longstanding close relationships with the fossil fuel industry. The PC government's appointments to university boards of governors were heavy with people tied to the industry. From at least 2001 to 2015, every chair of the board of governors at the University of Calgary worked in or with the fossil fuel business, including Douglas Black. The university's announcement of his appointment as chair in February 2011 noted his position as "president of the Energy Policy Institute of Canada [EPIC]."[474] The University of Alberta in Edmonton, one of the largest in Canada, boasted that "More than 1,000 U of A researchers collaborate on the oil sands and its environmental impact . . ."[475] For the University of Alberta, this was a success story, and valuable research was done for oil sands corporations on reducing water use, detoxifying tailings ponds, reclaiming land, and so on, but one way or another, it was all aimed at supporting oil sands production. The funds that flowed with the research helped stimulate the university's massive expansion of engineering laboratories and offices, but there was always a risk that research and funding on this scale could turn a university into a client of the petroleum industry. Universities are not immune to pressure, and their autonomy is not guaranteed.

A number of controversies at the University of Calgary reinforced this concern. In 2006, prominent faculty member Barry Cooper was caught channelling hundreds of thousands of dollars from donors — including petroleum companies and global warming deniers — through university research trust accounts, to support public campaigns that opposed the Kyoto Protocol. Many donors provided funds to the Calgary Foundation for tax receipts. The foundation, which kept donor names private, then donated the money to a university research account controlled by Cooper. In turn, Cooper would direct the money in the university research account to the anti-Kyoto Friends of Science organization to finance its campaigns. When the story broke in the national media, the university was forced to take corrective action.[476, 477]

In 2007, the University of Calgary set up the Canada School of Energy and Environment, which Bruce Carson joined in 2008. (See Chapters One and Two for an in-depth discussion.) CSEE showed how the boundaries of a university organization could get muddled, with its tangled mix of presidents and board chairs of three separate universities, plus staff, some of whom were paid by a university, some by industry, and some by both.

At about the same time, the University of Calgary also set up the School of Public Policy. As noted in Chapter One, the school was given a $1-million founding donation from Imperial Oil and the position of chair was endowed with $4 million from one of Alberta's senior oil investors, James Palmer.[478] The person recruited to fill that chair was Jack Mintz, an economist who also sat on the board of Imperial Oil. Imperial Oil was a major presence in Alberta. It had bought Calgary Petroleum Products from James Lougheed and R. B. Bennett in 1921, drilled the Leduc oilwell in 1947 that opened the modern petroleum era in Alberta, and was a major investor in the oil sands. Its controlling shareholder was the global giant Exxon/Mobil. Jack Mintz, you may recall, was the person to whom Bruce Carson reported for his U of C position as adjunct professor. Mintz published widely in both academic and popular media and was an unapologetic supporter of the Keystone

XL pipeline, writing in the *Financial Post* in February 2013 that "the American case for approving Keystone XL is unimpeachable."[479] Imperial Oil had been advocating for Keystone for years[480] and, a few weeks before Mintz's article, Imperial had been identified as a "winner" by market analysts if Keystone were approved, along with CNRL, Suncor, Baytex, and Cenovus.[481]

Imperial Oil's 2014 *Annual Report* indicated Mintz was paid $263,971 for serving on its board and had accumulated shares in Imperial Oil worth almost $1.4 million. Like all its board members, Mintz was obligated under the company's regulations to advance the interests of Imperial Oil,[482] which raised questions about his independence as a university official, unless the interests of the university were assumed to be the same as the interests of Imperial Oil. Mintz stepped out of his position at the School of Public Policy in 2015;[483] according to Imperial Oil's corporate filings, he could remain on the corporation's board until 2023.

The University of Calgary controversies just kept coming. In 2009, the oil industry launched EPIC, with Bruce Carson and U of C Board of Governors member Douglas Black on the payroll in leadership positions and a strategic goal of "engaging the academic community."[484] The documents at the Carson trial showed how hard EPIC and CSEE worked at this, drawing the presidents of the Universities of Alberta, Saskatchewan, Calgary, and Lethbridge into a process involving the most powerful federal and provincial civil servants and the wealthiest and most commanding executives of Canada's oil industry. (See Chapters 1 and 2.)

In 2012, the University of Calgary was embroiled in a controversy about its Institute for Sustainable Energy, Environment, and Economy (ISEEE), which had been established nine years before as a collaboration of government and the university with coal, oil, and natural gas companies. Allegations were made in 2012 that a researcher at the institute was removed at the request of pipeline company Enbridge, which Enbridge categorically denied.[485] The university issued a lengthy statement that included this as part of its explanation: "Balancing the views and interests of the academy, industry, government and non-governmental groups is not always easy, and often there are conflicts and disagreements."[486] This begged the question, was it the role of a university to balance the views and interests of academics with industry and other groups, or was this a sign the university was being captured by industry? Wasn't the role of a university to seek knowledge and truth, wherever they may lead?

The statement also said, "The University of Calgary values the support of our many industry partners, including Enbridge," and went on to say they were "proud to partner with Enbridge" on the "Enbridge Centre for Corporate Sustainability," which had been launched in the university's Haskayne School of Business in early 2012 with a $2.25 million contribution from Enbridge.[487]

In 2015, public controversy hit this program too. A series of emails written in 2011 and 2012, obtained by the CBC[488] and others, showed concerns by faculty members that Enbridge was having too much influence on the centre. The university had appointed Joe Arvai to be the Enbridge Centre's director. Arvai was a fast-rising American scholar who had served on President Obama's energy advisory group and had been recently appointed to two important American environmental boards, including the EPA's science advisory board. When the university delayed announcing these appointments, Arvai emailed a senior university official to ask why. The reply was blunt: "Len. He doesn't want to piss off Enbridge any more." The "Len" in question was Leonard Waverman, the dean of the business school.

Arvai was not pleased: "Making Enbridge happy is not on my radar . . . I know next to nothing about where we are in discussion with Enbridge. And I am the current director of the centre."[489]

Concerns were coming from other faculty too. As an email from Professor Harrie Vredenburg to Dean Waverman expressed it, "It sounds to me like a classic case of 'he who pays the piper calls the tunes' . . . Enbridge is doing too much tune-calling, in my view, to the point that the Centre's usefulness to HSB [Haskayne School of Business] academics is being sacrificed to Enbridge's PR objectives."[490] When the CBC story went public in 2015, Arvai, who by then had left the University of Calgary for the University of Michigan, described his experience in an article in the *Globe and Mail.* Saying the CBC had "done an exceptional job of getting the facts correct," he wrote:

> ... the CBC story correctly points to several instances where certain wishes expressed by officials at Enbridge, and ultimately granted by officials at the U of C, were incompatible with the mission of a new academic centre that needed to be built upon a foundation of academic and scholarly independence. In light of what I went through at the time, the post hoc suggestions by some that decisions made by the U of C in setting up the Enbridge Centre were transparent, legitimate and free of corporate interference or conflict-of-interest are as difficult for me to accept today as they were in 2012.[491]

Enbridge issued a statement calling the CBC story "unfair and false" and mounted an active defence, saying it was committed to "the principles of academic freedom" and there were "no strings attached" to its funding.[492]

The story was fuelled by emails and messages involving senior university leaders. When Professor Arvai raised concerns with Dean Waverman in January 2012 about Enbridge's perspective on the centre, the dean left a voice message saying, "If this goes belly up my ass is on the line and I won't feel happy with you either on this."[493] The dean may have felt even more pressure when he received an email from the university's president, Elizabeth Cannon, that August:

> They [Enbridge] have traditionally been strong supporters of U of A [University of Alberta in Edmonton] and this it

[*sic*] the first major gift to U of C. They are not seeing your leadership on this file and are feeling that once the funding was committed, the interest from you was lost. This is not good for the university.[494]

Then the story was taken further by the *Financial Post* and the CBC.[495, 496] They reported President Cannon was on the board of Enbridge Income Fund, which was approximately 90 per cent held by Enbridge. Cannon had been on the board since 2004, was paid $130,500 for the position in 2014, and owned 25,300 shares in the company valued at about $810,000 at the time. President Cannon said there was no conflict of interest with her intervention in the Enbridge Centre for Corporate Sustainability. "It was a simple reminder to him that when we get into an agreement he has to be held accountable for delivering back, but that does not contravene any conflict of interest," she said.[497]

The University of Calgary Board of Governors immediately hired a retired judge to review the allegations of conflict of interest against Cannon. The judge's report reviewed the situation and exonerated Cannon of any wrong-doing, saying "To put it simply, she was doing what Presidents do. Criticism of this intervention by Dr. Cannon can only be made by those lacking an understanding of a President's responsibilities."[498] The report was made public by Gord Ritchie, vice-chair of the board of governors. The chair of the board, Bonnie DuPont, had recused herself from the process: Before becoming chair, she had been a senior executive at Enbridge.[499]

The University of Calgary's Dean of Business Leonard Waverman left for McMaster University in 2012. In 2014, "Enbridge" was dropped from the name of the centre, and Enbridge's support was reduced by $1 million.[500] Cannon resigned from the Enbridge Income Fund Board of Directors in November 2015.[501] Controversy over the role of the energy industry at the University of Calgary, however, continued to simmer.[502]

* * *

Universities have a deeply ingrained tradition of independence supported by tenure agreements, a highly decentralized organizational
structure, and people who are prepared to speak out for it, such as
David Keith, Joe Arvai, and Harrie Vredenburg. A tenured professor
who expressed concern over global warming could not be fired in the
way David Swann was fired from his position as medical health officer.
The controversies at University of Calgary give blow-by-blow accounts
of the struggle to maintain the autonomy of an institution. They are an
expression of the spirit of democracy.

One of the only institutions for which autonomy is more vigorously
protected in Canadian democracy than universities is the court system.
In Alberta, anyone considered for a position as a judge has their application reviewed by an eminent committee that includes the chief justice of
Alberta, the chief justice of the Alberta Court of Queen's Bench, the chief
judge of the Provincial Court, the president of the Law Society of Alberta,
and two persons appointed by the minister of justice. A new twist was
introduced to this process by the PC government in 1999, when a second
committee was established to review the list of nominees approved by the
first committee. This second committee now made the final recommendation to the minister on who should be appointed as judges. Despite
its importance, this committee, called the Provincial Court Nominating
Committee (PCNC), kept an exceedingly low profile. Its terms of reference, budget, procedures, and minutes were not readily available, and its
membership was not listed on public government documents.

An investigation by the CBC in July 2013 identified nine of the
eleven members of the committee.[503] (Two positions appointed by the
minister of justice were vacant.) Of the six members appointed at the
discretion of the minister of justice, the chairman of the committee and
another member held volunteer positions in the PC Party and were
significant donors to the party and its candidates. Both were lawyers.
The law practice of the chairman featured oil and gas transactions and
regulatory matters.[504] A third appointee was a manager in a large petro-

leum company, and a fourth was a drill bit sales representative with an oilfield supply company.[505] A fifth appointee was a lawyer whose practice expertise included oil and gas issues.[506] The oil industry would seem to have had several supporters on the committee choosing judges for Alberta's provincial court.

Alberta's judges were disproportionately from the ranks of the PC Party. An investigation by *Alberta Views* magazine published in June 2014 found that "six of the 12 most recent appointments to the Alberta bench had donated to the PC party, PC constituency associations, PC candidates or PC leadership candidates, while none had donated to an opposition party."[507] The courts remained a keystone of democracy in Alberta and were making important decisions to protect due process. Nonetheless, the question must be asked: Were even Alberta's provincial courts being colonized by oil's deep state?

To the credit of the NDP government, the mandate and roles of the Provincial Court Nominating Committee were reviewed in 2016 and posted online, as were the names of committee members.[508] A new chair who wasn't from the fossil fuel industry was appointed, and a six-page code of conduct was posted, including as its first guiding principle "The actions and decisions of members are made to promote the public interest."[509] The terms of reference of the committee, however, were not public, and the government's website indicated several positions on the committee were vacant as of May 2017.[510]

This analysis is by no means exhaustive. It doesn't examine the media, the labour movement, or civil society organizations, and it skips over countless examples large and small,[511, 512] but by this point the pattern is clear: A diverse range of state and democratic institutions in Alberta had been captured to significant degrees by the oil industry. They had become instruments of the industry with a mantra of "what's good for oil is good for Alberta."

Does this mean Alberta is a petrostate and Canada or the United States are in danger of becoming ones? No. Petrostates arise where petroleum development begins before institutions of the modern state are established. When large petroleum resources are developed in countries with weak states, it forces a hurried incubation and growth of institutions that are alien to the local culture and become dysfunctional, imbalanced, and corrupt, as Venezuela's experience demonstrates.

In contrast, the oil deep state, which has a chokehold on Alberta and a grip on other parts of Canada and the United States, takes hold in societies that already have modern democratic institutions. For more than a century after its formation in 1670, the Hudson's Bay Company was both corporate monopoly and government in much of Canada, but at its headquarters in London, it was subject to the laws of the English parliament, the contracts of English lawyers, and the decisions of English courts. By 1840, modern institutions were spreading: Independent courts and judges were hearing cases in the Red River Settlement; the Royal Navy commanded the Pacific coast, where HBC had important interests; and in 1846, the Oregon Treaty between the United States and Britain drew Western Canada's national boundary along the forty-ninth parallel, putting a hard edge on the southern limits of HBC lands. Starting in the 1870s, the Government of Canada signed a series of treaties with the First Nations of the prairies, bringing the land under federal jurisdiction and securing it for the CPR and settlers. Government surveyors mapped the territory so it could be parceled out, and the Mounties were formed and dispatched to bring Ottawa's law and order to what was now western Canada. The North-West Rebellion was quashed in 1885, the same year that Donald Smith drove the last spike to complete the CPR.

Long before the Turner Valley oil field, then, the institutions of a modern state and democracy were well in place in Alberta, including elected governments, political parties, civil services, newspapers, schools, and a university. Most of the lands of HBC and the CPR had been sold by then, largely to farmers, who had established not a mineral economy but an agricultural one.

The wheat, barley, and canola produced by Alberta farmers were raw commodities sold for processing elsewhere, just like oil and coal. But farmers had a completely different legal, economic, and social relationship to their land than the miners, drillers, and company executives of the fossil fuel sector, and farms were dispersed across the province and owned and operated by, at their peak, hundreds of thousands of farm families. From before it became a province until the mid-1950s, a majority of Albertans lived in rural areas,[513] and farmers were a dominating political force. Until the giant oil and gas fields of central and northern Alberta were discovered in 1947, Alberta's petroleum and coal industries were too localized and small to control the province's economic and political agendas.

It took nearly a century for Canada's petroleum industry to grow to international significance. By global standards, the oilfield at Turner Valley was small and short-lived. Institutional capture in Alberta grew to deep state status gradually, in step with the long rise in oil and gas production that culminated with the oil sands.

Petrostates are *conceived in* petroleum, while oil deep states are *captured by* petroleum. The difference is fundamental. "Capture" suggests that a heritage of democracy survives inside the cage, a heritage that stands apart from oil and is ready to be released and renewed. The struggle over global warming will determine whether this release and renewal will happen, whether the life-and-death contest for the fossil fuel industry may prove also to be a life-and-death contest for modern democracy.

PART FOUR
RENEWAL

Chapter 17
Crossing the carbon divide

As we said at the outset, the purpose of this book is to answer the question, "Why have democratic governments failed to act to reduce carbon emissions despite dire warnings and compelling evidence of a profound and growing threat of global warming?" The question is important because the stakes are so high. The risks of emitting carbon into the atmosphere have been publicly raised since 1965, when the science advisory committee to the president of the United States warned President Lyndon B. Johnson that burning fossil fuels was producing so much carbon dioxide that "marked changes" were likely to occur in the atmosphere, leading to global warming, melting ice caps, and rising sea levels. Research in the 1970s and 1980s, some conducted by the petroleum industry itself, confirmed and strengthened this conclusion, and tremendous advances in research since have added to its certainty. The science was so strong by 1992 that more than a hundred heads of state gathered in Rio de Janeiro, Brazil, to sign a global treaty committing their countries to reduce emissions.

By then, the fossil fuel industry had realized reducing emissions meant reducing, and ultimately eliminating, the use of fossil fuels.

Global warming was a death knell for their industry, and they chose to damn the consequences and fight. Launching a permanent campaign of sometimes soul-scorching cynicism, the industry and its allies spent lavishly to spread misinformation, co-opt officials, entice politicians, mislead the public, and capture the institutions of democracy that might otherwise hold them to account. Efforts to reduce emissions were opposed by the industry, while consumption of fossil fuels rose and carbon dioxide in the atmosphere accelerated upward to levels unknown for millions of years. The campaign to oppose meaningful action on carbon emissions was a supreme triumph of self-serving public relations that swept up the public and many of its leaders. No doubt many in the industry believed their own positions, though the contrary evidence was readily at hand. Filled with hubris and ignorance, they made a Faustian bargain — some more aware than others — and staked the biosphere of the whole planet as their wager. It was a fool's wager for the public, and the industry's stake will be paid by the innocent for centuries to come.

It turned out there was a second peril as well, this one a threat to democracy. The substance of democracy is a system of institutions that make democratically accountable government possible and meaningful. To be effective, those institutions must be substantially autonomous, and they must have the resources and independence to pursue their own mandate in the public interest. They should not become instruments of private interests or outside groups. In the unending contests of democracy, though, they sometimes do. In other words, they are captured. In a healthy democracy, the few captured institutions are restored by the many institutions that remain autonomous. A central premise of this book is that when enough important institutions are captured and held long enough by the same private interest, the system becomes incapable of correcting itself. The captive institutions reinforce each other's captivity, and the capacity of democracy to function in the public interest is impaired. Democracy falls into the grip of a deep state.

Given the depth of science on the issue of global warming from the 1960s onward, one would expect a healthy democracy to have very active leadership across a majority of public institutions, aimed at meeting aggressive deadlines for an orderly phase-out of fossil fuels. This, in fact, *is* the leadership democracies were delivering in the lead-up to the 1992 Rio Earth Summit. The success of such leadership spurred a furious reaction from the fossil fuel industry that subverted democracy and led to the rise of a deep state.

Instead of the necessary action, we have the enfeebled response of a democracy substantially under the sway of the fossil fuel industry: a wide range of institutions that are compliant and sometimes complicit in the face of rising carbon emissions. The Liberal government in Ottawa could launch a plan to eliminate fossil fuel use by 2050, but it isn't. The Conservative opposition in Ottawa could demand the government drive down fossil fuel use, but it isn't. The NDP government in Alberta could be working to halt oil sands expansion, but it isn't. Environment Canada could take a strong stand and oppose projects that increase emissions, but it isn't. Universities could be pouring resources into ending the use of fossil fuels, but they aren't. Regulators could be including the impacts of carbon emissions in their assessments and rulings, but they are dragging their heels. Medical officers of health could be launching widespread carbon emission education programs as they do for so many health threats, but they have been silenced. This is not all coincidence.

The answer to the driving question of this book is clear: Democratic governments were failing to act to reduce carbon emissions in large part because the fossil fuel industry had worked relentlessly to prevent them from taking meaningful action. In the process, they captured so many institutions that they created their own deep state, operating through the relationships between democratic institutions and industry. The deep state superseded election cycles, and rather than being held to account by legislatures, political parties, and civil servants, it held *them* to account: "Serve us," it said, "or be gone."

Alberta has been our case study, but oil's deep state does not limit itself to that province alone. Global warming and weakened democracy are two aspects of the same problem, and they are widespread. From Calgary and Edmonton to Ottawa, and from Washington, DC, to the Gulf of Mexico, the fossil fuel industry and its allies have a long catalogue of efforts to defend their interests despite the clear and present hazards of global warming. These are not individual and isolated efforts; they are not "one-offs." The concepts of "institutional capture" and "deep state" allowed us to reframe this long list of incidents into a coherent story, a tragedy that is unfolding in the face of overwhelming evidence of its dangers. EPIC, the Koch network, and so many others represent determined efforts to gain and maintain power and privilege by shaping public thought, and by organizing the institutions of democracy and politics to suit their ends at the expense of those who will suffer the burdens of global warming, and the loss of nature, truth, and integrity. There is not a person on Earth today who will escape the effects of this deceit, nor will there be ever again.

Saskatchewan may be as firmly in the grip of oil's deep state as Alberta. Until its 2017 election, British Columbia, once a proud leader in weaning itself from fossil fuels and reducing carbon emissions, had frozen its carbon tax; endorsed pipelines; and was considering liquid natural gas developments that, when all their emissions are counted, may be dirtier than state-of-the-art coal-fired plants.[514] The federal government is certainly not immune to the deep state, as the Carson trial made clear. Whichever party controls parliament, the federal government mocks its own commitments to reduce emissions by approving pipelines and supporting oil and natural gas developments. Meanwhile, in the turbid waters of American politics, the front lines in the struggle over fossil fuels surge back and forth through court battles, state capitals, Congress, and the White House as the fossil fuel deep state fights for survival at all costs and marks large victories.

The energy produced by coal, oil, and natural gas made the contemporary world possible and shaped the rise of modern democracy.[515]

Fossil fuels powered machines that rendered slave labour obsolete and eased the rise of human rights and universal suffrage. Coal mines and steam railways gave birth to early industrial unions that impelled demands for better pay and democratic participation. Fossil fuels enabled the wealth that societies invested in universal education and public services. They made possible the idea of limitless economic growth, and they sustained cities, consumer lifestyles, factories, travel, politics, food production, and wars. Fossil fuels fed the model of a consumer society that is emulated worldwide. One sign of this was the roaring consumption of oil. It took from 1860 until the late 1980s — 130 years — for humanity to consume its first trillion barrels of oil; it took only twenty-two years more to consume the second trillion.[516] For all the dangers, there remains a great force of social and economic momentum in the flywheel of fossil fuel use. The end of fossil fuels will be difficult, but end they must.

The way forward will be different. Alberta and Canada are not petro-states; they are democracies captured to varying degrees by the fossil fuel industry, and this difference means everything. It shows the way to solutions: reclaiming political parties, legislatures, and civil services; reclaiming universities and regulators; drawing clear boundaries around democratic institutions. We do not need to build democracy from scratch. We need to take it back.

The state, through its institutions, is the only organization with the capacity to deal with global warming. This makes Charles Koch's call to "destroy the prevalent statist paradigm" particularly meaningful and menacing. Individuals acting alone can have a valuable symbolic effect in starting the movement away from carbon, but they cannot solve the problem. An effective state is the only organization with the capacity to impose limits on emissions; to demand higher standards for fuel economy and building codes; to tax carbon to reflect its full environmental cost; to impose penalties, rewards, incentives, permissions, restrictions, and enforcement. Inevitably, then, state institutions must be wielded to challenge the fossil fuel industry. The fossil fuel industry knows this, has pushed back hard, and so far has prevailed. It is a Pyrrhic victory: Medical officers can be fired, the Leap Manifesto can be shouted down, political parties can be tamed, and conditions can be placed on university funding. The laws of physics, however, cannot be cheated.

* * *

The Zero Emissions Movement

Any reader who has reached this point is probably deeply concerned about global warming and democracy, and so I'm writing these final paragraphs to you, the engaged reader and citizen. You and I and our society need to cross the divide between the high-carbon present and the post-carbon future with determination and speed. Science and truth are with us, but we'll have to work hard to get history on our side, for history is filled with societies that failed to act in the face of threats. There are many excellent resources on the Internet about personal actions you can take to address global warming. A good site that has links to many other resources is the Yale Program of Climate Change Communication (http://climatecommunication.yale.edu). Although global warming cannot be solved by individuals acting alone, the actions of individuals matter. As individuals, we can show others the path to change; we can pressure our governments to act; and we can sleep at night knowing we are living our values and are part of the zero emissions movement.

Wherever you live, global warming is underway and you can see its effects. It's personal for everyone. I live in Edmonton, the gateway to the oil sands and the northernmost large city in North America, famous for its cold winters. Like city governments around the world, Edmonton city council is studying how to cope with global warming and has commissioned research into the warming already underway. Edmonton's average winter temperatures warmed 4.5°C from 1915 to 2015, and there was an average of thirty-eight fewer days per year with temperatures below freezing.[517] If warming continues at its current rate, says the analysis, the average annual temperature in Edmonton by the 2060s will be similar to the warmest three years in the 20th century. In other words, the extreme will become the norm. The same research points out that temperatures are likely to rise even faster, because continuing emissions mean carbon dioxide and other greenhouse gases are accumulating in the atmosphere. So an entirely new climate — with new plants and insects, new patterns of rain, heat, and cold — is well on its way to Edmonton, and a variation of this is well on its way to where you live.

In 2017, the federal government had to redraw its map of climate zones for Canadian gardeners because climates have changed so much. Edmonton warmed up a zone,[518] which gardeners love: My wife's cousins now grow delicious apricots and tall bamboo in their yard. But global warming also means mountain pine beetles have been able to destroy vast tracts of Alberta forest; the risk of extreme flooding, such as the $5 billion flood in Calgary in 2013, is rising; and devastating wildfires will likely become more common. Edmonton was a primary evacuation centre for the thousands of people who fled the Slave Lake wildfire in 2011, and the tens of thousands who fled the Fort McMurray wildfire in 2016.

If these things are happening where I live, what is happening near you? You can see if you look, anywhere you live or visit. I began working on this book while at Western Sydney University in Australia; in February 2017, the temperature in a town not far from that campus hit 47°C,[519] hot enough to threaten death, and temperatures will get hotter and hotter in the future.

Individuals who are awake to these changes are taking their own actions, looking into their lives for ways to reduce emissions. In Edmonton and elsewhere, there is a movement of people designing and building "net zero energy" homes that generate as much energy as they use, and the expertise acquired from these is being applied to commercial buildings.[520] An engineer I know is considering installing solar panels on his garden shed to recharge an electric bike so he can commute emission free, riding through kilometres of river valley parks and avoiding traffic jams. In 2017, the community hall in my neighbourhood installed enough solar panels to offset its electrical needs, and a nearby church plans to do the same. These actions are more than economic and environmental statements; they are political statements, each one a tiny challenge to the dominant interests of the fossil fuel industry and its deep state.

Useful progress is being made on larger scales, sometimes in surprising places. Calgary's extensive light rail transit network is powered entirely through a contract for wind energy, "enabling zero-emissions door-to-door travel in Calgary" for its riders.[521] Dozens of new schools in Alberta are being equipped with solar electric panels thanks to funding from the Alberta government.[522] Ontario phased out the last of its coal-fired power plants in 2014, and by 2030 there will be few if any coal-fired power plants in Canada.[523] On April 21, 2017, the British electrical grid operated continuously for twenty-four hours without any coal-fired electricity for the first time, a sign of the country's trend away from coal.[524] Google fulfilled a five-year plan in 2017 to meet all its enormous electricity needs from renewable sources, and other leading tech companies are close behind.[525] The state government of California, backed up by a dozen other states, is defying the Trump administration and requiring the average fuel economy of new cars improve to 54.5 miles per gallon by 2025.[526] Even oil companies are adapting. Enbridge, one of the largest pipeline companies in North America, is making substantial investments in solar and wind energy,[527] and Shell is planning big forays into renewable energy.[528]

There are more confrontational pressures for change as well. Many First Nations are using the courts to oppose pipelines and other resource developments, and in New Brunswick, a coalition of First Nations and others used marches, protests, and sometimes violence to block fracking in that province. Vancouver and other cities in British Columbia's lower mainland are using legal and regulatory channels to oppose pipeline expansion because they fear rising ocean levels imperil the region's long-term viability.[529] They are right to worry: The Vancouver suburb of Richmond, home of Vancouver's international airport and 200,000 residents, sits one metre above sea level and is protected from the ocean by a system of dykes, making it highly vulnerable to rising sea levels. In the world of high finance, a global campaign is underway for pension and other investment funds to withdraw from fossil fuel companies, and includes among its supporters the

Rockefeller Brothers Fund, Stanford University, many religious groups, and dozens of municipal governments.[530]

For all this progress, many more things need to be done, and they need to be done quickly. The goal of humanity must be to reach zero emissions by mid-century, and even then we will need to brace for lifetimes of climate upheaval.

1. We must demand governments and regulators, with the support of universities and other agencies, plan an orderly phase-out of oil sand and conventional oil and gas production, so that production is completely ended by 2050 at the latest. If there isn't an orderly phase-out there will be a disorderly one that is far more costly, forced by global changes. The first priority for governments and regulators should be to stop issuing permits for increased production.

Serious planning for a complete fossil fuel phase-out will force several issues onto the public agenda. For example, the cost of reclamation of oil and gas wells and oil sands operations could jeopardize the finances of governments: over 400,000 conventional oil and gas wells have been drilled in Alberta, and most need to be reclaimed, at an average cost of $200,000 to $300,000 each.[531] That doesn't include the oil sands or wells in other provinces. The final bill seems certain to exceed $100 billion, far more than any province can afford.

Planning the orderly phase-out of fossil fuels will also force provincial governments to confront the reality that royalties from oil and gas are going to disappear, and it will encourage governments to support workers to transition out of the petroleum industry into other work.

2. The public must continue to demand an overhaul of regulatory agencies, including the National Energy Board

and the Alberta Energy Regulator. They must be fully independent from all energy industries; they need to be required to include climate change impacts in their decisions; and they should be given the explicit mandate to guide Canada toward an environmentally sustainable energy system as quickly as possible.

3. We must reject the argument that approving pipelines is a necessity of economics and interprovincial trade. Pipeline expansion is fundamentally an environmental issue; other arguments, including job creation, government revenues, and interprovincial trade must be secondary to moving Canada to a zero emissions energy system, which itself will create jobs, revenues, and trade.

4. The autonomy of our democratic institutions must be strengthened by reducing the influence of private interests on regulators, universities, civil servants, and political parties. This requires tight financial controls on political parties; full disclosure and strict regulation on funding to universities; and tougher restrictions on the movement of people among industries, the civil service, and regulators.

The fossil fuel industry has been brilliant and ruthless in campaigning for its self-interest. People like Charles Koch offer important lessons. He realized broad social change had to go beyond ordinary political action to become a social movement that included intellectuals, organizers, campaigners, think tanks, lobbyists, politicians, and more. He knew a range of institutions had to be targeted, and that launching a movement would take many years and careful strategy. He committed to his plan for his lifetime and made adjustments to its implementation as the years passed. He never lost focus, even when the odds seemed hopeless and his cause was on the margins.

As the Kochs show, perseverance means everything. EPIC stayed the course after Bruce Carson was arrested; Dan Gagnier emailed fossil fuel interests about pending changes in government before the 2015 federal election was even held; and the industry group "Protect the Patch" began organizing behind Alberta's Wildrose Party when the party's political profile was almost invisible and never quit.

The success of the deep state depends on avoiding public exposure; when capture is exposed, it is a setback for the deep state. For example, in August 2016, Canada's National Energy Board had to suspend its hearings into the Energy East pipeline when two board members were revealed to have met privately with former Quebec Premier Jean Charest, who was a paid consultant for TransCanada, the pipeline's backer.[532] The controversy forced several months of delay on the project. Remember that TransCanada had been a supporter of EPIC, and Dan Gagnier had been a vice-chair and president of EPIC and a chief of staff to Premier Charest, and also had ties to TransCanada. That's how the deep state works.

Advocates for the environment can learn from the successes of the fossil fuel industry, not in order to imitate them by undermining democracy, but in order to counter them by reasserting democracy. Zero emissions is a demanding goal, but it is consistent with the science and can be adapted to variations such as "zero emissions by 2050" or "zero emissions from fossil fuels." We can hold people to account for this goal, including ourselves. It cuts through the deceptive language of industry supporters who speak about "emissions intensity" or claim they support action on global warming while they increase fossil fuel use.

One hard lesson for the zero emissions movement is to never assume a political party, no matter its platform, will take action to reduce emissions unless it is kept under intense pressure for years at a time. This means challenging elected officials in their constituencies, legislatures, and parliaments; and putting them on the spot through visits, emails, social media, and letters. It means joining their parties and getting on their constituency boards. It might mean joining a political party you don't normally support, in order to engage with opponents on their home territory and attempt to change their party's positions. The deep state works with political parties of every stripe, and the zero emissions movement must as well.

The zero emissions movement can trace its origins to the Rio Earth Summit, and often much earlier. It has global leaders such as David Suzuki and Al Gore, and a network of deeply rooted organizations from the likes of Greenpeace, the Sierra Club, and 350.org; to university-based environmental law centres, First Nations, and landowner groups; to school environmental clubs. The zero emissions movement won't match the fossil fuel industry in dollars for a long time, but it can over-whelm them with its number of supporters.

Responding to global warming means ending CO_2 and other greenhouse gas emissions as quickly as possible, which in turn means an orderly phase-out of the fossil fuel industry. To achieve this, the power of the fossil fuel deep state must be broken. There is, then, a profound link between addressing global warming and strengthening democracy. The integrity of our environment depends on the integrity of our democracy. The people fighting to block the expansion of pipelines, to prevent fracking, to protect endangered species on lands leased by petroleum companies, and to close coal-fired power plants aren't just fighting to save the environment. Whether or not they realize it, they are fighting to save democracy. The biggest advances in addressing global warming will come from liberating our democratic institutions from their captors.

Notes

1. "RN Breakfast," Australian Broadcasting Corporation, March 21, 2014, accessed November 4, 2016, http://mpegmedia.abc.net.au/rn/podcast/2014/03/bst_20140321_0814.mp3.

2. Canadian Association of Petroleum Producers (CAPP), "Canada Oil Sands Expenditures 1997–2015," accessed November 3, 2016, http://statshbnew.capp.ca/SHB/Sheet.asp?SectionID=4&SheetID=202.

3. In 2012, Calgary Economic Development listed 111 oil and gas companies headquartered in Calgary with annual revenues of $100 million or more, including dozens with revenues in excess of $1 billion. "Calgary a Head Office Hub," *Calgary Herald*, May 8, 2012.

4. NASA updates their data monthly, with all of the information available online. NASA, "Global Land-Ocean Temperature Index in 0.01 Degrees Celsius Base Period: 1951–1980," http://data.giss.nasa.gov/gistemp/tabledata_v3/GLB.Ts+dSST.txt.

5. The margin of a hundredth of a degree Celsius is so small that it often disappears when NASA updates its monthly calculations, making July 1985 the last month below the baseline.

6. The White House, *Report of the Environmental Pollution Panel, President's Science Advisory Committee*, Appendix Y4, November 1965, pp. 126–27, accessed November 15, 2016, http://dge.stanford.edu/labs/caldeiralab/Caldeira%20downloads/PSAC,%20 1965,%20Restoring%20the%20Quality%20of%20Our%20Environment.pdf . This appendix is a substantial and remarkably far-sighted analysis of carbon dioxide emissions from burning fossil fuels.

7. United Nations, "UN Conference on Environment and Development (1992)," accessed March 17, 2017, http://www.un.org/geninfo/bp/enviro.html.

8. *United Nations Framework Convention on Climate Change* (1992), Article 4, Section 2(b), accessed March 18, 2017, http://unfccc.int/files/essential_background/background_publications_htmlpdf/application/pdf/conveng.pdf.

9. "The Keeling Curve," Scripps Institution of Oceanography, University of California at San Diego, accessed December 6, 2015, https://scripps.ucsd.edu/programs/keelingcurve/.

10. Svante Arrhenius, "On the Influence of Carbonic Acid in the Air upon the Temperature of the Ground," *The London, Edinburgh, and Dublin Philosophical Magazine and Journal of Science*, April 1986, 237–76, accessed March 17, 2017, http://www.rsc.org/images/Arrhenius1896_tcm18-173546.pdf.

11. George Marshall, *Don't Even Think about It: Why Our Brains Are Wired to Ignore Climate Change* (New York: Bloomsbury, 2014).

12. Brian Tashman, "James Inhofe Says Bible Refutes Climate Change," *Right Wing Watch*, March 8, 2012, accessed May 8, 2017, http://www.rightwingwatch.org/content/james-inhofe-says-bible-refutes-climate-change. See also Inhofe, The Greatest Hoax: How the Global Warming Conspiracy Threatens Your Future (WorldNetDaily Books, 2012).

13. Steve Rennie, "PM's Ex-Adviser Carson Has Chequered Past," *Globe and Mail*, August 23, 2012, accessed February 2, 2017, http://www.theglobeandmail.com/news/politics/pms-ex-adviser-carson-has-chequered-past/article596827/.

14. Andrew Nikiforuk, "Crash of 'the Mechanic': Oil Sands Flogger Bruce Carson Found Guilty," *The Tyee*, September 21, 2016, accessed February 2, 2017, https://thetyee.ca/News/2016/09/21/Bruce-Carson-Found-Guilty/.

15. Biographical information on Bruce Carson was obtained from the following sources: RCMP Commercial Crime Section, Ottawa, "Information to Obtain a Production Order," Police file #2012-1046508, November 21, 2013, prepared by Cst. Marie-Josee Roberts; "Bruce Carson to Lead Canada School of Energy and Environment," University of Lethbridge Notice Board, August 14, 2008, attached to letter from Guy Giorno, Chief of Staff to the Prime Minister, to Mary Dawson, Conflict of Interest and Ethics Commissioner, Parliament of Canada, January 23, 2009, document released under the *Access to Information Act* to Greenpeace, accessed December 4, 2015, http://www. greenpeace.org/canada/en/Blog/an-epic-battle-for-canadas-energy-future/blog/33239/; and "The Bruce Carson Controversy" *CBC News*, April 7, 2011, accessed December 4, 2015, http://www.cbc.ca/news/canada/the-bruce-carson-controversy-1.1012610.

16. Bruce Carson, *14 Days: Making the Conservative Movement in Canada* (Montreal: McGill-Queen's University Press, 2014).

17. Colin Perkel, "Ex-top Aide to Former PM Harper Guilty of Influence Peddling, Top Ontario Court Rules," *National Observer*, February 18, 2017, accessed March 19, 2017, http://www.nationalobserver.com/2017/02/18/news/ex-top-aide-former-pm-harper-guilty-influence-peddling-top-ontario-court-rules.

18. *R. v. Carson*, 2016 ONCJ 596, accessed May 13, 2017, http://canlii.ca/t/gv0fb.

19. *R. v. Carson*, 2016, p. 11.

20. *R. v. Carson*, 2016, p. 80, para. 233.

21. The termination date for EPIC comes from an article by Daniel Gagnier, "Canada's Economic-Energy Conundrum: EPIC's Contribution to a National Discussion," which appeared in the September/October 2014 issue of *Policy Magazine*. Available at http://policymagazine.ca/pdf/9/PolicyMagazineSeptember-October-14-Gagnier.pdf.

22. Information on EPIC's incorporation comes from RCMP Commercial Crime Section, Ottawa, "Information to Obtain a Production Order," Police file #2012-1046508, November 21, 2013, prepared by Cst. Marie-Josee Robert, p. 6.

23. University of Calgary, *Annual Report 2007–08.*

24. Biographic material on David Emerson is primarily from the entry under his name on Wikipedia, accessed May 29, 2017 at https://en.wikipedia.org/wiki/David_Emerson.

25. Information on Protti comes from several sources, including "Gerard Protti Biography," *Alberta Oil* magazine, May 2009, http://www.albertaoilmagazine. com/2009/05/gerard-protti-biography/; Alberta Energy Regulator (AER), "Gerry Protti," https://www.aer.ca/about-aer/governance/gerry-protti; and http://peel. library.ualberta.ca/boardofgovernors.html.

26. RCMP Commercial Crime Section, Ottawa, "Information to Obtain a Production Order," Police file #2012-1046508, November 21, 2013, prepared by Cst. Marie-Josee Robert.

27. Larry Clausen's LinkedIn account (https://ca.linkedin.com/in/larryclausen) on February 13, 2016, detailed the dates of his employment history: Executive VP, Cohn & Wolfe West, March 2014 to present February 2016 ; VP & Managing Partner Cohn & Wolfe West, January 2010–March 2014; Senior VP National Public Relations, May 2007–August 2009; President and CEO of Communications Incorporated, January 1989–May 2007. All positions were based in Calgary.

28. 2010 WPP Annual Report, p. 62, accessed May 23, 2017, http://www.wpp.com/ annualreports/2010/how-were-doing/reports-from-our-operating-brands/public-relations--public-affairs/index.html.

29. RCMP Commercial Crime Section, Ottawa, "Information to Obtain a Production Order," Police file #2012-1046508, November 21, 2013, prepared by Cst. Marie-Josee Robert, p. 8.

30. Thomas D'Aquino, "Biographical Notes," http://thomasdaquino.ca/biographical-notes/; "CCCE Backgrounder," June 25, 2009, http://thomasdaquino.ca/assets/CCCE_backgrounder_June_25_2009.pdf.

31. Ira Basen. "Dan Gagnier's departure from Liberal campaign highlights murky world of Ottawa lobbying." *CBC News*, October 16, 2015, accessed May 23, 2017, http://www.cbc.ca/news/politics/canada-election-2015-gagnier-lobbying-1.3274251.

32. Ira Basen. "Dan Gagnier's departure from Liberal campaign highlights murky world of Ottawa lobbying." *CBC News*, October 16, 2015, accessed May 23, 2017, http://www.cbc.ca/news/politics/canada-election-2015-gagnier-lobbying-1.3274251.

33. A copy of Gagnier's email was made available by CBC's Chris Carter, who uploaded the file to the website Document Cloud, accessed December 12, 2015, https://www.documentcloud.org/documents/2461454-gagnier-email.html.

34. Rebecca Penty, Hugo Miller, Andrew Mayeda, and Edward Greenspon, "How Alberta's Oil Patch Teamed Up with the 'Little Guys' for an End Run around Obama," *Financial Post*, October 7, 2014, accessed February 3, 2017, http://business.financialpost.com/news/energy/energy-east-keystone.

35. "By-law No.1 Being the General By-law of the Energy Policy Institute, Canada." Filed as part of *R. v. Carson*, 2016, as document 16-2.pdf with the Ontario Court of Justice, September 16, 2016, court file no. 14-20004.

36. "Energy Policy Institute, Canada (EPIC) Founding Meeting, Minutes. August 13, 2009," presented as evidence in *R. v. Carson*, 2016, in Ontario Court of Justice (East Region), Her Majesty in Right of Canada and Bruce Carson, court file number 14-20004, 2016.

37. Payments to Carson ended up much higher than this. EPIC paid a total of $160,000 to him from February 2010 to February 2011. RCMP Commercial Crime Section, Ottawa, "Information to Obtain a Production Order," Police file #2012-1046508, November 21, 2013, prepared by Cst. Marie-Josee Robert, paras. 101–7; see also p. 8.

38. RCMP Commercial Crime Section, Ottawa, "Information to Obtain a Production Order," Police file #2012-1046508, November 21, 2013, prepared by Cst. Marie-Josee Robert, p. 6.

39. Thomas D'Aquino, quoted in RCMP Commercial Crime Section, Ottawa, "Information to Obtain a Production Order," Police file #2012-1046508, November 21, 2013, prepared by Cst. Marie-Josee Robert, p. 7.

40. University of Alberta, Vice Provost (Information Technology), "CSEE," accessed February 3, 2017, http://www.vpit.ualberta.ca/completed/csee/.

41. "Agreed Statement of Facts between Her Majesty the Queen in Right of Canada and Bruce Carson," *R. v. Carson*, 2016, Ontario Court of Justice (East Region), court file no.: 14-20004, undated, para. 5. Also see RCMP Commercial Crime Section, Ottawa, "Information to Obtain a Production Order," Police file #2012-1046508, November 21, 2013, prepared by Cst. Marie-Josee Robert, p. 6.

42. Office of the Commissioner of Lobbying of Canada, "Monthly Communication Report 16637-77382," accessed February 3, 2017, https://lobbycanada.gc.ca/app/secure/ocl/lrs/do/cmmLgPblcVw?comlogId=77382.

43. University of Calgary, "Offer of Employment, Mr. Bruce Carson," June 27, 2008, presented as evidence in R. v. Carson, 2016, filed as document 5.pdf with the Ontario Court of Justice, September 16, 2016, court file no. 14-20004.

44. See University of Calgary, "School of Policy Studies," accessed October 15, 2016, http://www.ucalgary.ca/news/uofcpublications/oncampus/online/june14-07/publicpolicy.

45. Government of Alberta, "Premier Prentice Announces New Senior Staff," September 15, 2014, accessed May 23, 2017, https://www.alberta.ca/release.cfm?xID=37064D4DCE593-BBD5-E55E-454BF8B048DB4D52.

46. David Keith, "The Real Bruce Carson Scandal," *Toronto Star*, September 22, 2015.

47. RCMP Commercial Crime Section, Ottawa, "Information to Obtain a Production Order," Police file #2012-1046508, November 21, 2013, prepared by Cst. Marie-Josee Robert, paras. 101–7; see also p. 8. See also "Agreed Statement of Facts between Her Majesty the Queen in Right of Canada and Bruce Carson," *R. v. Carson*, 2016, Ontario Court of Justice (East Region) Court File No.: 14-20004, undated.

48. For example, see email from Mike Beale to Bruce Carson, July 16, 2009, subject: "re: Draft Report," Document released under the Access to Information Act. Available online May 23, 2017 at: https://drive.google.com/file/d/0B_0MqnZ4wmcMamwwTXRQNjdrYlU/view. The email does not specify Beale's title; other searches indicate he was a senior manager or associate assistant deputy minister with Environment Canada (see https://www.pipsc.ca/portal/page/portal/website/employers/departments/ec/pdfs/061420103.en.pdf).

49. Penni Stewart, "Collaborations: Are Universities Sacrificing Integrity?" *CAUT Bulletin* 28, no. 5 (May 2011), accessed December 7, 2015, https://www.cautbulletin.ca/en_article.asp?ArticleID=3253.

50. Thomas D'Aquino, quoted in RCMP Commercial Crime Section, Ottawa, "Information to Obtain a Production Order," Police file #2012-1046508, November 21, 2013, prepared by Cst. Marie-Josee Robert, p. 7.

51. RCMP Commercial Crime Section, Ottawa, "Information to Obtain a Production Order," Police file #2012-1046508, November 21, 2013, prepared by Cst. Marie-Josee Robert, p. 6.

52. Keith Stewart, "Bruce Carson Was the Godfather of Redford's 'National' Energy Strategy," Greenpeace Canada, July 27, 2012, accessed February 7, 2017, http://www.greenpeace.org/canada/en/blog/Blogentry/bruce-carson-was-the-godfather-of-redfords-na/blog/41581/.

53. Greg Weston, "PMO Warned Ethics Watchdog on Carson," *CBC News*, April 20, 2011, accessed February 7, 2017, http://www.cbc.ca/news/politics/pmo-warned-ethics-watchdog-on-carson-1.978276.

54. Email from Bruce Carson to Mike Beale, Bob Hamilton, and Ian Shugart, June 4, 2009, document released under the *Access to Information Act*.

55. "Scenario Brief, Meeting between Minister Prentice and Key Oil and Gas Industry Representatives, June 5, 2009," document released under the *Access to Information Act* to Greenpeace, p. 2.

56. "Scenario Brief, Meeting between Minister Prentice and Key Oil and Gas Industry Representatives," p. 3.

57. "Scenario Brief, Meeting between Minister Prentice and Key Oil and Gas Industry Representatives," p. 5.

58. This was Jim Ellis, who was deputy minister at Alberta Environment from 2008 to 2011, then deputy minister of Alberta Energy from 2011 to 2013, and then became CEO of the Alberta Energy Regulator (AER). See Alberta Department of Energy, "Jim Ellis," http://www.energy.alberta.ca/Org/pdfs/JimEllisBio.pdf, and AER, "Jim Ellis," https://www.aer.ca/about-aer/governance/jim-ellis.

59. "Scenario Brief, Meeting between Minister Prentice and Key Oil and Gas Industry Representatives," p. 5.

60. "Scenario Brief, Meeting between Minister Prentice and Key Oil and Gas Industry Representatives," p. 7.

61. *R. v. Carson*, 2016, pp. 17–19, paras. 52–55.

62. Collyer's list of desired participants included: Suncor (Rick George), Petro-Canada (Ron Brenneman), CNRL (Murray Edwards), Nexen (Marvin Romanow), Shell (John Abbott), Imperial Oil (Bruce March), Canadian Oil Sands Trust (Marcel Coutu), ConocoPhillips (Kevin Meyers), and Syncrude (Don Thompson). Email from Dave Collyer to Cassie Doyle, June 11, 2009, subject: "List of Participants for June 12th Meeting between the Clerk of the Privy Council and Oil Sands Industry Leaders," accessed December 16, 2015, http://www.greenpeace.org/canada/Global/canada/report/2012/07/Access%20to%20information-%20CAPP-NRCan%20emails%20re%20mtg%20with%20Clerk.pdf.

63. "Murray" seems to be Murray Edwards, head of CNRL, who is named at various places in the exchange and at one point is described as having a "keen interest in this subject."

64. Email from Dave Collyer to Cassie Doyle, June 11, 2009, subject: "List of Participants for June 12th Meeting between the Clerk of the Privy Council and Oil Sands Industry Leaders," accessed December 3, 2015, https://docs.google.com/a/greenpeace.org/file/d/0B_0MqnZ4wmcMRTlJS2FjajMxM0U/edit?pli=1.

65. Email from Cassie Doyle to Kevin Stringer and Sue Kirby, June 15, 2009, subject: "FW: Calgary Meetings," accessed May 23, 2017, https://docs.google.com/file/d/0B_0MqnZ4wmcMMjE4QlV1MEhXLUU/edit?pli=1.

66. Given that there is no mention in the minutes of solar, wind, or renewable energy, "clean energy" in this context undoubtedly refers to fossil fuels. It was, perhaps, a kind of psychological crutch to help everyone deny the reality of what they were discussing.

67. In 2010–11, the Government of Canada spent $270.5 billion. (Finance Canada, "Your Tax Dollar: 2010–2011 Fiscal Year," accessed February 14, 2016, http://www.fin.gc.ca/tax-impot/2011/html-eng.asp). The University of Alberta's total spending for the same year was $1.59 billion. ("2010–2011 University of Alberta Annual Report," (Edmonton: University of Alberta, 2012)).

68. "Scenario Brief, Meeting between Minister Prentice and Key Oil and Gas Industry Representatives," p. 32.

69. "Summaries of the Deputy Minister Meetings with Industry and the Alberta Government on Oil Sands Outreach and Communications," March 16, 2010, accessed December 17, 2015, http://climateactionnetwork.ca/wp-content/uploads/2011/10/62012456-Natural-Resources-Canada-Oilsands-advocacy-records.pdf.

70. Hansard of the Legislative Assembly of Alberta, March 16, 2010, 2:10 pm, exchange between Laurie Blakeman, MLA, Edmonton Centre, and Rob Renner, Minister of Environment. Full disclosure: I was an opposition member of the legislature at that time, but did not participate in this question.

71. "A Building Consensus: Moving Toward a Canadian Energy Strategy. Presentation to Federal, Provincial, and Territorial Energy Ministers," July 18, 2011, p. 5, accessed December 17, 2015, https://www.ppforum.ca/sites/default/files/Building_Consensus_Report_English_1.pdf.

72. Daniel Cayley-Daoust and Richard Girard, *Big Oil's Oily Grasp: The Making of Canada as a Petro-State and How Oil Money Is Corrupting Canadian Politics* (Ottawa: Polaris Institute, 2012), p. 3, accessed February 6, 2017, https://d3n8a8pro7vhmx.

cloudfront.net/polarisinstitute/pages/31/attachments/original/1411065312/
BigOil%27sOilyGrasp.pdf?1411065312.

73.   Forest Ethics Advocacy, "Who Writes the Rules? A Report on Oil Industry Influence,
      Government Laws, and the Corrosion of Public Process," n.d., p.1, accessed February
      6, 2017, https://issuu.com/forestethics/docs/who_writes_the_rules.

74.   Cited in Forest Ethics Advocacy, "Who Writes the Rules?" p. 1.

75.   *R. v. Carson*, 2016, p. 14., para. 43.

76.   *R. v. Carson*, 2016, pp. 88–89, paras. 252–53.

77.   *R. v. Carson*, 2016, pp. 89–90, para. 253.

78.   *R. v. Carson*, 2016, p. 98, para. 258.

79.   *R. v. Carson*, 2016, p. 11.

80.   EPIC, "A Strategy for Canada's Global Energy Leadership Progress Document," July
      2011, p. 3.

81.   Boyd Erman and Daniel LeBlanc, "Ex-Harper Chief of Staff Nigel Wright Rejoins
      Onex," *Globe and Mail*, June 4, 2014, accessed November 1, 2016, http://www.
      theglobeandmail.com/news/politics/ex-harper-chief-of-staff-nigel-wright-rejoins-
      onex/article18995914/#dashboard/follows/.

82.   Email from Bruce Carson to Nigel Wright, "Final Framework Document," September
      21, 2011, 10:44 pm. In *R. v. Carson*, 2016, filed as document 57.pdf with the Ontario
      Court of Justice, September 16, 2016, court file no. 14-20004.

83.   Email from Nigel Wright to Bruce Carson, "Final Framework Document," September
      22, 2011, 2:48 pm. In *R. v. Carson*, 2016, filed as document 58.pdf with the Ontario
      Court of Justice, September 16, 2016, court file no. 14-20004.

84.   For a book-length analysis of the Harper government's muffling of scientists, see
      Chris Turner, *The War on Science: Muzzled Scientists and Wilful Blindness in Stephen
      Harper's Canada* (Vancouver: Greystone Books, 2013).

85.   Brenda Heelan Powell, *An Overview of Bill C-38: The Budget Bill That Transformed Canada's
      Federal Environmental Laws* (Edmonton: Environmental Law Centre, n.d.), accessed
      February 7, 2017, http://elc.ab.ca/Content_Files/Files/Bill38AnalysisArticlefinal.pdf.

86.   Lorna Stefanick. "Alberta's Energy Paradigm: Prosperity, Security and the Environment,"
      p.128. Chapter 4 in Meenal Shrivastava and Lorna Stefanick, eds, *Alberta Oil and the
      Decline of Democracy in Canada.* (2013.) Athabasca University Press.

87.   For a good summary of the 2012 Bill C-38 and Bill C-45, see Powell, *An Overview of Bill
      C-38*, and *Back on the Omnibus with Bill C-45: Another Omnibus Budget Bill Drives More
      Change to Federal Environmental Law* (Edmonton: Environmental Law Centre, n.d.),
      accessed November 29, 2016, http://elc.ab.ca/Content_Files/Files/Bill_C_45.pdf.

88.   Heather Scoffield, "Pipeline Industry Pushed Environmental Changes Made in
      Omnibus Bill, Document Shows," *Globe and Mail*, February 20, 2013, accessed February
      6, 2017, http://www.theglobeandmail.com/news/politics/pipeline-industry-pushed-
      environmental-changes-made-in-omnibus-bill-documents-show/article8894850/.

89.   Michael Babad, "Joe Oliver Taints All with Talk of Environmentalists, Radicals," *Globe
      and Mail*, January 9, 2012, accessed December 18, 2015, http://www.theglobeandmail.
      com/report-on-business/top-business-stories/joe-oliver-taints-all-with-talk-of-
      environmentalists-radicals/article4085710/.

90.   Cited in Andrew Nikiforuk, "Oh Canada: How America's Friendly Northern Neighbor
      Became a Rogue, Reckless Petrostate," *Foreign Policy*, July-August 2013, p. 13.

91. Susana Mas, "Harper Won't Take No for an Answer on Keystone XL," *CBC News*, September 26, 2013, accessed December 18, 2015, http://www.cbc.ca/news/politics/harper-won-t-take-no-for-an-answer-on-keystone-xl-1.1869439.

92. Ipsos Reid, "Post-test Evaluation of the International Outreach Advertising Campaign — US Component," March 3, 2014, accessed October 31, 2016, http://epe.lac-bac.gc.ca/100/200/301/pwgsc-tpsgc/por-ef/natural_resources/2014/054-13/summary.pdf. See also "$24 Million Ad Campaign for Keystone Pipeline Has Little Impact: Survey," *CBC Business News*, August 21, 2014, accessed October 31, 2016, http://www.cbc.ca/news/business/24m-ad-campaign-for-keystone-pipeline-had-little-impact-survey-1.2742079.

93. "'I Want This Premier to Succeed' — Wildrose Leader Danielle Smith, Eight Other MLAs Join PCs," *Edmonton Metro News*, December 17, 2014, accessed February 7, 2017, http://www.metronews.ca/news/canada/2014/12/17/nine-wildrose-mlas-bolt-for-alberta-pc-party.html.

94. "Premier-designate Rachel Notley Tells Energy Industry It'll Be 'A-OK,'" *CBC News*, May 6, 2015, accessed December 18, 2015, http://www.cbc.ca/news/elections/alberta-votes/premier-designate-rachel-notley-tells-energy-industry-it-ll-be-a-ok-1.3063432.

95. Among the many sources on these issues, see the *Financial Post*, "Why Donald Trump's Election Boosts Canada's Oil Sands Pipelines," for information concerning the Keystone XL pipeline (http://business.financialpost.com/news/energy/why-donald-trumps-election-boosts-canadas-oilsands-pipelines?__lsa=23d6-ddf1); and *Time* on Trump's promise for the coal industry (http://time.com/4570070/donald-trump-coal-jobs/).

96. Gaurav Sharma, "Making American 'Crude' Again: U.S. Oil and Gas Industry Feels the Trump Effect," *Forbes*, January 27, 2017, accessed February 7, 2017, http://www.forbes.com/sites/gauravsharma/2017/01/27/making-america-crude-again-us-oil-and-gas-industry-feels-the-trump-effect/#661bd8622213.

97. AsiaPacific Foundation, "Canadian Oil: The Export Picture," accessed March 23, 2017, http://www.asiapacific.ca/sites/default/files/3_canadian_oil_exports.pdf.

98. Email from Peter Stokoe to rwhittaker@pco-bcp.gc.ca, subject: "WSHDC Oil Sands Workshop and Outreach Program- Apr. 23-24, 2009," May 21, 2009, 1:13 pm, document released under the *Access to Information Act* to Greenpeace, https://docs.google.com/a/greenpeace.org/file/d/0B_0MqnZ4wmcMWTNjOTcxMUh2d00/edit?pli=1.

99. See www.API.org.

100. Shannon Hall, "A Turning Point in Combating Climate Change May Be Here," *Scientific American*, December 14, 2015, accessed February 17, 2016, http://www.scientificamerican.com/article/a-turning-point-in-combating-climate-change-may-be-here/.

101. Among the most important is the report "Exxon: The Road Not Taken," prepared by a team of investigators and including copies of internal Exxon documents. Accessed February 18, 2016, http://insideclimatenews.org/content/Exxon-The-Road-Not-Taken.

102. Christine Wang, "SEC Investigating Exxon Mobil on Climate Change, Accounting Practices: Report," *CNBC*, September 20, 2016, accessed March 19, 2017, http://www.cnbc.com/2016/09/20/sec-investigating-exxon-mobil-on-climate-change-accounting-practices-report.html.

103. "For Decades, Exxon Mingled with the Climate Science Elite," *Inside Climate News*, September 22, 2015, accessed May 9, 2017, http://insideclimatenews.org/content/decades-exxon-mingled-climate-science-elite.

104. Neela Banerjee, Lisa Song, and David Hasemyer, "Exxon's Own Research Confirmed

Fossil Fuel's Role in Global Warming," *Inside Climate News*, September 16, 2015, accessed May 9, 2017, http://insideclimatenews.org/news/15092015/Exxons-own-research-confirmed-fossil-fuels-role-in-global-warming.

105. Banerjee, Song, and Hasemyer, "Exxon's Own Research Confirmed Fossil Fuel's Role in Global Warming."

106. The scope of Exxon's research plan can be seen in documents posted by *Inside Climate News*, available at http://insideclimatenews.org/sites/default/files/documents/Exxon%20Review%20of%20Climate%20Research%20Program%20%281981%29.pdf.

107. This memo can be read courtesy of *Inside Climate News*, http://insideclimatenews.org/sites/default/files/documents/%2522Consensus%2522%20on%20CO2%20Impacts%20%281982%29.pdf.

108. The documents are available online, courtesy of *Inside Climate News*, http://insideclimatenews.org/sites/default/files/documents/AQ-9%20Task%20Force%20Meeting%20%281980%29.pdf.

109. The film was posted on YouTube in early 2017, https://www.youtube.com/watch?v=0VOWi8oVXmo.

110. See the Calspace Course on climate change, "The Greenhouse Effect: The Radiation Balance," accessed May 15, 2017, http://earthguide.ucsd.edu/virtualmuseum/climatechange1/02_3.shtml.

111. Although we can only detect it as warmth, infrared energy can be "seen" by some creatures, such as snakes. See Janet Fang, "Snake Infrared Detection Unravelled," *Nature*, March 14, 2010, http://www.nature.com/news/2010/100314/full/news.2010.122.html.

112. A 2015 Toyota Camry has a seventeen-gallon tank, and each gallon produces about 19.8 pounds (8.9 kilograms) of CO_2. This information is based on US Environmental Protection Agency figures, accessed October 24, 2016, https://www.epa.gov/sites/production/files/2016-02/documents/420f14040a.pdf.

113. John Voelcker,"1.2 Billion Vehicles on World's Roads Now; 2 Billion by 2035: Report," *Green Car Reports*, July 29, 2014, accessed November 4, 2016, http://www.greencarreports.com/news/1093560_1-2-billion-vehicles-on-worlds-roads-now-2-billion-by-2035-report.

114. Based on "Carbon Emissions Calculator" provided by International Civil Aviation Organization at http://www.icao.int/environmental-protection/CarbonOffset/Pages/default.aspx.

115. IATA Press Release No. 72, December 31, 2013, accessed November 4, 2016, http://www.iata.org/pressroom/pr/Pages/2013-12-30-01.aspx.

116. The average household in Canada used 11,100 kilowatt hours (40 gigajoules) of electricity in 2007. Statistics Canada, "Households and the Environment: Energy Use," 2007, accessed October 24, 2016, http://www.statcan.gc.ca/pub/11-526-s/2010001/part-partie1-eng.htm.

117. Bituminous coal produces about 2.07 pounds of CO_2 to generate one kilowatt hour of electricity. US Energy Information Administration, "How Much Carbon Dioxide Is Produced per Kilowatthour When Generating Electricity from Fossil Fuels?" accessed October 24, 2016, https://www.eia.gov/tools/faqs/faq.cfm?id=74&t=11.

118. US Energy Information Administration, "Frequently Asked Questions," accessed November 4, 2016, online at: https://www.eia.gov/tools/faqs/faq.cfm?id=65&t=2.

119. According to data provided by the US National Oceanic and Atmospheric Administration (http://www.esrl.noaa.gov/gmd/ccgg/trends/). See also Greg and Tom Boden, "The Increasing Concentration of Atmospheric CO2: How Much, When, and Why?" Oak Ridge National Laboratory, Oak Ridge, Tennessee, December 2014, http://cdiac.esd.ornl.gov/epubs/other/Sicilypaper.pdf.

120. David Archer, *The Long Thaw: How Humans Are Changing the Next 100,000 Years of Earth's Climate* (Princeton, NJ: Princeton University Press, 2009), pp. 45, 1.

121. R.K. Pachauri, Leo Meyer, et al. (eds.), *Climate Change 2014 Synthesis Report*, accessed March 7, 2017, http://ar5-syr.ipcc.ch/ipcc/ipcc/resources/pdf/IPCC_SynthesisReport.pdf.

122. IPCC Working Group 1,"What Caused the Ice Ages and Other Important Climate Changes Before the Industrial Era?" in S. Solomon, D. Qin, M. Manning, Z. Chen, M. Marquis, K.B. Averyt, M. Tignor, and H.L. Miller (eds.), *Climate Change 2007: The Physical Science Basis. Contribution of Working Group I to the Fourth Assessment Report of the Intergovernmental Panel on Climate Change* (Cambridge: Cambridge University Press, 2007), accessed November 29, 2016, http://oceanservice.noaa.gov/education/pd/climate/factsheets/whatcause.pdf.

123. US Environmental Protection Agency Gulf of Mexico Program, "The Ice Age Pleistocene Epoch," December 15, 2014, http://www.epa.gov/gmpo/edresources/pleistocene.html.

124. Royal Society and US National Academy of Sciences, Climate Change: Evidence and Causes, 2014, p. 19.

125. During the last ice age, temperatures in Greenland were about 10°C colder than today, while temperatures in tropical areas were about 4°C lower. See Ahrens, C. Donald. (2012.) *Essentials of Meteorology: An Invitation to the Atmosphere.* Sixth Edition. Cengage Learning: Belmont California. p. 377.

126. Royal Society and US National Academy of Sciences, *Climate Change: Evidence and Causes*, 2014, p. 9.

127. Juyaid Laghari, "Climate Change: Melting Glaciers Bring Energy Uncertainty," Nature 502, no. 7473 (October 30/November 15, 2013), accessed December 29, 2014, http://www.nature.com/news/climate-change-melting-glaciers-bring-energy-uncertainty-1.14031.

128. Royal Society and US National Academy of Sciences, *Climate Change: Evidence and Causes.*

129. Pachauri, Meyer, et al. (eds.), *Climate Change 2014 Synthesis Report*, p. 16.

130. Royal Society and US National Academy of Sciences, *Climate Change: Evidence and Causes*, 2014.

131. Royal Society and US National Academy of Sciences, *Climate Change: Evidence and Causes*, 2014, p. 17.

132. Elizabeth Kolbert, *The Sixth Extinction* (New York: Henry Holt & Co., 2014), p. 118.

133. Royal Society and US National Academy of Sciences, *Climate Change: Evidence and Causes*, 2014, p. 18.

134. CSIRO, "Projections of Days over 35 Degrees to 2100 for All Capital Cities under a No-Mitigation Case," cited in Government of Australia, *The Garnaut Climate Change Review*, 2008, sec. 5, p. 117.

135. Pachauri, Meyer, et al. (eds.), *Climate Change 2014 Synthesis Report*, p. 12.

136. See, for example, D.B. Wake and V.T. Vredenburg, "Colloquium Paper: Are We in

the Midst of the Sixth Mass Extinction? A View from the World of Amphibians," *Proceedings of the National Academy of Sciences* 105 (2008), accessed December 28, 2014, http://www.pnas.org/content/105/Supplement_1/11466.full.

137. Kolbert, *The Sixth Extinction*, pp. 17–18.

138. Elahe Izadi, "The Gulf of Alaska Is Unusually Warm, and Weird Fish Are Showing Up," *The Washington Post*, September 15, 2014.

139. "Climate Change Pushing Lobster North, Study Says," *CBC News*, September 21, 2013, accessed December 23, 2014, http://www.cbc.ca/news/canada/nova-scotia/climate-change-pushing-lobster-north-study-says-1.1863271.

140. Pachauri, Meyer, et al. (eds.), *Climate Change 2014 Synthesis Report*, p. 13.

141. Pachauri, Meyer, et al. (eds.), *Climate Change 2014 Synthesis Report*, p. 69.

142. World Health Organization, "Climate Change and Infectious Diseases," accessed December 23, 2014, http://www.who.int/globalchange/climate/summary/en/index5.html.

143. Bob Marshall, "Losing Ground: Southeast Louisiana Is Disappearing Quickly," *Scientific American*, August 28, 2014, accessed October 24, 2016, https://www.scientificamerican.com/article/losing-ground-southeast-louisiana-is-disappearing-quickly/.

144. US Environmental Protection Agency, "Global Warming and the Coast," accessed October 24, 2016, https://www3.epa.gov/climatechange/Downloads/impacts-adaptation/saving_FL.pdf.

145. Royal Society and US National Academy of Sciences, *Climate Change: Evidence and Causes*, 2014.

146. Will Steffen, quoted on Australian Broadcasting Corporation, commenting on the report *Counting the Costs: Climate Change and Coastal Flooding*, Climate Council of Australia, accessed December 20, 2014, http://www.abc.net.au/lateline/content/2014/s4089069.htm.

147. Pachauri, Meyer, et al. (eds.), *Climate Change 2014 Synthesis Report*, 2014, p. 69.

148. The seminal work on "the commons" in political economy and environmental management is Garrett Hardin's essay "The Tragedy of the Commons," first published in *Science Magazine*, December 13, 1968, and easily available online. For a discussion on the commons and global warming, see Jouni Paavola's "Climate Change: The Ultimate 'Tragedy of the Commons'?" Paper No. 24, Sustainability Research Institute, School of Earth and Environment, University of Leeds, https://www.see.leeds.ac.uk/fileadmin/Documents/research/sri/workingpapers/SRIPs-24_01.pdf. Also see Elinor Ostrom et al., *The Drama of the Commons* (Washington, DC: The National Academies Press, 2002), and Elinor Ostrom, *Governing the Commons: The Evolution of Institutions for Collective Action* (New York: Cambridge University Press, 1990).

149. Coordination and Planning Division, Exxon Research and Engineering Company, "CO2 Greenhouse Effect, A Technical Review," April 1, 1982, accessed March 20, 2017, http://insideclimatenews.org/sites/default/files/documents/1982%20Exxon%20Primer%20on%20CO2%20Greenhouse%20Effect.pdf, pp. 4, 5, 12, 19, 20, and 21.

150. *Conservation Law Foundation Inc. v. ExxonMobil*, Massachusetts District Court, Case no. 1:16-cv-11950, filed September 29, 2016, http://www.clf.org/wp-content/uploads/2016/09/CLF-v.-ExxonMobil-Complaint.pdf.

151. PBL Netherlands Environmental Assessment Agency, "Trends in Global CO2 Emissions, 2015 Report,". Figure 2.2, accessed March 24, 2017, http://edgar.jrc.ec.europa.eu/news_docs/jrc-2015-trends-in-global-co2-emissions-2015-report-98184.pdf.

152. A major 2017 report forecasted that by 2050, oil demand must be at 45 per cent of the 2016 level, if global warming is to be kept to 2°C. International Energy Agency/ International Renewable Energy Agency, "Perspectives for the Energy Transition," p. 10, accessed April 3, 2017, https://www.energiewende2017.com/wp-content/uploads/2017/03/Perspectives-for-the-Energy-Transition_WEB.pdf.

153. "The White House and the Greenhouse," New York Times, May 9, 1989, accessed April 23, 2016, http://www.nytimes.com/1989/05/09/opinion/the-white-house-and-the-greenhouse.html.

154. The George C. Marshall Institute has been the subject of much critical analysis. A good introduction is Naomi Oreskes and Erik M. Conway, Merchants of Doubt: How a Handful of Scientists Obscured the Truth on Issues from Tobacco Smoke to Global Warming (New York: Bloomsbury Press, 2010).

155. Alison Mitchell, "G.O.P. Hopes Climate Fight Echoes Health Care Outcome," December 13, 1997, New York Times, accessed March 19, 2017, http://www.nytimes.com/1997/12/13/world/gop-hopes-climate-fight-echoes-health-care-outcome.html.

156. Wendy E. Franz, "Science, Skeptics and Non-state Actors in the Greenhouse," ENRP Discussion Paper E-98-18, Kennedy School of Government, Harvard University, 1998, accessed March 19, 2017, http://live.belfercenter.org/files/Science%20Skeptics%20 and%20Non-State%20Actors%20in%20the%20Greenhouse%20-%20E-98-18.pdf.

157. Franz, "Science, Skeptics, and Non-state Actors in the Greenhouse."

158. Images of the plan are widely available on the Internet, at addresses such as this website: http://www.euronet.nl/users/e_wesker/ew@shell/API-prop.html. The initial story was broken by John H. Cushman in the New York Times on April 26, 1998, under the headline "Industrial Group Plans to Battle Climate Treaty."

159. Based on disclosures provided to the US Federal Election Commission under US federal election financing laws. Compiled by Open Secrets Center for Responsive Politics, accessed October 31, 2016, https://www.opensecrets.org/industries/totals. php?ind=E01 and https://www.opensecrets.org/industries/totals.php?ind=E1210.

160. Condoleezza Rice, No Higher Honor (New York: Crown Publishers/Random House, 2011), p. 659.

161. Peter Wallsten and Tom Hamburger, "Cabinet Official Norton Resigns," LA Times, March 11, 2006, accessed February 23, 2016, http://articles.latimes.com/2006/mar/11/ nation/na-norton11.

162. The details of the day of the explosion are covered in wrenching detail in Deep Water: The Gulf Oil Disaster and the Future of Offshore Drilling by the National Commission on the BP Deepwater Horizon Oil Spill and Offshore Drilling (2011). See also: Josh Tickell and Rebecca Harrell Tickell (dirs.), The Big Fix (DVD; Green Planet Productions, 2012); Beyond Pollution (DVD; Swibble Films, 2012); Carl Safina, A Sea in Flames: The Deepwater Horizon Blowout (New York: Crown Publishers, 2011); and Abrahm Lustgarten, Run to Failure: BP and the Making of the Deepwater Horizon Disaster (New York: W.W. Norton, 2012).

163. See Safina, A Sea in Flames, pp. 108, 163, 181; and Lustgarten, Run to Failure, p. 291.

164. National Commission on the BP Deepwater Horizon Oil Spill and Offshore Drilling, Deep Water: The Gulf Oil Disaster and the Future of Offshore Drilling, 2011, accessed February 24, 2016, http://cybercemetery.unt.edu/archive/oilspill/20121210200431/ http:/www.oilspillcommission.gov/final-report.

165. In particular, Chapter Three of the final report is committed to the problems with regulatory oversight of the Gulf offshore drilling industry.

166. National Commission on the BP Deepwater Horizon Oil Spill and Offshore Drilling, *Deep Water: The Gulf Oil Disaster and the Future of Offshore Drilling*, p. 85.

167. National Commission on the BP Deepwater Horizon Oil Spill and Offshore Drilling, *Deep Water: The Gulf Oil Disaster and the Future of Offshore Drilling*, p. 225.

168. National Commission on the BP Deepwater Horizon Oil Spill and Offshore Drilling, *Deep Water: The Gulf Oil Disaster and the Future of Offshore Drilling*, p. 228.

169. National Commission on the BP Deepwater Horizon Oil Spill and Offshore Drilling, *Deep Water: The Gulf Oil Disaster and the Future of Offshore Drilling*, p. 224.

170. National Commission on the BP Deepwater Horizon Oil Spill and Offshore Drilling, *Deep Water: The Gulf Oil Disaster and the Future of Offshore Drilling*, p. 228.

171. National Commission on the BP Deepwater Horizon Oil Spill and Offshore Drilling, *Deep Water: The Gulf Oil Disaster and the Future of Offshore Drilling*, p. 225.

172. National Commission on the BP Deepwater Horizon Oil Spill and Offshore Drilling, *Deep Water: The Gulf Oil Disaster and the Future of Offshore Drilling*, p. 71.

173. National Commission on the BP Deepwater Horizon Oil Spill and Offshore Drilling, *Deep Water: The Gulf Oil Disaster and the Future of Offshore Drilling*, p. 71.

174. National Commission on the BP Deepwater Horizon Oil Spill and Offshore Drilling, *Deep Water: The Gulf Oil Disaster and the Future of Offshore Drilling*, p. 72.

175. National Commission on the BP Deepwater Horizon Oil Spill and Offshore Drilling, *Deep Water: The Gulf Oil Disaster and the Future of Offshore Drilling*, p. 72.

176. Earl Devaney, Office of Inspector-General, United States Department of the Interior, Memorandum to Secretary Kempthorne, September 9, 2008, accessed April 17, 2015, http://media.mcclatchydc.com/smedia/2008/09/10/18/Gordon-OIG-Cover-Letter.source.prod_affiliate.91.pdf.

177. Mary L. Kendall, Office of Inspector-General, United States Department of the Interior, Memorandum to Secretary Salazar, May 24, 2010, accessed April 17, 2015, http://abcnews.go.com/images/Politics/MMS_inspector_general_report_pdf.pdf.

178. For more information, see the Council's website: https://www.whitehouse.gov/administration/eop/ceq/about.

179. For coverage of the House of Representatives probe into this issue, see https://web.archive.org/web/20070927222003/http://www.whistleblower.org/content/press_detail.cfm?press_id=838&keyword=.

180. Andrew C. Revkin, "Bush Aide Softened Greenhouse Gas Links to Global Warming," *New York Times*, June 8, 2005, http://www.nytimes.com/2005/06/08/politics/bush-aide-softened-greenhouse-gas-links-to-global-warming.html?_r=0.

181. Safina, *A Sea in Flames*, p. 74.

182. Revkin, "Bush Aide Softened Greenhouse Gas Links to Global Warming."

183. Images of parts of the memo are available at various websites, including *Mother Jones* (https://www.motherjones.com/files/LuntzResearch_environment.pdf). For further analysis on this issue, see Anthony Leiserowitz et al., "What's in a Name? Global Warming versus Climate Change," Yale Project on Climate Change Communication, May 2014, pp. 132, 137, 138, and 142.

184. Jennifer Lee, "A Call for Softer, Greener Language," *New York Times*, March 2, 2003, accessed February 16, 2016, http://nyti.ms/1iBFuvr.

185. Interview in *Beyond Pollution* (DVD; Swibble Films, 2012).

186. Dan Eggen and Kimberly Kindy, "Three of Every Four Oil and Gas Lobbyists Worked for Federal Government," *Washington Post*, July 22, 2010, accessed April 21, 2015, http://www.washingtonpost.com/wp-dyn/content/article/2010/07/21/AR2010072106468.html.

187. Anne C. Mulkern, "Oil and Gas Interests Set Spending Record in 2009," *New York Times*, February 2, 2010, accessed April 21, 2015, http://www.nytimes.com/gwire/2010/02/02/02greenwire-oil-and-gas-interests-set-spending-record-for-l-1504.html?pagewanted=all.

188. Jen DeGregorio, "Some Question Whether Louisiana Is too Dependent on Oil, Gas Revenues," *The Times-Picayune*, August 2, 2009.

189. State of Louisiana Office of the Governor, June 2, 2010, letter from Governor Bobby Jindal to President Barack Obama and Secretary of State Ken Salazar, accessed April 18, 2015, http://www.huffingtonpost.com/2010/06/03/bobby-jindal-obama-letter_n_599226.html.

190. The list of financial contributions was compiled by a consortium that included Deep South Center for Environmental Justice, Global Green, League of American Woman Voters, Louisiana Bucket Brigade, and the Sierra Club. See Mark Schleifstein, "Jindal Opposes Coastal Erosion Lawsuit due to Oil Industry Contributions, Environmental Groups Say," *The Times-Picayune*, August 28, 2013, accessed April 22, 2015, http://www.nola.com/environment/index.ssf/2013/08/environmental_groups_say_jinda.html.

191. Louisiana Association of Business and Industry, "Senator Robert R. Adley," accessed April 18, 2015, http://labi.org/legislature-info/legislator-detail/adley-robert.

192. Michael Hiltzik, "Bobby Jindal's Huge Favor to His Pals in the Oil and Gas Industry," *Los Angeles Times*, June 6, 2014.

193. Josh Tickell and Rebecca Harrell Tickell (dirs.), *The Big Fix* (DVD; Green Planet Productions, 2012).

194. The program is described at the Gulf State Marine Fisheries Commission's website (http://www.gsmfc.org/odrp.php).

195. Debbie Elliott, "5 Years after BP Oil Spill, Effects Linger and Recovery Is Slow," *NPR*, April 21, 2015, accessed February 25, 2016, http://www.npr.org/2015/04/20/400374744/5-years-after-bp-oil-spill-effects-linger-and-recovery-is-slow.

196. Patrick Barkham, "Oil Spills: Legacy of the *Torrey Canyon*," *The Guardian*, June 24, 2010.

197. Jane Mayer, *Dark Money* (New York: First Anchor Books, 2017), pp. 221–27.

198. Robert J. Brulle, "Institutionalizing Delay: Foundation Funding and the Creation of U.S. Climate Change Counter-Movement Organizations," *Climatic Change*, 2013, accessed February 11, 2017, https://johncarlosbaez.wordpress.com/2013/12/23/who-is-bankrolling-climate-change-countermovement/.

199. "Canadian Federal Election, 2011," *Wikipedia*, https://en.wikipedia.org/wiki/Canadian_federal_election,_2011. See the subsection "Election Spending."

200. Mayer, *Dark Money*, pp. 34–38.

201. "Koch Industries Canada Facts," March 2014, accessed February 16, 2017, https://www.kochind.com/files/canadafacts.pdf.

202. Steven Mufson and Juliet Eilperin, "The Biggest Foreign Lease Holder in Canada's Oil Sands Isn't Exxon Mobil or Shell, It's the Koch Brothers," *Washington Post*, March 20, 2014, accessed February 16, 2017, https://www.washingtonpost.com/news/wonk/wp/2014/03/20/the-biggest-land-owner-in-canadas-oil-sands-isnt-exxon-mobil-or-

conoco-phillips-its-the-koch-brothers/?utm_term=.3f0353ed82ff.

203. Mayer, *Dark Money*, p. 106.

204. Charles Koch, "The Business Community: Resisting Regulation," *Libertarian Review* 7, no. 7 (August 1978), 30–35. Quotes from pp. 32, 33, and 34.

205. Mayer, *Dark Money*, pp. 69–70.

206. Mayer, *Dark Money*, pp. 172–74.

207. Mayer, *Dark Money*, p. 447.

208. Mayer, *Dark Money*, pp. 189, 448.

209. Leigh Ann Caldwell, "Charles Koch Explains to Donors Why He Won't Support Trump," August 1, 2016, accessed February 20, 2017, http://www.nbcnews.com/politics/2016-election/charles-koch-explains-donors-why-he-won-t-support-trump-n620621.

210. Mayer, *Dark Money*, pp. 452–53.

211. Mayer, *Dark Money*, p. 426.

212. Mayer, *Dark Money*.

213. Accessed February 19, 2017, http://www.resistingthegreendragon.com.

214. Daniel Tencer, "Koch Brothers, Tea Party Billionaires, Donated to Right Wing Fraser Institute, Reports Show," *Huffington Post*, April 26, 2012, accessed February 26, 2017, http://www.huffingtonpost.ca/2012/04/26/koch-brothers-fraser-institute_n_1456223.html.

215. Mayer, *Dark Money*, pp. 246–47.

216. See http://www.devonenergy.com/featured-stories/nichols-earns-apis-top-lifetime-achievement-honor.

217. Mayer, *Dark Money*, p. 245.

218. The non-partisan research group Open Secrets reported that the oil and gas industry donated $73.4 million in the 2012 US election cycle, 90 per cent of which went to Republicans. Cited in Alexander Panetta, "Stalled Keystone XL a DC Cash Cow," *Canadian Press*, May 9, 2014.

219. Mayer, *Dark Money*, p. 337.

220. Mayer, *Dark Money*, p. 386.

221. Mayer, *Dark Money*, p. 386.

222. Mayer, *Dark Money*, p. 388.

223. "The Full List of the Richest People in America," *Forbes*, 2009, 2016, accessed February 17, 2017, http://www.forbes.com.

224. Mayer, *Dark Money*, p. 453.

225. Mayer, *Dark Money*, p. 455.

226. Mayer, *Dark Money*, p. 454.

227. Dana Bash, "McConnell, the Democrats, and the Limits of a Secret Tape," *CNN*, August 28, 2014, accessed February 20, 2017, http://www.cnn.com/2014/08/27/politics/mitch-mcconnell-kentucky-race/.

228. Paul Barrett and Jim Rowley, "Mitch McConnell and the Coal Industry's Last Stand," *Bloomberg News*, December 23, 2015, accessed February 20, 2017, https://www.bloomberg.com/politics/articles/2015-12-23/senator-mitch-mcconnell-and-the-coal-industry-s-last-stand.

229. Coral Davenport, "McConnell Urges States to Help Thwart Obama's 'War on Coal,'" *New York Times*, March 19, 2015, accessed February 20, 2017, https://www.nytimes.com/2015/03/20/us/politics/mitch-mcconnell-urges-states-to-help-thwart-obamas-war-on-coal.html?_r=0.

230. Brandon Smith, "Indiana Joins Lawsuit Against EPA's Clean Power Plan," *Indiana Public Media*, October 23, 2015, accessed February 23, 2017, http://indianapublicmedia.org/news/indiana-joins-lawsuit-epas-clean-power-plan-88849/.

231. Dominique Mosbergen, "Scott Pruitt Has Sued the Environmental Protection Agency 13 Times. Now He Wants to Lead It," *Huffington Post*, January 17, 2017, accessed February 23, 2017, http://www.huffingtonpost.com/entry/scott-pruitt-environmental-protection-agency_us_5878ad15e4b0b3c7a7b0c29c.

232. Among the many sources of Donald Trump quotes on global warming is *Snopes*, accessed November 28, 2016, http://www.snopes.com/donald-trump-global-warming-hoax/.

233. Caldwell, "Charles Koch Explains to Donors Why He Won't Support Trump."

234. Caldwell, "Charles Koch Explains to Donors Why He Won't Support Trump."

235. Mayer, *Dark Money*, pp. xvi, xvii.

236. Gaurav Sharma, "Making American 'Crude' Again: U.S. Oil and Gas Industry Feels the Trump Effect."

237. Victoria Hermann, "I Am an Arctic Researcher. Donald Trump Is Deleting My Citations," *TheGuardian.com*, March 28, 2017, accessed March 28, 2017, https://www.theguardian.com/commentisfree/2017/mar/28/arctic-researcher-donald-trump-deleting-my-citations.

238. Robinson Meyer, "As the Planet Warms, Trump's EPC Pick Hedges," *The Atlantic*, January 19, 2017, accessed February 7, 2017, https://www.theatlantic.com/science/archive/2017/01/as-the-planet-warms-senators-shrug/513746/.

239. Tom DiChristopher, "Scott Pruitt Is Great Pick to Lead EPA, Says Pruitt-Ally Harold Hamm," *CNBC News*, December 8, 2016, accessed February 24, 2017, http://www.cnbc.com/2016/12/08/scott-pruitt-is-great-pick-to-lead-epa-says-pruitt-ally-harold-hamm.html.

240. Philip Elliott, "Why the Koch Brothers Are Worried about President Trump," *Time*, January 30, 2017, accessed February 20, 2017, http://time.com/4654523/donald-trump-koch-brothers-worries/.

241. Drew Doggett, "Following the Money behind Mike Pence," The Sunlight Foundation, July 25, 2016, accessed February 20, 2017, https://sunlightfoundation.com/2016/07/25/following-the-money-behind-mike-pence/.

242. Mayer, *Dark Money*, p. xviii.

243. Mayer, *Dark Money*, p. xv.

244. Mayer, *Dark Money*, p. xiv.

245. Damian Carrington, "Green Movement 'Greatest Threat to Freedom,' Says Trump Adviser," *The Guardian*, January 30, 2017, accessed February 20, 2017, https://www.theguardian.com/environment/2017/jan/30/green-movement-greatest-threat-freedom-says-trump-adviser-myron-ebell.

246. Amber Jamieson and Adam Vaughan, "Keystone XL: Trump Issues Permit to Begin Construction of Pipeline," *The Guardian*, March 24, 2017, accessed March 24, 2017, https://www.theguardian.com/environment/2017/mar/24/keystone-xl-pipeline-permit-trump-administration.

247. Evan Lehman and Emily Holden, "Trump Budget Cuts Funds for EPA by 31 Percent," *Scientific American*, March 16, 2017, accessed March 24, 2017, https://www.scientificamerican.com/article/trump-budget-cuts-funds-for-epa-by-31-percent/.

248. Shawn McCarthy and Greg Keenan, "Trump Targets Fuel-Efficiency Standards," *Globe and Mail*, March 16, 2017, A1.

249. Dominic Rushe, "Top Coal Boss Robert Murray: Trump Can't Bring Mining Jobs Back," *The Guardian*, March 27, 2017, accessed March 27, 2017, https://www.theguardian.com/environment/2017/mar/27/us-coal-industry-clean-power-plan-donald-trump.

250. In her book *Understanding Institutional Diversity* (Princeton, NJ: Princeton University Press, 2009), Elinor Ostrom provides a definition of the full concept of institution that is representative of the general literature on institutions: "Broadly defined, institutions are the prescriptions that humans use to organize all forms of repetitive and structured interactions including those within families, neighborhoods, markets, firms, sports leagues, churches, private associations, and governments at all scales. Individuals interacting within rule-structured situations face choices regarding the actions and strategies they take, leading to consequences for themselves and for others" (p. 3). I use a specific subset of institution in this book, formal organizations that have important roles in the democratic function of society, and I only look at a handful of these, mostly political parties, government departments, regulators, universities, and courts.

251. *Department of Natural Resources Act* (1994), S.C., c. 41, Section 6, subsections (a), (e), and (h).

252. *Department of Environment Act* (1985), R.S.C., c. 14 (2nd Supp.), Section 4(1), subsection (a).

253. Samuel P. Huntington, *Political Order in Changing Societies* (New Haven, CT: Yale University Press, 1968), p. 20.

254. Valerie Bunce, "Comparative Democratization: Big and Bounded Generalizations," *Comparative Political Studies* 33 (August/Sept 2000), 714.

255. David Held, *Models of Democracy*, 3rd ed. (Stanford, CA: Standford University Press, 2006), p. 263.

256. Held, *Models of Democracy*, p. 261.

257. This is adapted from Daniel Carpenter and David Moss, "Introduction," in Daniel Carpenter and David Moss (eds.), *Preventing Regulatory Capture: Special Interest Influence and How to Limit It*, (New York: Cambridge University Press, 2014), p. 13.

258. *ICC v. Chicago, R.I. & Pac. Ry. Co.*, 218 U.S. 88, 103 (1910), cited in Samuel P. Huntington, "The Marasmus of the ICC: The Commission, the Railroads, and the Public Interest," *Yale Law Journal* 61, no. 4 (April 1952), 467–509, p. 509.

259. Mark Philp, "Corruption and State Capture: An Analytical Framework," Department of Politics and International Relations, University of Oxford, 2001, accessed August 25, 2016, http://siteresources.worldbank.org/INTWBIGOVANTCOR Resources/1740479-1149112210081/2604389-1149265288691/2612469-1149265301559/prague_corrupt_capture.pdf.

260. See Philp, "Corruption and State Capture," p. 2: "Regulatory capture is not necessarily illegal, nor it is necessarily corrupt. It is corrupt only where the regulators and/or those who pass the regulation they enact, serve the interests of the industry (C) because of a bribe, inducement or threat. Such cases need to be demarcated sharply from those in which there is a process of interest representation in the design of legislation."

261. Correspondence from Mary Dawson, Conflict of Interest and Ethics Commissioner, to Bruce Carson, Senior Legislative Adviser to the Prime Minister of Canada, July 9, 2008. Tabled in court as evidence in Carson's trial.

262. Auditor-General of Alberta, *Annual Report of the Auditor General of Alberta, 2006–2007* (Edmonton: Queen's Printer of Alberta), p. 91.

263. Government of Alberta, "Budget 2011, Building a Better Alberta," February 4, 2011, accessed May 11, 2017, http://www.finance.alberta.ca/publications/budget/budget2011/energy.pdf, p. 54.

264. Daniel Carpenter and David Moss (eds.), *Preventing Regulatory Capture: Special Interest Influence and How to Limit It* (New York: Cambridge University Press, 2014), p. 18. In the Carpenter and Moss volume, see also James Kwak, "Cultural Capture and the Financial Crisis," pp. 71–98.

265. Jeffrey Jones, "'Our pipeline': Notley's Elusive Holy Grail," *Globe and Mail*, May 31, 2017, p. B1.

266. Adapted from Daniel Carpenter, "Detecting and Measuring Capture," in Daniel Carpenter and David Moss (eds.), *Preventing Regulatory Capture: Special Interest Influence and How to Limit It* (New York: Cambridge University Press, 2014), pp. 57–68.

267. Carpenter, "Detecting and Measuring Capture," p. 62.

268. Environment and Climate Change Canada, "Greenhouse Gas Emissions," https://www.ec.gc.ca/indicateurs-indicators/default.asp?lang=en&n=FBF8455E-1.

269. Environment and Climate Change Canada, "Greenhouse Gas Emissions by Province and Territory," https://www.ec.gc.ca/indicateurs-indicators/default.asp?lang=en&n=18F3BB9C-1.

270. Canadian Judicial Council, *Ethical Principles for Judges*, p. 4, accessed May 25, 2016, https://www.cjc-ccm.gc.ca/cmslib/general/news_pub_judicialconduct_Principles_1998_en.pdf.

271. Mehta Soyler, *The Turkish Deep State: State Consolidation, Civil-Military Relations and Democracy* (New York: Routledge, 2014). See also Patrick H. O'Neil, *The Deep State: An Emerging Concept in Comparative Politics*, Department of Politics and Government, University of Puget Sound, January 2015; Dexter Filkins, "The Deep State," The New Yorker, March 12, 2012; and Peter Dale Scott, *The U.S. Deep State: Wall Street, Big Oil, and the Attack on U.S. Democracy* (Lanham, MD: Rowman and Littlefield, 2014).

272. Philip, "Corruption and State Capture: An Analytical Framework."

273. Franz Wild, "Gupta's Grip: State Captive to Networks of Patronage," *Mail & Guardian*, December 17, 2015, accessed November 1, 2016, http://mg.co.za/article/2015-12-17-guptas-grip-state-captive-to-networks-of-patronage. See also "Wheels Coming off Zuma's South Africa, Says Nelson Mandela Foundation," *Associated Press*, November 1, 2016, accessed November 1, 2016, https://www.theguardian.com/world/2016/nov/01/nelson-mandela-foundation-jacob-zuma-south-africa.

274. George Monbiot, *Captive State: The Corporate Takeover of Britain* (London: Pan Books/Macmillan, 2000), pp. 4, 5, 11.

275. Scott, *The American Deep State*, p. 13.

276. Janine R. Wedel, *Unaccountable: How Elite Power Brokers Corrupt Our Finances, Freedom, and Security* (New York: Pegasus Books, 2014).

277. Mike Lofgren, *The Deep State: The Fall of the Constitution and the Rise of a Shadow Government* (New York: Viking, 2016), p. 4.

278. *R. v. Carson*, 2016, p. 11.

279. For instance, in April 2016, the world's largest oil company, Saudi Aramco, owned by the Saudi government, was valued at just over $2 trillion US, more than three times the value of the world's largest publicly traded company, Apple Computers. *Globe and Mail Report on Business*, April 26, 2016, p. B1.

280. For an early example see Gobind Nakani, "Development Problems of Mineral Countries," World Bank, August 1979.

281. J.D. Murray, "Is There a Commodity Curse?" in David Ryan (ed.), *Boom and Bust Again* (Edmonton: University of Alberta Press, 2013).

282. Dylan Moeller, "Canada's Trade Performance," CRD Working Paper, August 1, 2012 (Ottawa: Export Development Canada).

283. "A Capital Opportunity: A Global Market for Mining Companies" and "A Capital Opportunity: A Global Market for Oil & Gas Companies," Toronto Stock Exchange, 2015, accessed June 11, 2016, http://www.tsx.com/resource/en/193 and http://www.tsx.com/resource/en/194.

284. Toby Schneider, "Alberta GDP Attributable to Oil & Gas Activity (Direct & Indirect) by Industry (2011)," slide from *Alberta: The Road to a Strong and Diversified Economy*. Presentation for FMI, February 9, 2017, Edmonton. Alberta Ministry of Economic Development and Trade.

285. Pascal Tremblay, "Alberta's Merchandise Trade with the World," Library of Parliament Research Publications, 2013, accessed May 6, 2014, http://www.parl.gc.ca/Content/LOP/ResearchPublications/2013-32-e.htm.

286. Stuart Landon and Constance Smith, "Government Revenue Volatility in Alberta," in David Ryan (ed.), *Boom and Bust Again* (Edmonton: University of Alberta Press, 2013). The calculation of this percentage excludes the value of federal government transfers to the Alberta government.

287. Adapted from Terry Lynn Karl, *The Paradox of Plenty: Oil Booms and Petro-States* (Berkeley, CA: University of California Press), p. 17.

288. A Caterpillar model 797B mining dump truck costs $5 million; Syncrude operates a fleet of ninety of these at its oil sands mine near Fort McMurray, Alberta.

289. Karl, *The Paradox of Plenty*, pp. 3–22.

290. National Commission on the BP Deepwater Horizon Oil Spill and Offshore Drilling, *Deep Water: The Gulf Oil Disaster and the Future of Offshore Drilling*. See, in particular, Chapter Three.

291. National Commission, *Deep Water*, p. 56.

292. National Commission, *Deep Water*, p. 64.

293. Nancy Birdsall and Arvind Subramaniam, "Saving Iraq from Its Oil," *Foreign Affairs*, July/August 2004, accessed June 7, 2016, https://www.foreignaffairs.com/articles/iraq/2004-07-01/saving-iraq-its-oil.

294. Karl, *The Paradox of Plenty*, Chapter 2.

295. Johannes Alvarez and James Fiorito, "Venezuelan Oil Unifying Latin-America," Ethics of Development in a Global Environment, Stanford University, June 2, 2005.

296. Karl, *The Paradox of Plenty*, Part Two, Chapters 4–8.

297. Karl, *The Paradox of Plenty*, p. 7.

298. Karl, *The Paradox of Plenty*, p. 44, italics in original.

299. Karl, *The Paradox of Plenty*, p. 239.

300. An important source for information on the history of Alberta's petroleum industry is Alberta Culture and Tourism, "Alberta's Energy Resources Heritage," accessed June 1, 2016, http://history.alberta.ca/energyheritage/.

301. Albertasource.ca, "Canadian Royalite," accessed June 18, 2016, http://wayback.archive-it.org/2217/20101208163042/http:/www.albertasource.ca/petroleum/industry/companies_canadian_royalite.html.

302. Alberta's Energy Heritage, "Royalite No. 4 Era: 1924–1936," Alberta Culture and Tourism, accessed November 29, 2016, http://history.alberta.ca/energyheritage/oil/the-waterton-and-the-turner-valley-eras-1890s-1946/turner-valley-period-1914-1946/royalite-era-1924-1936/default.aspx.

303. Biographical information on James Lougheed comes primarily from *Dictionary of Canadian Biography*, University of Toronto, http://www.biographi.ca/en/index.php; and Donald B. Smith, *Calgary's Grand Story* (Calgary: University of Calgary Press, 2005).

304. Smith, *Calgary's Grand Story*, p. 182-183.

305. Allan Hustak, *Peter Lougheed: A Biography* (Toronto: McClelland & Stewart, 1979), p. 15.

306. Lougheed House, accessed June 16, 2016, http://www.lougheedhouse.com/house-history/.

307. Hustak, *Peter Lougheed*, p. 10.

308. John Richards and Larry Pratt. *Prairie Capitalism: Power and Influence in the New West* (Toronto: McClelland and Stewart, 1979), p. 152.

309. Smith, *Calgary's Grand Story*, p. 42.

310. For the basic biographic details of Belle Lougheed's early life, see *The Free Library*, "Isabella Clarke Hardisty Lougheed: First Lady of the North-West," accessed March 10, 2017, https://www.thefreelibrary.com/Isabella+Clarke+Hardisty+Lougheed%3A+First+Lady+of+the+North-West.-a0424620187.

311. General historic information on HBC is primarily from *The Canadian Encyclopedia*, Vol. II (Edmonton: Hurtig Publishers, 1985); and Peter C. Newman, *Company of Adventurers*, Vol. I. (Markham, ON: Viking/Penguin Books, 1985).

312. Richard Hardisty's wife was Eliza McDougall, daughter of Methodist missionary George McDougall, who played a prominent role in the settlement of Alberta.

313. This is stated in the entry for James Lougheed in the *Dictionary of Canadian Biography*.

314. The biographical details on Donald Smith are taken largely from the *Dictionary of Canadian Biography* and the print edition of the *Canadian Encyclopedia*.

315. Merrill Dennison, *Canada's First Bank: A History of the Bank of Montreal*, Vol. Two (Toronto: McClelland & Stewart, 1967).

316. Hustak, *Peter Lougheed*, pp. 9–10.

317. There is an extensive collection of readily available biographic material on Peter Lougheed. A very good source for his early years is Hustak, *Peter Lougheed*.

318. David G. Wood, *The Lougheed Legacy* (Toronto: Key Porter Books, 1985), p. 138.

319. Hustak, *Peter Lougheed*, p. 145.

320. Wood, *The Lougheed Legacy*, pp. 147, 157.

321. Glenbow Museum, Calgary, "Oil Sands Oral History Project," interview with

Peter Lougheed, April 13, 2011, p. 2, http://www.glenbow.org/collections/search/findingAids/archhtm/extras/oilsands/Lougheed_Peter.pdf.

322. The original brick power plant building still stands, now in the centre of the campus and converted to a student bar and lounge in 1978.

323. Alberta Culture and Tourism, "Oil Sands: Alberta's Energy Heritage — Karl Clark," accessed November 15, 2016, http://www.history.alberta.ca/energyheritage/sands/unlocking-the-potential/the-scientific-and-industrial-research-council-of-alberta/karl-clark.aspx. Also see Adriana Davies, "Petroleum History Society," accessed November 21, 2016, http://www.petroleumhistory.ca/oralhistory/OilSandsFondsUofA_Archives.pdf.

324. InnoTech Alberta, "Alberta Research Council," accessed November 15, 2016, http://www.albertatechfutures.ca/corporate/history/albertaresearchcouncil.aspx. Also see Oil Sands Discovery Centre, "Facts about Alberta's Oil Sands and Its Industry," http://history.alberta.ca/oilsands/docs/facts_sheets09.pdf, p. 11, accessed November 15, 2016.

325. Among the many sources on the history of oil sands development, see the National Task Force on Oil Sands Strategies of the Alberta Chamber of Resources, "The Oil Sands: A New Energy Vision for Canada," 1995, for a good summary of the early years. In addition, see the Alberta government's Tourism and Culture "Energy Heritage" website (http://www.history.alberta.ca/energyheritage/sands/default.aspx).

326. For an extensive discussion of market regulation in the 1960s and 1970s, see Alan J. MacFadyen and G. Campbell Watkins, *Petropolitics: Petroleum Development, Markets, and Regulations: Alberta as an Illustrative History* (Calgary: University of Calgary Press, 2014). Chapter Six is especially relevant.

327. For a more detailed discussion, see MacFadyen and Campbell Watkins, *Petropolitics*, pp. 309-316.

328. For a general overview of the "energy wars" the Alberta government faced in the 1970s and 1980s, see Chapter Eight of Wood, *The Lougheed Legacy*. For a much deeper analysis of the economic aspects of the energy wars, see MacFadyen and Campbell Watkins, *Petropolitics*.

329. Lougheed explained this approach in an interview with *Policy Options*, "Sounding an Alarm for Alberta," September 1, 2006, accessed May 23, 2017, http ://policyoptions.irpp.org/magazines/the-fiscal-imbalance/sounding-an-alarm-for-alberta-interview/.

330. CAPP, "Canadian Crude Oil Production 1971–2009," accessed December 5, 2016, http://statshbnew.capp.ca/SHB/Sheet.asp?SectionID=3&SheetID=76.

331. Wood, The Lougheed Legacy, pp. 114-115.

332. Hustak, Peter Lougheed, p. 178.

333. Macrotrends, "Crude Oil Prices — 70 Year Historical Chart," accessed March 8, 2017, http://www.macrotrends.net/1369/crude-oil-price-history-chart. Prices are for West Texas Intermediate oil.

334. Statistics Canada, "Unemployment Rates in Alberta and Canada," accessed March 8, 2017, http://www.statcan.gc.ca/daily-quotidien/160205/cg-a003-eng.htm.

335. Ratehub, "5 year Mortgage Rate History, 1973–Today," accessed March 8, 2017, https://www.ratehub.ca/5-year-fixed-mortgage-rate-history.

336. Alvin Finkel (ed.), *Working People in Alberta: A History* (Edmonton: Athabasca University Press, 2012), pp. 192-193.

337. "Zeidler Recalls City Workers after Bitter 5-Year Strike," *Edmonton Journal*, May 28, 1993, B1.

338. Alberta Federation of Labour, "United They Fell: The Gainers Meatpacking Strike 25 Years Later," June 13, 2011, accessed March 9, 2017, http://www.afl.org/united_they_ fell_the_gainers_meatpacking_strike_25_years_later.

339. Alan Boras, "Province Sells off Syncrude," *Calgary Herald*, October 11, 1995, A1.

340. The ministers were Patricia Black/Nelson, Jim Dinning, Mel Knight, Shirley McClellan, Greg Melchin, Rick Orman, and Murray Smith. At different times, Patricia Black/ Nelson served as both minister of energy and of finance.

341. Gordon Laird, "Oil in Government: Unresolved Ethical Issues Haunt Provincial Tories," *Parkland Post* (Winter 2000), accessed December 18, 2006, http://www. ualberta.ca/-parkland/post/Vol-IV-No1/09laird.html.

342. "An Update on the Economy of the Calgary-Edmonton Corridor: More Action Needed for the Tiger to Roar," Topic Paper, TD Economics of TD Bank Financial Group, October 3, 2005, pp. 2–3.

343. "The Tiger That Roared across Alberta," Special Report, TD Economics of TD Bank Financial Group, September 27, 2007, pp. i, 2.

344. See Kevin Taft, Mel McMillan, and Junaid Jahangir, *Follow the Money* (Calgary: Detselig Enterprises, 2012).

345. PennWest Exploration, "Notice of 2012 Annual and Special Meeting and Management Proxy Circular," p. 28.

346. Baytex Energy Corp., "Notice of Annual and Special Meeting of Shareholders to Be Held on Thursday, May 15, 2014," pp. 7, 14.

347. Energy Efficiency Branch, Alberta Department of Energy, *A Discussion Paper on the Potential for Reducing CO2 Emissions in Alberta, 1988–2005: Executive Summary*, September 1990. Alberta Legislature Library Sessional Paper 547/2002.

348. Shortened versions of the quote are widely available on media websites. The full quote, according to Wikipedia, is, "You know, my science is limited to the fact that I know that eons ago there was an ice age. I know that for sure. I know that at one time, the Arctic was the tropics. And I guess I wonder what caused that? Was it dinosaur farts? I don't know."

349. Employment and Social Development Canada, *Indicators of Well-being in Canada, Environment — Greenhouse Gases*, accessed March 23, 2015, http://www4.hrsdc. gc.ca/.3ndic.1t.4r@-eng.jsp?iid=64#M_4.

350. Government of Canada, "A Climate Change Plan for the Purposes of the Kyoto Protocol Implementation Act," accessed November 24, 2016, http://www.climatechange.gc.ca/ default.asp?lang=En&n=4D57AF05-1.

351. PEI, Nova Scotia, New Brunswick, Quebec, and Ontario met or surpassed the Kyoto goals, while Manitoba and Newfoundland/Labrador had modest increases, according to Environment Canada, "National Inventory Report 1990–2014: Greenhouse Gas Sources and Sinks in Canada — Executive Summary, Section ES-5, Table S-4," accessed November 2016, https://ec.gc.ca/ges-ghg/default.asp?lang=En&n=662F9C56-1#es-5.

352. CAPP, "Industry across Canada," accessed November 21, 2016, http://www.capp.ca/ canadian-oil-and-natural-gas/industry-across-canada.

353. Environment Canada, "National Inventory Report 1990–2014: Greenhouse Gas Sources and Sinks in Canada — Executive Summary."

354. Glenbow Museum, Calgary, "Oil Sands Oral History Project," interview with Patricia Nelson, http://www.glenbow.org/collections/search/findingAids/archhtm/oilsands.cfm, pp. 2, 6.

355. Most biographical material on Patricia Black/Nelson is drawn from Glenbow Museum's interview with her, as part of their "Oil Sands Oral History Project."

356. Glenbow Museum, interview with Patricia Nelson, p. 12.

357. The dates were derived from Wikipedia, "List of Alberta Provincial Ministers," https://en.wikipedia.org/wiki/List_of_Alberta_provincial_ministers#Minister_of_Energy.

358. J. David Hughes, "Oil Sands Growth 1984–2011," *The Tyee*, January 12, 2012, accessed November 16, 2016, http://thetyee.ca/News/2012/01/12/2011-Oil-Sands-HUGHES.pdf.

359. Glenbow Museum, Calgary, "Oil Sands Oral History Project," interview with Eric Newell, former CEO of Syncrude, http://www.glenbow.org/collections/search/findingAids/archhtm/oilsands.cfm.

360. BP, *BP Statistical Review of World Energy*, June 2002, p. 6, accessed December 6, 2016, http://www.griequity.com/resources/industryandissues/Energy/bp2002statisticalreview.pdf.

361. See Lieutenant-Governor of Alberta, "Anne McLellan," https://www.lieutenantgovernor.ab.ca/Aoe/community-service/anne-mclellan/index.html. Also see Glenbow Museum, Calgary, "Oil Sands Oral History Project," interview with Anne McLellan, http://www.glenbow.org/collections/search/findingAids/archhtm/extras/oilsands/McLellan_Anne.pdf.

362. The task force was formed in 1991, but wasn't active until 1993. See Glenbow Museum, interview with Eric Newell, former CEO of Syncrude, p. 18.

363. The organizational structure and membership of the task force is presented in detail on pp. 50 and 51 of the task force's final report, "The Oil Sands: A New Energy Vision for Canada," published by the Alberta Chamber of Resources in 1995. Accessed November 22, 2016, http://www.acr-alberta.com/Portals/0/projects/PDFs/The%20Oil%20Sands%20A%20New%20Energy%20Vision%20for%20Canada.pdf?ver=2015-07-15-164525-940.

364. Glenbow Museum, Calgary, "Oral History of the Oil Sands Project," interview of Paul Precht, transcript lines 359–62, accessed December 6, 2016, http://www.glenbow.org/collections/search/findingAids/archhtm/extras/oilsands/Precht_Paul.pdf.

365. For detailed accounts of the political efforts of the National Oil Sands Task Force, see the interview transcripts available at the Oil Sands Oral History Project of the Glenbow Museum, including, for example, those of Eric Newell, former CEO of Syncrude, and Anne McLellan, former minister of Natural Resources Canada, http://www.glenbow.org/collections/search/findingAids/archhtm/oilsands.cfm.

366. Glenbow Museum, interview with Anne McLellan.

367. An analysis of donations to the Alberta PC Party conducted by *Alberta Political Scan* shows that of fourteen donors that gave $25,000 or more in total from 1993 to 1995, seven were petroleum companies. *Alberta Political Scan*, Issue 132 (April 12, 1996).

368. See p. 27 of the National Oil Sands Task Force final report.

369. I've had personal acquaintance with a number of task force members, and I know from direct conversation that at least one of them bluntly rejected the role of CO_2 in atmospheric warming.

370. Glenbow Museum, Calgary, "Oil Sands Oral History Project," interview with Howard Dingle, p. 18, http://www.glenbow.org/collections/search/findingAids/archhtm/extras/oilsands/Dingle_Howard.pdf.

371. Glenbow Museum, interview with Howard Dingle, p. 13.

372. Glenbow Museum, interview with Patricia Nelson, p. 12.

373. See *Market Wired,* "Anne McLellan Joins Nexen's Board of Directors," http://www.marketwired.com/press-release/anne-mclellan-joins-nexens-board-of-directors-tsx-nxy-602477.htm.

374. Transcription of tapes of presentation by Alberta Energy Minister Murray Smith to the Austin Annual Meeting General Session, October 16, 2006, Austin, Texas. In author's possession.

375. Alberta Chamber of Resources, "The Oil Sands: A New Energy Vision for Canada," p. 5.

376. "Alberta Energy Facts and Statistics," accessed November 24, 2016, http://www.energy.alberta.ca/Oilsands/791.asp. Also see Pembina Institute, "Oil Sands Fever," November 2005, accessed November 24, 2016, https://www.pembina.org/reports/OilSands72.pdf.

377. Canadian Energy Research Institute, "Canadian Oil Sands Supply Costs and Development Projects," August 2015, p. 30, accessed November 24, 2016, http://resources.ceri.ca/PDF/Pubs/Studies/Study_152_Full_Report.pdf.

378. "Alberta Energy Facts and Statistics."

379. The largest construction project in Toronto in 2012 was the Eglinton Crosstown transit line, with an average expenditure of $510 million a year for ten years. "Eglinton Crosstown FAQs," accessed November 24, 2016, http://thecrosstown.ca/the-project.

380. Bob Weber, "Pressure Builds for Pause in Oil Sands Development," *Toronto Star,* January 2, 2007, accessed March 12, 2017, https://www.thestar.com/business/2007/01/02/pressure_builds_for_pause_in_oilsands_development.html. Also see Charles Frank, "Oilsands Party Hits a Bump," *Calgary Herald,* September 30, 2006, accessed March 12, 2017, https://www.pressreader.com/canada/calgary-herald/20060930/282428459674415.

381. Brent Wittmaer, "Life in a Northern Work Camp: Huge 'Shadow Population' of Oil Workers Flies in, Flies out," *Edmonton Journal,* January 7, 2014, accessed November 24, 2016, http://www.edmontonjournal.com/business/Life+northern+work+camp+Huge+shadow+population+workers+flies+flies/9219752/story.html.

382. Among the many sources on this, see, for example, Statistics Canada, "Exports of Goods on a Balance-of-Payments Basis, by Product," http://www.statcan.gc.ca/tables-tableaux/sum-som/l01/cst01/gblec04-eng.htm; and Patrick Cain, "Link between Canadian Dollar and Oil Prices Coming Undone," *Global News Online,* August 17, 2016, http://globalnews.ca/news/2885196/link-between-canadian-dollar-and-oil-prices-coming-undone/. For the correlation between the price of oil and the value of the Canadian dollar, see David Rosenberg, "A Stronger Loonie Ahead," *Canadian Business,* accessed November 25, 2016, http://www.canadianbusiness.com/economy/canadas-50-most-important-economic-charts-for-2016/.

383. Alberta Energy, "Alberta Resource Revenues: Historical and Budget," accessed November 25, 2016, http://www.energy.alberta.ca/About_Us/2564.asp.

384. Alberta Energy Regulator (AER), "Oil Sands Bitumen Upgrading (2009–2015)," accessed November 25, 2016, http://www.energy.alberta.ca/About_Us/1701.asp.

385. Macrotrends, "Crude Oil Price History Chart," http://www.macrotrends.net/1369/crude-oil-price-history-chart.

386. CAPP, "Capital Investment in Canada Oil and Gas Industry down 62 Per Cent in 2 Years," http://www.capp.ca/media/news-releases/capital-investment-in-canada-oil-and-gas-industry-down-62-per-cent-in-2-years.

387. Melissa Gilligan, "Calgary Unemployment Rate Remains Highest in Canada," *Global News,* http://globalnews.ca/news/2930267/calgary-unemployment-rate-remains-highest-in-canada/.

388. Robson Fletcher, "Calgary Office Vacancy Nears 25%, says Re/Max," *CBC News*, September 28, 2016, http://www.cbc.ca/news/canada/calgary/calgary-office-vacancy-25-percent-july-remax-1.3781916.

389. Gillian Steward, "Shelve Constitution, Solve Big Problems; Out of the West," *Edmonton Journal*, January 2, 1992, A11.

390. Anthony Johnson and Alan Boras, "Klein Stands Firm on 'Carbon' Threat," *Calgary Herald*, May 21, 1994, p A1.

391. Allyson Jeffs, "Legal Challenge on Emissions Pondered," *Edmonton Journal*, December 4, 1997, A6; and Larry Johnsrude, "Alta. to Fight Greenhouse Gas Targets; We Were Betrayed by Ottawa —West," *Edmonton Journal*, December 2, 1997, A1.

392. "Sounding an Alarm for Alberta," *Policy Options*, September 1, 2006. Also see Glenbow Museum, interview with Peter Lougheed, pp. 5–7.

393. Glenbow Museum, Calgary, "Oil Sands Oral History Project," interview with Allan Warrack, accessed December 7, 2016, http://www.glenbow.org/collections/search/findingAids/archhtm/extras/oilsands/Warrack_Allan.pdf.

394. "Sounding an Alarm for Alberta," *Policy Options*, September 1, 2006.

395. Claudia Cattaneo. "Canadianization Of Oilsands Has Aligned Interests: Suncor CEO," *Edmonton Journal*, April 28, 2017, B3.

396. Glenbow Museum, interview of Paul Precht, transcript lines 337-343.

397. "Canada Southern Petroleum Ltd. Elects Mr. Myron Kanik a Director," *PR News Wire*, April 30, 2002, accessed March 9, 2017, http://www.prnewswire.com/news-releases/canada-southern-petroleum-ltd-elects-mr-myron-kanik-a-director-77185972.html.

398. Wilson Center Canada Institute, "David Manning Bio," accessed March 9, 2017, https://www.wilsoncenter.org/person/david-manning.

399. Canada School of Energy and Environment, "Canada School of Energy and Environment Appoints Interim Executive Director," April 21, 2011, accessed March 12, 2017, http://www.newswire.ca/news-releases/canada-school-of-energy-and-environment-appoints-interim-executive-director-508077681.html.

400. Sheila Pratt, "Peter's Principles," *Alberta Views*, March 2007, p. 30.

401. All figures from *Alberta Political Scan*, October 26, 2012, p. 6. Analysis based on statements filed with the chief electoral officer of Alberta, Alberta Legislature Library. See also Elections Alberta's "final reports" at http://efpublic.elections.ab.ca/efParty.cfm?MID=FP_8&PID=8.

402. The Harper government banned political contributions from corporations and unions to all federal parties and candidates in 2007, a move duplicated by the NDP government in Alberta in 2015. Before that, Alberta allowed personal, corporate, and union donations up to $15,000 per year, and double that in election years. While these donations were publicly reported, it can be difficult to know the full picture.

403. Elections Alberta Campaign 2012, effective date March 26, 2012–June 23, 2012. Elections Alberta, "Contributions Data," accessed November 1, 2016, http://efpublic.elections.ab.ca/efCXDataExtract.cfm?MID=CX_DATA.

404. "Oil Patch Loaded with Lame Duck CEOs," *Calgary Herald*, April 3, 2012, accessed November 1, 2016, http://calgaryherald.com/business/energy/oilpatch-loaded-with-lame-duck-ceos.

405. Cassie Doyle to Kevin Stringer and Sue Kirby, subject "FW: Calgary Meetings," June 15, 2009, 10:56 am, document released under the *Access to Information Act* to Greenpeace,

https://docs.google.com/file/d/0B_0MqnZ4wmcMMjE4QlV1MEhXLUU/edit?pli=1.

406. *Insight Into Government* 26, no. 29 (March 30, 2012), in the collection of Alberta Legislature Library.

407. Fukuyama, *Political Order and Political Decay*, p. 478.

408. A copy of the letter is in the author's possession.

409. Darcy Henton, "Alta. Wildrose Leader Has Doubts about Science on Climate Change," *Calgary Herald*, April 15, 2012, accessed May 7, 2016, http://www.calgaryherald.com/health/alta+wildrose+leader+doubts+about+science+climate+change/6468221/story.html.

410. One indication of this subversion was an infamous series of emails attacking Stelmach, sent in September 2009 by Hal Walker, a prominent PC Party organizer. Walker deliberately showed the vast list of people to whom he sent the emails, including ministers in Stelmach's cabinet, reporters, PC Party organizers, and oil industry leaders. Emails in author's possession.

411. Darren Campbell, "Alison Redford's Energy Outlook Could Be a Game-Changer," *Alberta Oil*, February 1, 2012, accessed May 5, 2015, http://www.albertaoilmagazine.com/2012/02/evolutionary-road/.

412. Ira Basen. "Dan Gagnier's departure from Liberal campaign highlights murky world of Ottawa lobbying." *CBC News*, October 16, 2015, accessed May 23, 2017, http://www.cbc.ca/news/politics/canada-election-2015-gagnier-lobbying-1.3274251.

413. Alison Redford, "Keystone Is Responsible Oil Sands Development," *USA Today*, February 25, 2013.

414. Bill Graveland, "Alberta Budget: Alison Redford Says Energy Royalties Won't Change," *Canadian Press*, April 7, 2013.

415. "Alison Redford, Al Gore Discuss Oilsands — Doesn't End Well for Alberta Premier," *Canadian Press*, January 29, 2014, updated March 31, 2014.

416. Joanna Slater, "Alberta's Redford Takes Pipeline Pitch to Manhattan," *Globe and Mail*, June 19, 2013, accessed May 7, 2016, http://www.theglobeandmail.com/report-on-business/industry-news/energy-and-resources/albertas-redford-takes-pipeline-pitch-to-manhattan/article12693243/.

417. Claudia Cattaneo, "Prentice's Return to Politics May Leave behind Unfinished Northern Gateway Business," *Financial Post*, April 30, 2014, accessed May 6, 2016, http://business.financialpost.com/news/energy/jim-prentices-return-to-politics-may-leave-behind-unfinished-northern-gateway-business?__lsa=6d24-5483.

418. Susana Mas, "Enbridge Taps Jim Prentice to Rescue Northern Gateway First Nations Talks," *CBC News*, March 5, 2014.

419. Allan Maki and Carrie Tait, "Why Jim Prentice Is Unfamiliar to Average Alberta Voters," *Globe and Mail*, September 5, 2014, accessed May 6, 2016, http://www.theglobeandmail.com/news/politics/why-jim-prentice-is-unfamiliar-to-the-average-alberta-voters/article20380993/.

420. Dean Bennett, "Danielle Smith Resigns as Wildrose Leader, Joins Alberta PC Party," *Canadian Press*, December 16, 2014.

421. James Wood, "NDP Candidates Won on the Cheap against Big-Spending Tories in Alberta Election," *Calgary Herald*, September 10, 2015, accessed May 8, 2016, http://calgaryherald.com/news/politics/ndp-candidates-won-on-the-cheap-against-big-spending-tories-in-alberta-election.

422. "'Orange Is the New Blue': New NDP Candidate in Medicine Hat Riding," *Canadian Press*, April 14, 2015, accessed May 8, 2016, http://www.nationalnewswatch. com/2015/04/14/orange-is-the-new-blue-new-ndp-candidate-in-medicine-hat-riding/#.Vy-Ic6tK4_Y.

423. Government of Alberta, "Oil Sands Advisory Group," accessed March 20, 2017, https://www.alberta.ca/oilsands-advisory-group.aspx.

424. Darcy Henton, "Notley Issues Fiery Stance on Pipeline Proposition in First NDP Question Period," *Calgary Herald*, June 16, 2015, http://calgaryherald.com/news/ politics/notley-issues-fiery-stance-on-pipeline-position-in-first-ndp-question-period.

425. "Alberta's Climate Change Strategy Targets Carbon, Coal, Emissions," *CBC News*, November 22, 2015, accessed May 8, 2016, http://www.cbc.ca/news/canada/ edmonton/alberta-climate-change-newser-1.3330153.

426. Andrew Leach et al., *Climate Leadership: Report to Minister*, p. 8, November 20, 2015, accessed May 13, 2016, http://www.alberta.ca/documents/climate/climate-leadership-report-to-minister.pdf.

427. "The Leap Manifesto," accessed May 8, 2016, https://leapmanifesto.org/en/the-leap-manifesto/.

428. Julia Parrish, "Naïve, Tone-Deaf: Premier's Reaction to Leap Manifesto," *CTV News*, April 11, 2016, accessed May 8, 2016, http://edmonton.ctvnews.ca/naïve-tone-deaf-premier-s-reaction-to-leap-manifesto-1.2854855.

429. Justin Giovanetti, "Alberta Minister Calls Federal NDP's Proposed Climate Plan 'a Betrayal'," *Globe and Mail*, April 8, 2016.

430. "Leap Manifesto: Alberta NDP 'Had Nothing to Do with This Nonsense," *CBC News*, April 11, 2016, accessed May 8, 2016, https://ca.news.yahoo.com/leap-manifesto-alberta-ndp-had-114700860.html.

431. Gary Mason, "Alberta, B.C. Discuss Deal to Swap Pipeline for Electricity," *Globe and Mail*, April 20, 2016, accessed May 8, 2016, http://www.theglobeandmail.com/news/ national/alberta-bc-discuss-deal-to-swap-pipeline-for-electricity/article29702997/.

432. Yadullah Hussein. "Enbridge seeks three-year extension to revive stalled Northern Gateway project." *Financial Post*, May 6, 2016, accessed May 23, 2017,.http://business. financialpost.com/news/energy/enbridge-partners-ask-national-energy-board-for-3-year-extension-on-northern-gateway-pipeline.

433. Andrew Leach et al., *Climate Leadership: Report to Minister*, November 20, 2015, accessed May 13, 2016, http://www.alberta.ca/documents/climate/climate-leadership-report-to-minister.pdf.

434. Canada's international commitments were to reduce emissions 17 per cent below 2005 levels by 2020; 30 per cent below by 2030. See Environment Canada, *Canada's Second Biennial Report on Climate Change*, February 10, 2016, Section 3, accessed May 13, 2016, https://www.ec.gc.ca/GES-GHG/default.asp?lang=En&n=02D095CB-1.

435. Trevor Robb, "Wildrose Blog Post That Compares Carbon Tax to Ukrainian Genocide Requires Apology, NDP Cabinet Minister Says," *Edmonton Journal*, June 3, 2016, accessed June 6, 2016, http://edmontonjournal.com/news/politics/wildrose-blog-post-that-compares-carbon-tax-to-ukrainian-genocide-requires-apology-ndp-cabinet-minister-says.

436. There are many sources on Alberta's relative prosperity during the oil sands boom. One such report is "The Tiger That Roared across Alberta," Special Report, TD Economics of TD Bank Financial Group, September 27, 2007.

437. AER, "Cassie Doyle," accessed May 13, 2016, http://www.eub.gov.ab.ca/about-aer/governance/cassie-doyle.

438. AER, "What We Do," accessed May 16, 2016, http://aer.ca/about-aer/what-we-do.

439. AER, "Jim Ellis," accessed May 16, 2016, http://aer.ca/about-aer/governance/jim-ellis.

440. Government of Alberta, "Public Sector Body Salary Disclosure Table," 2016, p. 144, accessed November 1, 2016, http://www.alberta.ca/public-sector-body-compensation-disclosure-table.cfm.

441. According to public sector salary disclosures reported by the CBC in 2014, the deputy minister of Alberta cabinet in 2013 was paid $342,630. Accessed November 3, 2016, http://www.cbc.ca/news/canada/edmonton/alberta-releases-first-sunshine-list-of-government-salaries-1.2519097.

442. Carrie Tait, "Alberta's Sunshine List Offers Clear Look at Public Sector Salaries," *Globe and Mail*, June 25, 2016, accessed November 1, 2016, http://www.theglobeandmail.com/news/alberta/albertas-sunshine-list-offers-clear-look-at-public-sector-salaries/article30619479/.

443. "Summaries of the Deputy Minister Meetings with Industry and the Alberta Government on Oil Sands Outreach and Communications," March 16, 2010, accessed May 16, 2016, https://drive.google.com/file/d/0B46zsDD7Xqu3NzIxNmVhYmEtMTQ0NC00NzVkLTk0ZDgtMGJiYThmNzA1ZWQz/view?pli=1.

444. See, for example, Kai Nagata, "Will Michael Chong Become Canada's Next Conservative Leader?" *The Tyee*, http://thetyee.ca/Opinion/2016/03/05/Michael-Chong-Next-Conservative-Leader/.

445. Douglas Black, Bill Gilliland, Nick Kangles, et al., "Significant Developments in the Canadian Energy Industry – March 2006," accessed May 16, 2016, http://www.mondaq.com/canada/x/39630/Utilities/FMCs+Overview+of+Significant+Developments+in+the+Canadian+Energy+Industry+March+2006.

446. RCMP Commercial Crime Section, Ottawa, "Information to Obtain a Production Order," Police file #2012-1046508, November 21, 2013, prepared by Cst. Marie-Josee Robert, p. 22.

447. Government of Alberta, accessed May 16, 2016, http://www.alberta.ca/release.cfm?xID=36649E591A272-9F98-C659-41BDFCC1B520F8D5; and National Energy Board, "Board Members," https://www.neb-one.gc.ca/bts/whwr/rgnztnndstrctr/brdmmbr/brdmmbr-eng.html.

448. National Energy Board, "Responsibilities," accessed May 16, 2016, https://www.neb-one.gc.ca/bts/whwr/rspnsblt/index-eng.html.

449. Grant Sprague, LinkedIn profile, accessed May 16, 2016, https://ca.linkedin.com/in/grant-sprague-qc-a2057559.

450. Deborah Yedlin, "Alberta Energy Losing Key Player," *Calgary Herald*, May 3, 2016, accessed May 31, 2016, http://calgaryherald.com/business/energy/yedlin-alberta-energy-losing-key-player.

451. Bow Valley College, "Board of Governors: Member Profiles," http://bowvalleycollege.ca/about-bvc/offices-and-governance/board-of-governors/member-profiles.html.

452. FirstEnergy, accessed May 31, 2016, http://www.firstenergy.com.

453. Government of Alberta, "Climate Leadership Plan Will Protect Albertans' Health, Environment and Economy," news release, November 22, 2015, accessed May 31, 2016, http://www.alberta.ca/release.cfm?xID=38885E74F7B63-A62D-D1D2-E7BCF6A98D616C09.

454. For an excellent account of this, see Chapters Two and Three of David H. Breen's major book *Alberta's Petroleum Industry and the Conservation Board* (Edmonton: University of Alberta Press, 1993).

455. J.P. Prince, "Requiem for a Regulator," 2013. Unpublished paper.

456. Sheila Pratt, "Staff Flock to Industry-Paid Watchdog," Edmonton Journal, December 23, 2013, A3.

457. *Pembina Institute v. Alberta (Environment and Sustainable Resources Development)*, 2013 ABQB 567.

458. *Pembina Institute v. Alberta (Environment and Sustainable Resources Development)*, 2013.

459. Pachauri, Meyer, et al. (eds.), *Climate Change 2014 Synthesis Report*, p. 75.

460. World Health Organization, "Climate Change and Health," Fact Sheet No. 266, updated September 2015, accessed May 25, 2016, http://www.who.int/mediacentre/factsheets/fs266/en/.

461. World Health Organization, "Climate and Health Country Profiles — 2015: A Global Overview," p. 9, accessed May 25, 2016, http://www.who.int/globalchange/resources/country-profiles/climatechange_global_overview.pdf.

462. James Wood, "Health Officials Call for Kyoto Ratification," *Medicine Hat News*, September 26, 2002; Kelly Cryderman, "Accord Good for Health, Says Expert," *Calgary Herald*, September 26, 2002, p. 18.

463. "Alberta Liberals Wonder If Health Officer Let Go over Kyoto; Tories Say No," *Moose Jaw Times Herald*, October 4, 2002, p. 18.

464. Full disclosure: I was an Opposition member of the legislature at this time and was one of the first to speak with Dr. Swann about the situation. Some examples of the media coverage of the case are available at http://injusticebusters.org/index.htm/Swann_David.htm.

465. Deborah Yedlin, "CAPP Chose Wrong Tactic on Kyoto," *Globe and Mail*, November 29, 2002, accessed May 16, 2016, http://www.theglobeandmail.com/report-on-business/capp-chose-wrong-tactic-on-kyoto/article1337153/.

466. "Canada Takes Fight over Kyoto Treaty to Russia," *Associated Press*, October 1, 2003, accessed May 19, 2016, http://en.ccchina.gov.cn/Detail.aspx?newsId=34165&TId=97.

467. "Alberta Launches Campaign against Kyoto," *CBC News*, September 18, 2002, accessed May 19, 2016, http://www.cbc.ca/news/canada/alberta-launches-campaign-against-kyoto-1.349305.

468. Steven Chase, "Albertans Support Kyoto Accord, Poll Says," *Globe and Mail*, May 31, 2002, accessed November 3, 2016, http://www.theglobeandmail.com/news/national/albertans-support-kyoto-accord-poll-says/article4135778/.

469. Ipsos Reid, "Canadian's Stance on the Kyoto Accord," *The Public Policy Landscape* Vol 17, no. 4 (November-December 2002), accessed November 3, 2016, http://www.ipsos.ca/common/dl/pdf/tr/publicpolicylandscape1102.pdf.

470. Richard Schneider, "Alberta's Natural Subregions Under a Changing Climate: Past, Present and Future," Biodiversity Management and Climate Change Adaptation Project, Department of Biological Sciences, University of Alberta, Edmonton, October 29, 2013.

471. Mayer, *Dark Money*, p. 69.

472. James Piereson. "Planting Seeds of Liberty," *Philanthropy Magazine*, May/June 2005, accessed March 27, 2017, http://www.philanthropyroundtable.org/topic/excellence_in_philanthropy/planting_seeds_of_liberty.

473. Mayer, *Dark Money*, p. 447.

474. University of Calgary, "New Board of Governors Chair Appointed," February 25, 2011, accessed May 24, 2016, http://www.ucalgary.ca/news/utoday/february25-2011/chair.

475. University of Alberta, "Research," http://why.ualberta.ca/ualbertafacts/Research.

476. SourceWatch, "Friends of Science," http://www.sourcewatch.org/index.php?title=Friends_of_Science.

477. SourceWatch, "University of Calgary Auditor Report," April 14, 2008, accessed May 24, 2016, http://sourcewatch.org/images/4/4b/U_of_C_Auditor%27s_Report_April_14_2008.pdf.

478. University of Calgary, "Former C. D. Howe President to Launch Flagship School of Policy Studies in Calgary," June 14, 2007, accessed May 15, 2017, http://www.ucalgary.ca/news/uofcpublications/oncampus/online/june14-07/publicpolicy.

479. Jack Mintz, "Jack Mintz: The Absolute Case for Why the U.S. Should Approve Keystone XL," *Financial Post*, February 19, 2013, accessed May 26, 2016, http://business.financialpost.com/fp-comment/jack-mintz-the-absolute-case-for-why-the-u-s-should-approve-keystone-xl.

480. *Wall Street Journal*, quoted in "Imperial Oil CEO Backs Keystone Pipeline Expansion," Mining.com, March 11, 2011, accessed May 26, 2016, http://www.mining.com/imperial-oil-ceo-backs-keystone-pipeline-expansion/.

481. Claudia Assis, "Keystone Pipeline: Who Wins When the Oil Flows?" *MarketWatch*, January 25, 2013, accessed May 26, 2016, http://www.marketwatch.com/story/keystone-pipeline-who-wins-when-the-oil-flows-2013-01-25.

482. See Appendix B of Form 10-K filing to the Securities Exchange Commission in New York, pp. 140–44, accessed May 24, 2016, http://www.imperialoil.ca/Canada-English/Files/2014_10k.pdf.

483. University of Calgary, "Jack Mintz Appointed President's Fellow at the School of Public Policy," November 14, 2014, https://www.ucalgary.ca/utoday/issue/2014-11-14/jack-mintz-appointed-presidents-fellow-school-public-policy.

484. Thomas D'Aquino, quoted in RCMP Commercial Crime Section, Ottawa, "Information to Obtain a Production Order," Police file #2012-1046508, November 21, 2013, prepared by Cst. Marie-Josee Robert, p. 7.

485. "Scientist Calls University of Calgary Energy Centre a Failure," *CBC News*, January 28, 2013, accessed May 15, 2017, http://www.cbc.ca/news/canada/calgary/scientist-calls-u-of-c-energy-centre-a-failure-1.1337139.

486. "Scientist Calls University of Calgary Energy Centre a Failure," *CBC News*.

487. University of Calgary, "Enbridge Centre for Corporate Sustainability," Community Report 2012, March 28, 2012, accessed May 25, 2016, http://www.ucalgary.ca/report2012/44.

488. Kyle Bakx and Paul Haavardsrud, "How the University of Calgary Enbridge Relationship Became Controversial," CBC News, November 2, 2015, accessed May 25, 2016, http://www.cbc.ca/news/canada/calgary/university-calgary-enbridge-sponsorship-1.3286369.

489. This email exchange is described in James Turk, "University Debased," *Alberta Views*, September 2016, pp. 28–32. See p. 30 for this exchange.

490. The email is reproduced in full in Bakx and Haavardsrud's CBC article, accessed

May 25, 2016, http://www.cbc.ca/news/canada/calgary/university-calgary-enbridge-sponsorship-1.3286369.

491. Joe Arvai, "Enbridge, the University of Calgary, and Me," *Globe and Mail*, November 6, 2015, accessed May 25, 2016, http://www.theglobeandmail.com/opinion/enbridge-the-u-of-c-and-me/article27150560/.

492. Enbridge Media Center, "Enbridge's Partnership with the University of Calgary and the Centre for Corporate Sustainability," November 2, 2015, accessed May 25, 2016, http://www.enbridge.com/media-center/media-statements/enbridges-partnership-with-the-university-of-calgary-and-the-centre-for-corporate-sustainability.

493. Bakx and Haavardsrud, "How the University of Calgary Enbridge Relationship Became Controversial."

494. Bakx and Haavardsrud, "How the University of Calgary Enbridge Relationship Became Controversial."

495. Annalise Klingbeil and Matt McLure, "University of Calgary President, Who Intervened in Research Centre Funded by Enbridge, Defends Her Role Despite Sitting on Related Board," *Financial Post*, November 3, 2015, accessed May 25, 2016, http://business.financialpost.com/news/energy/enbridge-university-of-calgary?__lsa=6d24-5483.

496. Bakx and Haavardsrud, "How the University of Calgary Enbridge Relationship Became Controversial."

497. Klingbeil and McLure, "University of Calgary President, Who Intervened in Research Centre Funded by Enbridge, Defends Her Role Despite Sitting on Related Board."

498. *Report by the Honourable Terrence F. McMahon to the Board of Governors of the University of Calgary*, accessed November 3, 2016, http://www.ucalgary.ca/secretariat/files/secretariat/final_independent_review_report_2015-12-18.pdf.

499. "University of Calgary to Review Enbridge Relationship after CBC Probe," *CBC News* Calgary, November 6, 2015, accessed April 2, 2017, http://www.cbc.ca/news/canada/calgary/university-calgary-launches-review-of-enbridge-relationship-1.3308043.

500. Bakx and Haavardsrud, "How the University of Calgary Enbridge Relationship Became Controversial."

501. "Enbridge Income Fund Holding Inc. Announces Resignation of Dr. Elizabeth Cannon from Board of Directors," *Globe and Mail*, November 6, 2015.

502. Christopher Adams, "Teachers Investigate Whether University of Calgary Is in Bed with Big Oil," *National Observer*, August 10, 2016, accessed November 3, 2016, http://www.nationalobserver.com/2016/08/10/analysis/teachers-investigate-whether-university-calgary-bed-big-oil.

503. "Who Picks Alberta's Provincial Court Judges," *CBC Edmonton*, accessed March 30, 2015, http://www.cbc.ca/edmonton/interactive/judicial-appointments/.

504. See the entry for "Michael B. Niven" at the website of Carscallen, LLP, accessed on March 30, 2015, http://www.carscallen.com/our-people/.

505. Jennie Russell, "Appointment of Judges Politically Biased in Alberta, Critics Say," *CBC News*, July 25, 2013.

506. See "Suzanne M. Porteous" at the Carscallen, LLP website, accessed March 30, 2015, http://www.carscallen.com/our-people/suzanne-m-porteous/.

507. Darcy Henton, "Friends in High Places," *Alberta Views*, June 2014, p. 30.

508. 507 PCNC, "Mandate," accessed March 30, 2017, https://justice.alberta.ca/programs_services/about_us/Documents/PCNC-Mandate.pdf.

509. PCNC, "Code of Conduct," accessed March 30, 2017, https://justice.alberta.ca/programs_services/about_us/Documents/PCNC-Code-of-Conduct.pdf.

510. The Government of Alberta website for committees, accessed May 26, 2017, https://www.alberta.ca/public-agency-list.cfm.

511. For example, unpublished research by Robert Ascah shows the reach of the PC Party into the boards of four important institutions in Alberta: the University of Alberta, the Alberta Securities Commission, Alberta Treasury Branches (the equivalent of a state-owned bank), and AIMCO, the Alberta government's investment manager, responsible for about $90 billion in 2016. Of the 138 individuals on the boards of these agencies from 2003 to 2015, sixty-three were associated with the PC Party. See Ascah, "Board Appointments and Executive Compensation: A Survey of Four Alberta Provincial Agencies," Institute for Public Economics, University of Alberta, June 26, 2016, accessed March 31, 2017, https://albertarecessionwatch.files.wordpress.com/2016/06/board-appointments-and-executive-compensation.pdf.

512. Dean Neu, David Cooper, and Jeff Everett provide a published account and theoretical analysis of reactions that a column they wrote, critiquing the Alberta government in the 1990s, drew from newspapers, a think tank, the auditor-general of Alberta, CAPP, and the University of Alberta. See their article "Critical Accounting Interventions" in *Critical Perspective on Accounting*, 12 (2001), 735–62.

513. Statistics Canada, "2011 Census: Population, Urban and Rural, by Province and Territory, Alberta," accessed October 23, 2016, http://www.statcan.gc.ca/tables-tableaux/sum-som/l01/cst01/demo62j-eng.htm.

514. Among several reports indicating this is David J. Hughes, "A Clear Look at BC LNG," Canadian Centre for Policy Alternatives BC Office, May 2015.

515. A good analysis of the relationship of fossil fuels to democracy is provided by Timothy Mitchell in *Carbon Democracy* (London: Verso, 2011).

516. Mitchell, *Carbon Democracy*, p. 260.

517. Climate Resilience Consultants, "Climate History for the City of Edmonton: A Reconstruction of Trends in Precipitation, Temperature and Indices of Climate Extremes over the Last 100 Years," Final Report, December 20, 2016, pp. 4, 5.

518. Adrienne Lamb and John Robertson, "Warm Weather Puts Edmonton Gardeners in the (New) Zone," *CBC News*, February 25, 2017, accessed May 4, 2017, http://www.cbc.ca/news/canada/edmonton/warm-weather-edmonton-gardeners-1.3997875.

519. Information accessed May 4, 2017, http://weather.mla.com.au/climate-history/nsw/penrith. Also see "Heatwave to Send Temperatures Past 45C in Western NSW," *ABC News*, January 8, 2017, accessed May 4, 2017, http://www.abc.net.au/news/2017-01-09/heatwave-expected-to-send-temperatures-past-45c-in-western-nsw/8169124.

520. For example, see information about the Mosaic Centre in Edmonton (http://themosaiccentre.ca).

521. City of Calgary, "Transportation Report to SPC on Transportation and Transit," March 15, 2017, p. 6, accessed May 7, 2017, http://agendaminutes.calgary.ca/sirepub/cache/2/monh4fzws01em25dougd1303/51793505072017030501706.PDF.

522. Government of Alberta, "Solar Panels to Be Featured in Alberta's New Schools," media release, October 26, 2016, accessed May 7, 2017, https://www.alberta.ca/release.cfm?xID=436961ac661cd-df8f-5721-666c7b634e826188.

523. Shawn McCarthy, "Ottawa to Phase out Coal, Aims for Virtual Elimination by 2030," *Globe and Mail*, November 21, 2016, accessed May 7, 2017, http://www.theglobeandmail.

com/report-on-business/industry-news/energy-and-resources/ottawa-to-announce-coal-phase-out-aims-for-virtual-elimination-by-2030/article32953930/.

524. Georgia Brown, "British Power Generation Achieves First Coal-Free Day," *The Guardian*, April 21, 2017, accessed May 7, 2017, https://www.theguardian.com/environment/2017/apr/21/britain-set-for-first-coal-free-day-since-the-industrial-revolution.

525. Adam Vaughn, "Google to Be Powered 100% by Renewable Energy from 2017," *The Guardian*, December 6, 2016, accessed May 7, 2017: https://www.theguardian.com/environment/2016/dec/06/google-powered-100-renewable-energy-2017.

526. Hiroko Tabushi, "California Upholds Auto Emissions Standards, Setting Up Face-Off with Trump," *New York Times*, March 24, 2017, accessed May 8, 2017, https://www.nytimes.com/2017/03/24/business/energy-environment/california-upholds-emissions-standards-setting-up-face-off-with-trump.html?_r=0.

527. Enbridge, "Renewable Energy," May 7, 2017, https://www.enbridge.com/about-us/our-work/renewable-energy.

528. Terry Macalister, "Shell Creates Green Energy Division to Invest in Wind Power," *The Guardian*, May 15, 2016, accessed May 7, 2017, https://www.theguardian.com/business/2016/may/15/shell-creates-green-energy-division-to-invest-in-wind-power.

529. Elizabeth McSheffrey, "Nine B.C. Mayors Urge Trudeau to Put Brakes on Kinder Morgan Pipeline," *National Observer*, September 29, 2016, accessed May 8, 2017, http://www.nationalobserver.com/2016/09/29/news/nine-bc-mayors-urge-trudeau-put-brakes-kinder-morgan-pipeline.

530. For examples, see 350.org (https://350.org/category/topic/divestment/).

531. Geoffrey Morgan, "Putting Alberta's Idle Wells to Work Could Heat Up the Energy," October 20, 2016, *Financial Post*. June 23, 2017, http://business.financialpost.com/commodities/energy/putting-albertas-idle-wells-to-work-could-heat-up-the-energy-patch/wcm/cfc8dae5-7063-4c18-a464-041b92a758cc.

532. Shawn McCarthy, "Energy East Hearings Put on Hold over Complaints against NEB Members."

Index